William Adams

Thanksgiving

Memories of the day: Helps to the habit

William Adams

Thanksgiving
Memories of the day: Helps to the habit

ISBN/EAN: 9783743347052

Manufactured in Europe, USA, Canada, Australia, Japa

Cover: Foto ©ninafisch / pixelio.de

Manufactured and distributed by brebook publishing software (www.brebook.com)

William Adams

Thanksgiving

THANKSGIVING:

MEMORIES OF THE DAY: HELPS TO THE HABIT.

BY WILLIAM ADAMS, D.D.

καὶ τανῦν παραινῶ ὑμᾶς εὐθυμεῖν.

ST. PAUL.

If thou be a severe, sour-complexioned man, then I here disallow
thee to be a competent judge.

IZAAK WALTON.

NEW YORK

CHARLES SCRIBNER'S SONS

1887

CONTENTS.

INTRODUCTORY.

MEMORIES AND HABITS.

THE beginning of this world's history was a song: its end will be a doxology.

The secret of all rational contentment is revealed in that inspired direction which ought to be written on every heart, as a compendious rule of life. " Be careful for nothing ; but in *everything,* by prayer and supplication, WITH THANKSGIVING, let your requests be made known unto God. And the peace of God, which passeth all understanding, shall keep your hearts and minds thro' Christ Jesus."

While the cultivation of a thankful spirit is at all times commended by reason and religion, it would be affectation to attempt any concealment of the fact, that the substance of this volume was prepared with special reference to that day in the calendar which bears the familiar name of THANKSGIVING.

In the cathedral of Limerick there hangs a peal of bells which was manufactured for a convent in Italy, by an enthusiast who fixed his home for many years near the convent cliff to enjoy their daily chimes. In some political convulsion the bells and their manufacturer were swept away to another land. After a long interval, the course of his wanderings brought him to Ireland. On a calm and beautiful evening, as the vessel which bore him floated along the broad stream of the Shannon, he suddenly heard the bells peal forth from the cathedral tower. They were the long-lost treasures of his memory. Home, happiness, friends, all early recollections were in their sound. Crossing his arms on his breast, he lay back in the boat. When the rowers looked round, they saw his face still turned to the cathedral—but his eyes had closed forever on the world.* Such a tide of memories had swept over the sympathetic cords of his heart, that they snapped under the vibration. Who has not experienced the power of association in its milder and happier forms? The return of an anniversary, the melody of a tune, the swinging of a church bell, will set memory in motion, and unveil the pictures which hang on her sacred walls. Because memory is clad in sober and russet garb, many associate her form with sadness. But it is a sadness from which we never wish to be divorced. Peace, quietness, and " cherub contemplation," come in her train. Memory is the mother of gratitude. Mirth and frivolity are born of present excitements ; but there cannot be deep and serene happiness in the absence of all memories of the past.

The bare mention of the word, the Old Thanksgiving Day—what a power has it to revive the pleasantest reminiscences, and recall the brightest scenes of other days in

* Quarterly Rev., Oct., 1854.

many hearts! It transports them to the home of their childhood. It takes them at once into the presence of the father and mother who, it may be, for many years have been sleeping in the grave. It recalls their smiles of affectionate greeting, their tones of cheerful welcome; tones and smiles such as none but they could give. Every image of peace, contentment, competence, abundance, and joy, comes back spontaneously on each return of the grateful festival. It is a day not indeed heralded and emblazoned, like the corresponding festivals in our ancestral land, in all the pomp and glory of song. It has not been celebrated like Christmas, by the imperial song of Milton, the dove-like notes of Herbert, or the classic beauty of Keble. Connected with it are no superstitious rites handed down from time immemorial; no revellings in baronial halls; no decorations of churches or houses with garlands or evergreens; no wassailings; no shoutings; no carols; no riotous dissipation. Simpler in its nature, humbler in its pretensions, better suited to a people of a more recent origin, it is set apart to the exercise of those home-bred affections, those " honest fireside delights," which are greener than laurel or fir-tree, and which, from a natural affinity, most closely harmonize with the sweet sanctities of our holy religion. As the day drew on, anticipation was busy in the young and the old. The aged pair, from beneath whose shelter their children, one after the other, had gone forth into the world, leaving them alone, looked forward with delight to the prospect of being surrounded once more by their numerous progeny on a day of gladness ; and children separated widely apart, and already grown familiar with life's perplexities and cares, hailed with pleasure the "yearly sacrifice,' when they should all rally again around the paternal hearth, and renew their faith and affection among the long-cherished scenes of their childhood. Happy was the venerable sire, who went up that day to the house of God, in company with his children and children's children, and who sat down to the table of plenty with his whole household, in health, peace, and contentment. If any were detained from the gathering by stern necessity, places were prepared for them as if they were present, in order that all might feel how closely they were linked by invisible sympathies ; and the absent ones, wherever on sea or land they roamed, were as " a bird wandering from his nest," or crippled in the time of migration, looking far away, and longing to join himself unto his fellows.

Though this particular day has been designated by the civil authorities, it should be borne in mind that in the one only national organization which had God for its author, several days in the year were set apart by Divine institution for religious festivities. Spring, summer, and autumn had each its festal symbolism ; the most joyous of which, called the Feast of Tabernacles, was an annual Thanksgiving—not only in memory of ancestral favors, but for the ingathering of the harvests. Nothing can be conceived more beautiful than the manner of its observance. Booths were erected in the open air, with branches from the palm and willow, within which families were gathered, to eat together before the Lord ; so that the occasion was sacred to the reunion of friends, the enjoyment of hospitality, the interchange of kindness, the expression of generous regard for the stranger, the widow, and the fatherless.   Nor was it lawful for a Jew so much as to taste of ear or parched corn, or bread of the new harvest, till a nation had borne a sheaf of barley or wheat and waved it before God, in token of their gratitude. Are we charmed by the picture which the imagination paints of that national spectacle, when the glens of the vine and olive gave forth their happy inhabitants, to flow together into the court of the Lord, with chanting of psalms and waving of sheaf and branch?   But when did the sun ever look down upon such a scene as has been spread often beneath his eye on this Western Continent, a land unknown and undreamed of when Hebrew feasts were instituted, when many States have agreed to devote one and the same day for Thanksgiving to our common Father for his abundant goodness?   What millions of well-clad, well-fed, well-taught, and, if they would but believe it, happy people, within the temples of religion, and the homes of health, comfort, and plenty!   As the mind traverses over the extended scene, it rests not so much on metropolitan affluence, on gatherings in stately mansions and tapestried walls, where sumptuous fare is of daily occurrence, as on the humbler habitations of rural life, where man is brought by earth, sky, and season, in closer contact with God.   Toil is at rest and contented with its rewards.   Plough and flail are exchanged for recreation. If nature is more silent than in earlier months, when birds and beasts are full of jocund music and life, it is the silence of peaceful contentment.   The rich autumn sunlight bathes the sere and yellow stalks and husks of corn still standing in the field, reduced to the undress of the year, yet testifying of the golden wealth they have yield·

ed to man ; barns bursting with plenty ; the cattle chew-
ing the cud with mute thankfulness ; families reassem-
bled in the old homestead ; mirth in the voices of the
young, and placid delight warming the ashy hue of age ;
what images of serene satisfaction are those which are
presented by this day of happy memories !

Thanksgiving Day has a history attached to it. Like
the Latin word "virtus," it is a history which runs
through the entire life of a people. We cannot afford to
lose reverence for ancestral memories. It is to be regretted that Mr. Irving, our American Goldsmith, has
expended so much time and labor in the prolix exagge-
ration of the peculiar habits of the early Dutch colonists.
When Diedrich Knickerbocker extends an extravaganza
through two volumes over that portion of our history, we
confess to a feeling somewhat painful, mingling with the
keenest relish of the humorous. We need more, not less
of filial respect and gratitude in our national character.
Shem and Japheth, with their mantle of charity, did a
nobler service than their brother who laughed at the
shame of their common parentage. In that transition
period through which we are passing, it is well to think
of the primitive strength which is beneath us, and upon
which a fruitful surface invites and rewards our toil. The
origin of this day was with a people who were exiles for
the sake of truth and liberty, and who gave a soul to the
scattered colonies of the Western Hemisphere. "Te
Deums" had been chanted in the cathed als of the Old
world by royal decree, at the birth of princes, the coronation of kings, and the issue of great battles ; but the
voluntary appointment of a day, by a whole people, for

the distinctive purpose of rendering thanks to the Al
mighty for his manifold blessings, civil and religious,
national and domestic, marks an epoch in history.—
Thanksgiving day is the festival of religious liberty.
Removed to a distance from all tyranny, passing from
suffering, which called for brave defiance and patience,
into success and enlargement which inspired gratitude,
religion, finding its freedom in the New World, poured out
its carols at the very gate of heaven.

Among the many proclamations issued by the Gover-
nors of the several States in the autumn of 1857, appointing the Thanksgiving for that year, was one couched
in these words :

" Since I have been in office, I have, in each year, as
governor of the State, without any authority of law, but
sustained by ancient custom, appointed a day of thanksgiving.   Thursday, the 19th day of this month, is the day
now appointed, and I trust it will be observed.   There
is, certainly, some super-ruling Providence which has
brought us into existence, and which will ultimately accomplish the ends for which we were created, not only as
individuals, but as a people.   Nothing can, therefore, be
lost by recognizing the obligation which we owe to the
Supreme Being—by it much may be gained."   With all
respect for magistracy, I call that an extraordinary
document.   He is not altogether confident about it, but
on the whole is inclined to think that " some super-ruling
Providence " may be addressed with thanks, especially
since nothing can be lost, and something may be gained
by the act!   The idea of " making something " out of
Thanksgiving carries our national propensity quite to a

1*

ludicrous extreme ; and the words "loss " and "gain," if they do not convey the nicest sense of religious obligation, certainly suggest an eye to the "main chance," as an apology for the rendering of thanks !

We are certainly a most astonishing nation ! We are very tenacious of our old British privilege of *grumbling*. If weather and business and politics kept along smooth and prosperous all the time, very many would be thrown out of occupation. Croaking is their profession, and making themselves unhappy is their habit. A man ought to have a very steady head who reads nothing but American newspapers. He becomes familiar with excitement and apprehension, and is all the while wondering what will come to pass next. Mr. Miller, who, a few years ago, broached the theory that the world was nigh its end, and like " Judas of Galilee, in the days of the taxing, drew away much people after him," could have succeeded with this notion nowhere else so well as in these United States of America. Such things are indigenous to our soil. A country like our own, stretching over so many degrees of latitude and longitude, through such varieties of climate, hot and cold, dry and wet, with such diversities of interest and manners among a heterogeneous population, and with such artificial facilities for flashing the report of everything which occurs on a vast continent backwards and forwards, and bringing it, every few minutes, upon the retina of every man's eye ; why one might be excused who should live in a constant expectation of the world's catastrophe. Rumors of a comet whisking its fiery tail among the stars and certain to demolish our planet upon such a day of the calendar ; a tornado upsetting houses, fences and forests ; corn in the last of June, all over the West, not more than three inches high, when it should have been as many feet, alarming the country with the certainty of a famine ; now a drought which bakes the furrows and burns up the pastures ; now rains, excessive and continuous beyond all the memories of the " oldest inhabitant ;" a tremendous inundation of the Mississippi ; a cold snap in May, which kills all the fruit ; a popular election, when the very foundations of society are moved, the sea upturning its discolored depths; mobs in Baltimore and New York, bringing out the military ; senators, counsellors, judges—names so venerable in the beginning—accused of corruption and venality ; good old philanthropic and ecclesiastical bodies rent asunder; Shem, Ham, and Japheth pelting one another with hard recriminations, and the air filled with all the menaces and terrors of the old prophets ; to-day, a plethora of money, eager to buy up the whole continent, and all the islands and countries which lie adjacent thereto ; and to-morrow, a " panic " before which the bags of gold in all the bank-vaults collapse and shrivel up, like those of wind which Eolus sent to Homer's hero ; verily, one might think the world was coming to an end, twenty times in the course of a twelvemonth ! But in some way, I know not how it is, we get along marvellously well. The sun rises and sets ; the stars are not jostled out of their steady orbits ; the months are not thrown out of step in their orderly procession ; the seasons follow each other serenely and honestly ; the sign of the covenant is in the heavens, bright and beautiful as when the mothers from the ark lifted their babes aloft to "bless the bow of God ;" all the heathenish signs in the Zodiac do not prevent the mighty monarch of day from bringing the year about, "filling our hearts with food and gladness;" and on Thanksgiving Day, in the golden autumn, multitudes of people, in the temples of religion and in their homes, meet together with more reason and occasion for gratitude—if they were wise enough to know it—than any nation upon the face of the earth. "The Lord hath done great things for us, whereof we are thankful." If there is one peril more than another which threatens our prosperity, it is that indifference to our mercies which might provoke God to withdraw them. May God incline us more and more to that unambitious, unselfish, contented, cheerful, thankful temper, which is at once a medicine and a feast, an ornament and a protection.

One of the chief advantages, we are told, of the national festivity of the Hebrew, was that, by friendly intercourse between different tribes, it promoted a spirit of common patriotism. If Thanksgiving would but be observed in a becoming spirit, how much would it accomplish in the way of purifying and strengthening the sentiment of nationality, which was fostered by ancestral memories, cemented by the blood of our fathers, and wrought into the structure of our continent by the hand of God, in the flow of rivers, the clasp of lakes and ridges, and the embracing arm of an unbroken sea-board.

An excellent minister of my acquaintance is in the habit of selecting the texts of his Thanksgiving sermons out of the Book of Lamentations. The elegies of the weeping prophet are a part of the Sacred Volume, and frequent enough are the occasions when they may be used with utmost pertinency. But so it happens that "Thanks-giving"—the only day in our calendar of the kind—is the one in which dirges are not so appropriate as carols. Its true design is not to furnish the pulpit with an opportunity for pelting the civil magistracy, nor for indulging in lugubrious complaints and apprehensions as to the condition and prospects of political affairs ; but specifically to rehearse those acts of the Divine goodness which should inspire us with gratitude and incline us to a cheerful expression of thanks. That man who, in the worst condition of affairs, cannot discover material enough for praise, is already in a morbid and most deplorable state.

This festival was first appointed by a people proverbially parsimonious in the designation of holidays. With the exception of " Election Day," and the " Fourth of July," it was the one only holiday of the year. " New Year " came and passed in the New England States with no recognition, save in the present of a new primer, and a vague impression that it was the time for a boy to make good resolutions. But the last Thursday in November gathered to itself all fragrant and pleasant associations. What extraordinary sermons ; what extraordinary anthems, on that day in the old " Meeting House ! " * Without reproof, one could smile, on that day, at the wonderful performances of the choir in those old fugue tunes in which the several parts were perpetually chasing each other in a hard race, till they came in at the close, with a general making up on satisfactory terms ; and even at the

---

* This name for a church is not of New England origin, as is generally supposed, for the classic Addison uses it in the Spectator.

sermon too, when the minister—that man of black—did not seem so ghostly as in other days, but descending from high mysteries, talked of passing events and familiar things, in a style which kept his hearers awake without the aid of physical appliances ; and so the day which went forth with joy was led in at night with peace.

The reader will infer that the foundations of the author's mind were laid in happy memories and associations with the Day and the Habit of Thanksgiving.

Sufficiently compensated will he be if anything shall be found in these pages, which may serve as a few grains of frankincense on that oblation which, he trusts, will burn pure and bright on all our altars and our hearths, on each return of THANKSGIVING DAY.

DAILY MARVELS.

Blessed be the Lord, who *daily* loadeth us with benefits.

Ps. 68 : 19.

Ημέρα τη ἡμέρα ερευγεται ρημα.

ψαλ. ιη.

I.

DAILY MARVELS.

In one of those books from the pen of Mrs. Barbauld, and her accomplished brother, Dr. Aiken—" Evenings at Home "—once the delight of childhood, is a chapter entitled, " *Travellers' Wonders.*" The children of a family group are represented as urging their father to recite to them some stories of the wonderful things he had seen in his many voyages. They had themselves read the famous travels of Mr. Gulliver, and the Adventures of Sinbad the Sailor, and, of course, their ears were erect to hear of something not less remarkable than " The Loadstone Mountain," the " Valley of Diamonds," or the people of Lilliput and Brobdingnag. Complying with their request, he gave them a minute description of a certain country he had once visited, of the habits of the people—their dwellings, their dress, their food, their manners, and customs; and it was not till the evening was far advanced that the listeners detected that, under that thin pretence and disguise of marvel, they had been entertained with an accurate account of themselves, and their own native land.

Something akin to this I now propose. I mount no telescope through which to observe what Jeremy Taylor has called the "great constellations of God's goodness ;" let us look at objects nearer to ourselves, assured that the greatest marvels in the universe are those which fail to strike us as marvels, because of their commonness. The truly great things of the Divine goodness are not to be sought for in the affairs of empires, or in the *extraordinary* events of our own lives, but in those manifold arrangements which are essential to our *daily* existence, but which, because of their constancy, are too commonly left out of our enumeration. How many things, if we would sum them up, must conspire to put us in a state of ease ! How many things, which must all go right, and that for all the time, to keep our bodies and minds in moderate comfort ! Let what we call a misfortune, an accident befall us, it becomes the topic of remark, the occasion of sympathy, for it is an *extraordinary* thing, thereby reminding us that it is the exception to that common course of providential dealing, to which we become sensible only by an occasional interruption.

Instead of straining after what is remote and uncommon, suppose that we should begin the day, and mention over a few of those many blessings which compose the usual course of our personal life.

The morning has come, and we awake, refreshed and invigorated by *sleep*. Did we pause to consider how great a benefit is healthful sleep? The inspired Psalmist, amid the many imperial mercies which crowned him as king, forgot not the mention of this : " I laid me down, and slept ; I awaked ; for the Lord sustained me." Again, amid the many afflictions which burdened him, this one is specified as very great : " Thou holdest mine eyes *waking*."

Any one who has been in the course of his life, from any cause, subject to protracted vigils, will understand this language. The eye held waking, the eye-ball hot and hard, and the brain strung to its tightest tension ; the clock tolling off the hours, the day at length returning, and no sleep ! An occasional loss of this great restorer is followed by temporary inconvenience, but let it be protracted beyond all relief, and madness and death ensue. Consider how many causes might intrude to deprive you of your customary sleep. Bodily pain, mental agitation, convulsions of nature, perils from fire, and violence ; the sickness and suffering of others.

> The careful Betty the pillow beats,
> And airs the blankets, and smooths the sheets,
> And gives the mattress a shaking—
> But vainly Betty performs her part,
> If a ruffled head and a rumpled heart,
> As well as the couch, want making !

Neither is it by any effort or skill of our own that sleep visits our eyelids. Pursue it, strive to overtake it, and it flees from you. The best account we can give of it, when sound and sweet, is this : " I laid me down, and slept." It is the gift of a beneficent Providence. It is His own hand which draws the curtain, subdues the glare of the sun, and hushes all the noise of the world. The involuntary functions of life go on more calmly, more smoothly than ever. The lungs heave, the heart keeps on without your thought or care ; startled by no alarm, agitated by no peril, you lie quietly in the soft mystery ; the exhausted energy of life is recruited ; that which is wasted is supplied, that which was wearied is restored, and you awake like a strong man to run a race. As Bunyan's Pilgrim, in the large chamber which looked to the sunrising, and was called Peace, awoke and sung, leave not your chamber without an ascription of gratitude to the world's great Watchman for the gift of sound and refreshing *sleep*.

And how were you awakened? The light of the sun gently touched your eyelids and they opened. The *light* —the light of day—the common light of the morning, what shall we say of its beauty, its wondrous composition, its value, and its blessing? Wonder not that Milton, detained so long in that obscure sojourn with " the Stygian council," in the opening books of his immortal epic, should begin the book which follows with the apostrophe :

Hail, holy light, offspring of heaven, first-born !

For if, by some sudden interruption of nature, for which we could not account, a horror of great darkness, like that which plagued the land of Egypt in the day of divine wrath, should settle upon us ; if, when clock and chronometer announced that the time for sun-rising had returned, no sun should appear, and slow-paced hours and days should follow one after another, and neither sun nor moon nor stars should break the frightful gloom, and panic should seize the world, as certainly it would, and business should come to an end, and life lose its motion, and men's hearts had failed from looking for what was coming to pass; if, after such an extraordinary and terrific withdrawa' of the light, it should again break upon the world, kissing the hill-tops, and then come pouring over into valleys, illuminating every recess, and bathing the globe with its joy, how would the world's population together lift up their shouts of gladness for the return of such a visitant! *Light*—image of beauty, image of gladness— how wondrously is it compounded—painting everything it touches in such variety of colors. How remote its birth-place, how long its journey of kindness! Yet though it travels so far, and so fast, accumulating power as it goes, it is so soft, so safe, that it impinges not on the delicate eye, nor inflicts mischief on the most sensitive surface. To give us this cheerful illumination, to furnish light for the poor man's toil, what a vast and costly machinery is employed! The whole planetarium of the heavens is pre- served in proper equilibrium, attraction, and motion—the sun, like a mighty monarch, leading forth his train of at- tendant orbs, and scattering joy in his path. "Truly, the light is sweet ; and a pleasant thing it is to behold the sun." Let us not forget the blessing and the wonder.

Shut out by no walls, penetrating into the tightest compartment, on fleetest wings, invisible to the eye, comes another visitor, the vital tonic *air*. So curiously is it composed that, if there were the slightest deviation from the right proportions, we must gasp and die. Many seem to be afraid of it, just as they shun others of their best friends, but it does not resent the insult ; it follows us with its kindly offices, tripping down to the lowest cell of the lungs, playing scavenger to the blood ; throwing in fuel to the flame of life ; and verily, if we did not put so many slights on this aerial visitant which has come so far to see us, trying so hard as we do to avoid it or con-

taminate it, fewer hard words would be spoken in this
irritable world; fewer infirmities of body and mind
would there be, and much more heart and tone to our
daily and annual thanksgiving.

The bare mention of *water*—the water which we drink,
the water in which we bathe, suggests a world of wonders.
Two invisible spirits, travelling alone, each intent on
burning up the world, meet in the upper air, agree to
forget their direful purpose, enter into partnership and
descend together in a new form, to refresh and bless the
world and its inhabitants.   We waste it, we throw it away,
we despise it, we count it the meanest and cheapest of
all things, but it is one of the greatest wonders in God's
laboratory.   When we stop to think of it, pleasant sights
and pleasant sounds are associated with it.   In the drip
of the rain, the glitter of the dew, the tinkling of the fountain, the splash of the brook, the coolness of the well, the
tumble of the cascade, the thunder of the cataract, the
mirrored surface of the lake, the spirit of the mist, the
expanse of the ocean, we will never see it, touch it, use
it again without a thought of wonder and of gratitude.

Refreshed by these constant visitants, sleep, light,
air, and water, you invest yourself with suitable and
comfortable clothing.   There is not an article you wear
which has not in it a lesson of advanced civilization.   The commonest pin reminds you that you have
conveniences which would have astonished kings and
queens dependent on the product of the thorn-bush.   It
would be too much to assert that our habiliments are not
sometimes grotesque and absurd; that fashion will not
now and then inaugurate some appendage not altogether

the most picturesque or comfortable; but look at a Hot-tentot or a New Zealander, scantily clad, horribly disfigured with plaited grasses and coarsest skins, and then at your own persons clad in garments so curious in material, excluding cold without impeding motion, befitting in shape, that savages almost invariably imagine the dress of a civilized man to be a part of the man himself. The skins of herds which roam on other continents, subjected to the processes of chemistry; the little pod bursting with its snowy treasure, growing in the States of the South, the transportation of which employs countless fleets, and in the price of which the variation of a penny a pound affects the commerce of the world; the fleeces of the flock, the manufacture of which into cloth, by the nimble fingers of steam and machinery, bring before you the sources of national wealth; the little worm which weaves its own shroud and tomb of silk, bequeathing to us a moral lesson, of consuming ourselves in weaving garments for others; the little instrument compounded of wheels and springs, of steel, and jewels and gold, and a few numerals figured on its face, which you put in your pocket, and which promises to tell you, while you are busy, what the sun is about, and how fast the nimble-footed hours, minutes, and seconds are tripping away; all these and a thousand other things, combined in our daily raiment, suggest the marvels which are connected with our commonest conveniences.

You descend from your chamber, and will you not bestow one thought of gratitude for the use of your *limbs* and *senses?* I ask for nothing quite so elaborate as that argument for the goodness of God which you will find drawn out in the treatises of Paley, on the articulation of the joints, and the structure of the eye ; or by Sir Charles Bell on the vital endowments of the hand.

You comprehend the joy of the lame man, healed at the gate Beautiful, by the Apostle ; he ran and leaped, and praised God. How natural his joy! his ankles receiving strength, and he jumping and running in the use of his new-found liberty. And yet, you have had the use ot your limbs for the whole of life. Instead of being a cripple, carried by others from place to place, when you were a child, your footsteps were on the hill, in the wood, along the brook, across the fields, and this very morning, your limbs bore you up and down the stairs, very likely more than one at a step.

Painters have studied long and hard to catch the expression which must have overspread the face of Blind Bartimeus, at the very moment when he was restored to sight by the miraculous touch of Christ. First wonder, then confusion ; men and trees blended promiscuously ; at length a quick bright flash of ecstacy—for he saw clearly, saw the face of his Lord, saw the faces of friends, and all at last was the glow of serene and unmingled gratitude. But which is the greater mercy—to be restored to sight after long blindness, or never to have known what it was to be blind at all?

You join the family group and interchange friendly salutations. What a wonder is that which just entered your ear, and fell from your mouth—*Articulate speech !* Sometimes a transatlantic stranger will visit our country to exhibit his skill upon a musical instrument, and cities are agape at the tripping trills and brilliant bravuras which burn under his fingers. Boast not of that adroitness in the use of finger and thumb on keys of ivory, till you have considered more the flexibility, variations and compass of the instrument which God has created for the utterance of language, and the many years which are requisite in learning to play upon it. With what delight does the ear of a child catch the first intelligent sounds which are made by the wonderful organ it has just discovered in its throat! He breathes on it again, more than ever delighted at each experiment; now with this tone and now with that, becoming familiar with every stop and string, pleased whenever it acquires the utterance of a new note or word, till at length it will coo, and chatter, and hum, and talk and sing, like a popinjay twittering about the eaves, and all for the simple pleasure which it finds in its own proficiency. Think it not strange that a child talks as it does with little regard to sense. It is tuning that instrument which God has called the "glory" of our frame, and years will be necessary before it comes out a master of the great and wonderful art of talking. The body is not the tomb or the prison of the soul. "Ear-gate" and "mouth-gate" are open, words pass and repass, tones become the vehicle of sentiment, society is established, and in the power of communicating thought lies the great bond and cement of life.

And *what* were the words which first greeted you this morning? Kindly inquiries after your *health*. And you were able to reply, with thanks for the question, that you were *well—very well*. Hold that word a moment. It drops from your lips many times a day. Do not think the time wasted which is spent in inquiries and answers, whenever you meet a friend, in regard to health ; for now we touch what is absolutely essential. Sickness overtakes you, the heart works irregularly, the lungs heavily, the nerves are sensitive and irritable, digestion enfeebled, the brain plethoric and excitable, and pain gnaws in the marrow and the joints. What shall be done that health may be restored ? No exertion is spared, no expenditure of money is deemed extravagant ; all medical skill is summoned, voyages planned, every healing spring and genial clime are visited, and all that by some means health may be regained. Yet how many years of uninterrupted health have you enjoyed, when it was not necessary for you to watch the clouds, or analyze your food, or weigh your clothing, or take exercise by rule ; when you were not conscious that such a thing as a nerve existed, or a stomach either, save from the satisfaction with which its simple and healthy wants were supplied. That illness should occasionally enfeeble us, is not half so wonderful as this, that we should pass through so many vicissitudes of heat and cold, moisture and drought, labor and leisure, without detriment ; that we should carry this delicate harp of a thousand chords through all the roughness, violence, and collisions of the world without breaking it. Never reply again to a kind morning inquiry after your *health*, that you are *well, very well*—without an emphasis on the word which intends a special gratitude to the Almighty.

And *who* were those with whom you interchanged this morning's salutations? The living reduplications of yourself. Father, mother, son, daughter, husband, wife, brother, sister, friend. Those who know you, trust you, love you. Those who are identified with your interests, interwoven with your life ; who understand you as no others can, who give you their sympathy and confidence as no others will. These are they who make up that endeared circle of *home*, never to be thought of without a gentler and happier mood. ·It was your own child who gave you a morning kiss, your own parent who gave you a cordial blessing. It is not strange that you begin each day with such a good heart and courage, for you have a home which recruits the motives of daily life, to which weariness will return for repose, care come back for composure ; the retreat where gloom is chased away by smiles, and your heart feasts on those nameless, numberless acts of kindness, which are the more to be valued because unbought and unpretend-ing. Think what a hard, uncouth, rough, coarse, vulgar drudge you would be, without those kind and gentle companionships which now soften and mould your character. It is not strange that the great metaphysician, Jonathan Edwards, should have written so profoundly on *disinterested benevolence.* The only wonder is, that the severity of his style did not oftener relax into something like humor ; when he, the greatest thinker of his age, had for his wife one whom he has himself described after this manner : " You could not persuade her," writes he, " to do anything wrong or sinful, if you could give her all the world. She is of wonderful gentleness, calmness, and universal benevolence of mind. She will sometimes go about from place to place, singing sweetly ; and seems to be always full of joy and pleasure, and no one knows for what. She loves to be alone, walking in the fields and groves, and seems to have some one invisible always conversing with her." The metaphysician metamorphosed into the poet, without his knowing it. Such is the alchemy of home, that we are led into many virtues by means of our pleasures.

And *where* was it, that amid all these other mercies of Providence you began this day? Within your *own dwelling*, with its innumerable conveniences and comforts. A house is not a home, but a home implies that there is a house. The style of human dwellings is an index of the varied stages of civilization. Nomadic tribes make use of movable tents; savages have holes or huts, execrable with filth. The " House of Diomede," as it is called, at Pompeii, by its very structure, with so much of court and corridor, and so little room within, reveals the idea of Roman life—out of doors and public, with small domestic conveniences. Erasmus accounts for the prevalence of the plague in England, in his day, by the condition of the houses. Very few in all the kingdom had chimneys for the passage of the smoke. Rushes and straw covered the floors, accumulating discomfort, day and night. It is not strange that in such circumstances Lord Bacon brought his imperial imagination to contrive whatever was desirable in domestic architecture. In the remarkable description from his pen of the " House of Solomon," in the New Atlantis, which was received by his contemporaries as a mere rhodomontade, we have what has since been proved to be the far-reaching vision of science, for there is scarcely a contrivance there imagined for warming, lighting, ventilating, and furnishing a human habitation, which is not in common use in our own dwellings. Observe the house where you live, arranged for convenience, divided off into separate compartments; it is

not a hermit's cell nor yet a tavern ; privacy without soli-
tude, society without turnpike publicity. By a beautiful
combination of sand and an alkali, your windows are furnished with that transparent material through which the
light passes but not the cold. The world is seen but not
admitted. Philosophy and art, no longer divorced, find
their true dignity in discovering, inventing, and arranging
those many conveniences which contribute to the warmth,
economy, and healthiness of human habitations. When
the ancients lost their fire from their hearths and altars,
they lighted it again, by means of lenses, from the sun.
Some may remember that when the same calamity befell
a family in olden time, resort was had to that one of the
household who had acquired the knack of eliciting and
catching the welcome spark from flint and steel. As to
that great convenience which modern chemistry has
given us, so economical of time and patience, by which
light and fire are afforded us in a second, there is but one
drawback to gratitude. In ancient times, the smoking of
a pipe by an old man, in the chimney-corner, was the very
image of cosy comfort ; but the convenience of portable
fire, carried in the pocket, in all places, seems to have
suggested certain habits, even to the children, suddenly converting a whole generation into peripatetic
chimneys.

Two things, in the domestic arrangements of our metropolitan life, are greatly to be missed and regretted—
a *fireplace* and a *barn*. A city stable is an adjunct of
wealth ; an appendage of luxury, set apart for horses, and
grooms, and footmen. That is not the idea at all. The
place we speak of was a part of *home*. There was it that

we grew familiar with the " honest faces of animals ; " there was the meadow-sweet scent of the hay ; there was the bright golden corn stripped from its overcoat of felt, and its underdress of silk ; there was the thud of the thresher's flail ; there rung the merry laugh of boyhood and girlhood in their holiday freedom—alas ! how many of those clear, sweet voices were silent years ago in their small graves, while we are now men and women.   There, on the south side of that old, weather-beaten, unpainted barn, the sun would shine brighter and warmer than any-where else, and we and the cattle chewed together the cud of contentment.

To many of the children of our day the *fireside* is rather an allegorical expression.   To others, it is an ac-tual history.   A hole in the wall, through which the heat passes, attaches to itself no ideas of sociability.   The old fireplace, with its generous supply of clean, honest wood, its crackling blaze, its ample room, symbolized the dwelling-place of cheerfulness, the home of love, and the altar of religion.   There was it, when the twilight shadows had come, and candle and lamp were as yet un-lighted, and the reflection of the flame was dancing on the wall, that you sat and mused—and if, perchance, as the wood sizzled on the hearth, your mind fell upon some sad and pensive train, some gleam of the mystery of life, you laid your head upon your mother's lap, and was calm ; and when the evening had gone, the large ruddy coals of the log, brighter than those of England's Christ-mas Yule, were laid in their bed of ashes, and the gray-haired sire commended the group to heaven for protec-tion ; love, peace, comfort, joy and prayer, all beside that old fireplace, where the gray-haired love and pray no more.

Animals feed alone, greedily crunching each his own bone and portion. To eat in silence is a sign of barbarism. The table where you sat this morning is not the crib and rack where you eat what is necessary to support life. It is the focus of all courtesy, the symbol of all hospitality. Not to speak of the coarse and disgusting articles of food which those in the most abject condition of poverty have been compelled to resort to for the sustenance of life, compare the delicate, nutritious, palatable food upon your family table this morning, with the beef and the beer which composed the breakfast of Queen Elizabeth and her nobility. While thousands upon thousands have actually perished from starvation, you never knew what it was to be hungry and in want all your life. You have had enough and to spare. Over and above all that is needful, as if to give us special proofs of His goodness, Divine Providence has spread before us, every day, whatever would give a pleasure to the palate. The cup of which Cowper sang, which "cheers but not inebriates," China's fragrant leaf; the juices of the tropical cane crystallized into sparkling lumps; the corn which you watched in its summer growth, with its ribbons of green, and its tassels of yellow floss; the wheat which you paused to admire while it was yet green, the wind passing over it, and bending it in graceful waves as if it were a sea of life; all the "treasures hid in the sand," these and whatever other material there may be in the sea, the air, the stall and the field, suited to the use and pleasure of man—all these are your daily aliment in this land of God's exuberant bounty.

While you were sleeping during the night, so completely divorced from the world, the great world itself was at work to prepare for you one of its greatest wonders. It lies waiting for you upon your breakfast-table—so common and worthless a thing after it has been read, that it will be crumpled up and burned, or serve to wrap the refuse meat which is dropped into the beggar's basket. Yet in fact it is a microcosm, the world made smaller, and brought within the compass of the newspaper now in your hands.* The fleet steamers upon the ocean, the ships on every river and sea, the camels and dromedaries of the East, the swift-footed trapper of the West, the ponderous engines which tramp across the land, the electric wires which throb over the land, and beneath the surges of the Atlantic—every instrument, every agent, every vehicle that can convey intelligence—explorers, adventurers, politicians, thinkers, speakers, actors, dreamers, advertisers, all at the top of their speed, and huddling together the world's wisdom and the world's folly, all that this world has done, and spreading it out before your eyes in that reeking sheet, as if it were a moving panorama of the whole earth. Cowper has inimitably described the marvel in his lines upon the daily newspaper.

> This folio of four pages, happy work !
> Which not e'en critics criticise ; that holds
> Inquisitive attention, while I read,
> Fast bound in chains of silence, which the fair,
> Tho' eloquent themselves, yet fear to break :

* See Essay by H. L. Tuckerman.

What is it but a map of busy life,
Its fluctuations, and its vast concerns ?
Here runs the mountainous and craggy ridge
That tempts *Ambition.*   On the summit see
The seals of office glitter in his eyes ;
He climbs, he pants, he grasps them !   At his heels—
Close at his heels, a demagogue ascends,
And with a dexterous jerk soon twists him down,
And wins them, but to lose them in his turn.
Here rills of oily eloquence in soft
Meanders lubricate the course they take :
The modest speaker is ashamed and grieved
To engross a moment's notice ; and yet begs,
Begs a propitious ear for his poor thoughts,
However trivial all that he conceives.
Sweet bashfulness ! it claims at least this praise :
The dearth of information and good sense,
That it foretells us, always comes to pass.
Cataracts of declamation thunder here ;
There forests of no meaning spread the page,
In which all comprehension wanders lost :
While fields of pleasantry amuse in these
With merry descants on a nation's woes.
The rest appears a wilderness of strange
But gay confusion ; roses for the cheeks,
And lilies for the brows of faded age,
Teeth for the toothless, ringlets for the bald,
Heaven, earth and ocean, plundered of their sweets—
Nectareous essences, Olympian dews,
Sermons, and city feasts, and favorite airs,
Ethereal journeys, submarine exploits,
And Katerfelto, with his hair on end
At his own wonders, wondering for his bread.

Loquacious as we have been—many as are the marvels which have passed under our notice, we have not yet
2*

stepped out of our own dwelling. Our catalogue must somewhere find a limit. But should you take the hand of your child on his way to school, perhaps you might be thinking that philosophies which centuries ago were as lofty and remote as the clouds, are now dripping in rain and dew, producing fruits and food. When you receive your letters from the post-office, if not too much pressed and worried with affairs, perhaps you might bestow a thought upon this cheap wonder, than which nothing is more amazing to uncivilized man—the thinkings of other minds, the affections of other hearts made portable by means of paper and pen, and packed away in leathern pouches, to talk in lieu of the absent and remote ; or, if business should take you of a sudden to a neighboring State, do not accomplish your hundred miles and back before your evening meal without observing that what was once described as the wildest freak of fancy in the Arabian Nights Entertainments, has actually come to pass ; for if I remember the dream aright, it was but to seat yourself upon a certain mechanical horse, and pull a plug, and away you were transported through the air with the velocity of the wind.

But the greatest blessing and wonder of all is reserved for the latest mention. Before you left your dwelling this morning you opened a book—a veritable book, with pages and covers, paper and type—a book, haloed round about, if it was an old family copy, with a thousand domestic memories, and within inscribed all over with the lessons of celestial truth. The God who made us has so condensed and concentrated therein all his wisdom, and all his love, that it was needful to make but one book, and that one he calls *the* Book—the Bible. That book, for the preparation of which the Spirit who brooded over the great deep to form this world of order and brightness hath moved the minds of holy men, guiding and inspiring their diamond pens ; that book which has been transcribed with slow and consummate care by cloistered men, counting every word and syllable and letter, as if each were a royal jewel ; that book, which in ancient times was esteemed so rare and costly, that for a single copy men bartered away their castles and their herds, but which is now so cheap and common, that it is multiplied and scattered about, thick as the " leaves of Vallambrosa ; " that book which despotism has tried to kill, tearing, burning, burying it, but which, like the milk-white hind of the fable, has come out pure and brave from blood and fire and battle, carrying in its train all the light and liberty and hope of the world ; that book which, like a chart, lays down your safe and happy course, day by day, furnishing you with all the wisdom you need for this life, and all the promises for the life to come ; which inspires hope, pardons sin, comforts sorrow, diffuses light, invigorates toil, prompts to duty, illuminates the grave, and points to immortality ; this one incomprehensible gift of God, wondrous as if it were given us to-day, fresh and sparkling with the dews and fragrance of heaven; precious beyond gold and rubies, rich and costly enough in itself to wake the thanksgivings of the world ; this book lies in every room of your dwelling, and more is it for us than if an angel sat in our chamber, and walked at our sides, to direct us in the way. That book, which pours its light alike into the rich man's mansion, the poor man's cottage, the arches of the cathedral, the cloisters of great monasteries, and the pauper's attic; if there had been but one man on the earth who possessed it, how would the world's population encircle him with wonder and envy! You have read it to your children, that you might catch the key-note of an endless thanksgiving. We have begun with the commonest, the cheapest blessings of our existence, and from waking in the morning, with light and air, and food and raiment, and health and reason, and soundness of limb and sense, with home and speech and friends, and blessings innumerable, our feet, ere we have stepped out into the great world, crowded with benefits, public, political, and national, have touched that bridge of Christian Revelation, which connects the humblest habitation on the earth with the palace of the Great King, resplendent with light, and resounding with the anthems of praise. Why is it that, with so much given, whatever be withheld— with so much spared, whatever be withdrawn, perpetual thanks are not exhaling from our hearts? Why do we not go bounding along the undulating surface of life, duty, trial, care, privilege, with joys playing through us like a sparkling sea? "Bless the Lord, O my soul, and all that is within me, bless his holy name."

EXUBERANT GOODNESS.

καθ' ὑπερβολὴν εἰς ὑπερβολήν.—ST. PAUL.

2 Cor. iv. 17.

II.

EXUBERANT GOODNESS.

In the eighth chapter of the Book of Proverbs we
have a most lively personification of Wisdom. The
poetry of all languages furnishes nothing more spirited
or pleasing. Before the mountains were settled, and the
hills brought forth ; when there were no fountains and no
depths ; when as yet the earth and the fields and the
firmament were not ; "then," says Wisdom, "I was with
the Almighty as one brought up with him ; and I was
daily his delight, rejoicing always before him. Rejoicing
in the habitable part of the earth, and my delights were
with the sons of men." In this most animated description there is one sentiment too beautiful to lie concealed
in an imperfect translation. It occurs in that word which
represents Wisdom as *rejoicing* in the presence of the
Creator and throughout the world which he has made.
In the original the image is that of a child playing in excess of glee and sportiveness, in the company of its own
parent. That is the word—playing ! Some translators,
aiming at great exactness, have rendered it " dancing,"
and " laughing ;" but the authors of our English version,
deeming the literal translation unsuited to the dignity of
the personification, have contented themselves with the

more quiet word—*rejoicing;* but the image which the word presents is that of a child, the object of parental delight, leaping and running in exuberance of spirits, unable to express all its overflowing pleasure. And this is the figure which represents the creative power by which the world was made; the pleasure of the Almighty when he swept the graceful curves of the globe, sloped the swell of the hills, wove the tresses of the woods, and gave to the sea its easy swing. This is the form which descends also to the habitable parts of the earth, as if it could not find room enough for its illimitable delights, playing—we must retain the word—like the sweet-flowings of the air all over the world it would bless, and making expressions, in every way, of its own boundless pleasure. The only living and true God is not like Brahma, cold, indifferent, and passionless, sleeping upon the stars; the ocean is not so full of currents as is the heart of our Maker with delight, in the contemplation of his own works.

Dr. Paley has constructed an admirable argument in proof of the goodness of God, from the evident design of what he has made. Excellent for its own purposes as the treatise is, its only defect is that it is set to a key too low. It is necessarily scholastic, and, to a certain degree, frigid. It might have had more of poetic fervor without impairing its logic, or diluting its sound and wholesome sense. The lenses of the eye and the articulations of the bones furnish, indeed, a resistless proof of the Divine goodness; but mere utility does not describe the principles on which the Almighty has employed his creative skill. Delight was in his own mind, and how much has he done to confer delight upon others. He has trans-

cended all the conditions of a bare and frigid necessity.
Ten thousand things has he made, ten thousand things
has he given, which were never necessary at all, the expressions of his own superabundance, and the proof that he
seeks our special pleasure. The genius of Jeremy Taylor,
exuberant as a vine spreading all over the courts of the
Lord, was better suited to discourse on such a theme than
was William Paley, even though the excellent Dean was
the embodiment of all cheerfulness and good humor.

Mr. Carlyle has somewhere said, that a man should
put himself at zero, and then reckon every degree ascending from that point as an occasion for thanks. Precisely
on this scale do the Scriptures compute our mercies.
Demerit places us at the very nadir. Every step we take
from the point where conscious unworthiness would
consign us, should call for an offering of gratitude, whatever envied heights may tower, unreached, above us.
" It is of the Lord's mercies that we are not consumed."
" Why should a *living* man complain ? " So begins the
anthem of thanks, at its lowest note of all, " We are
alive—we are not consumed." We are all of us far, far
above the extremest point ; therefore, let each, from the
place where he stands, strike in with his own melody, till
the accumulated song rises higher and higher, like the
lark circling towards the skies. " Bless the Lord, O my
soul, who forgiveth all thine iniquities, who healeth all thy
diseases, who redeemeth thy life from destruction, who
satisfieth thy mouth with good things, who crowneth thee
with loving-kindness and tender mercies."

Standing on the very lowest conditions of contentment, in possession of life, food, and raiment, every rea-

son have we for gratitude ; how much more when we consider the acts of God's goodness which are OVER AND
ABOVE all that is necessary, designed solely and expressly
for our pleasure.

The point to which we look, is not so much the pleasure which God enjoys in the exercise of his own powers,
the expression of his own goodness ; though this were a
noble theme by itself. Great delights must have thrilled
the heart of Raphael when he had finished his immortal
picture of the Transfiguration ; Canova and Thorwaldsen
must have felt a joy beyond all the pleasures of sense,
when they had brought out from the marble block the
statues of the great and good : but this satisfaction was
as a drop to the sea, compared to the delight of God
when he created such minds as Milton and Newton and
Pascal and Fénélon and Melanchthon and Herbert, or
when he made manifestation of himself in the gospel
of Jesus Christ, waking the harmonies of the skies,
sweeter and louder than on the morning of creation.
This would be a glorious theme by itself, and useful
withal, since it would correct the theology of those who
misunderstand the saying that God made all things for
his own glory, as if that were ignoble, forgetting that
what is the vanity of display in man, in God is but the expression of Infinite Love, and the pleasure which attends
its exercise.

This, however, is not our theme just now, so much as
its sister and counterpart—the manifold objects which God
has made for our pleasure merely, above all the demands
of necessity. The goodness of a parent is justified when
he provides all that is useful and indispensable for his

child ; but how many things he bestows upon that child, for his special gratification, which are not needful at all. If we set out upon this course of thought, language will confess its inadequacy to measure the "miracles of this infinity." "The little drops which run over, though they be not much in themselves, yet they tell that the vessel is full, and can express the greatness of the shower no otherwise but by spilling, and in artificial expressions and runnings over."* Our cup runneth over. Sometimes we fall into depression, when we can hardly see that anything good remaineth ; we travel from Dan to Beersheba and say that it is all barren, but if we only had an eye to discern what is good and beautiful, we should be astonished at the exuberance and profusion with which our Maker has furnished and decorated the world we live in. There are some people, good in their way, who never hear the word " *beauty* " without a revulsion, and *taste* is something to be looked upon with suspicion. It is, indeed, greatly to be lamented that beauty and taste have so often been perverted by irreligious associations ; but did it never occur to persons of such a temper to wonder why God has lavished such profuseness of beauty in all his works ? He has not left the walls and the rafters of the earth bare and sightless, but has decorated them all over with divine skill, and the attributes of our Maker seem not to have reached the region of highest joy till, passing the rugged acts of necessity, they disport in the free play of affluent generosity.

Let us not imitate Baillie Jarvie, who could not look upon a sparkling lake without pronouncing it a pity that

* Jeremy Taylor.

so much good soil should lie useless under the water; who never could see a wood, without computing how much lumber it would make; or a moss-covered rock, without forecasting how much building stone it would turn out; or a cataract like Terni or Niagara, without satisfying himself how much water-power it would supply for manufacturing. It is scarcely credible how few people, even in what are called the educated classes, enjoy anything. A recent writer in the London Quarterly tells the story of Lord Melbourne and a young guardsman going with some ladies to an entertainment. Next day the guardsman complained that the evening had been stupid, and that there had been nothing to see. " Nothing to see !" exclaimed the good-tempered nobleman. "Were there not the lobsters in the fish-shops to look at as we went along?" Melbourne was one of the few men who *knew how to enjoy;* and if every man would only educate his eye to discern beauty in common objects, and when he had detected it would take his wife and children to see it too, this world would be very different from what it now is.

There are the *flowers*, wee things, clad in glory which shames the robes and regalia of kings. There was no *necessity* for their brilliant beauties, or their luxurious perfume; but God has scattered them with a liberal hand all over the earth, precisely as you hang a gem on the person of your child, simply and solely for her special gratification.

God might have made the earth bring forth
  Enough for great and small,
The oak-tree and the cedar-tree,
  Without a flower at all.

> We might have had enough, enough
>   For every want of ours,
> For luxury, medicine and toil,
>   And yet have had no flowers.
>
> The ore within the mountain mine
>   Requireth none to grow,
> Nor doth it need the lotus-flower
>   To make the river flow.
>
> The clouds might give abundant rain,
>   The nightly dews might fall,
> And the herb which keepeth life in man
>   Might yet have drunk them all.
>
> Then wherefore, wherefore, were they made,
>   All dyed with rainbow-light,
> All fashioned with supremest grace,
>   Upspringing day and night :
>
> Springing in valleys green and low,
>   And on the mountains high,
> And in the silent wilderness
>   Where no man passes by ?
>
> Our outward life requires them not—
>   Then wherefore had they birth ?
> To minister delight to man,
>   To *beautify* the earth."

Distrust and despondency there cannot be, when one has taught his eye to read the beautiful lesson of the flowers ; for thus it runneth: " He that careth enough for me to bestow such inimitable luxuries, surely will not withhold what is absolutely necessary."

So of the *fruits*, so pleasant to the eye and to the taste. God might have withheld them all, and yet no imputation be cast upon his generosity. The commonest esculent necessary for subsistence cannot grow without its blossom; as if beauty invariably waited on utility. The homely potato cannot begin its under-ground usefulness till it has sent up into the air a flower of delicate hue, to promise its coming; and the corn hangs out its tassels of softest silk, and when the southwest wind plays through its tresses and banners, they wave and flaunt as if they had delight in the grace of motion. But when all the sober and honest vegetables and grains which we are accustomed to regard as the necessaries of life are bestowed, above and beyond them all are the *fruits*, which, for the delight they afford our every sense, must be esteemed as designed to afford us a special pleasure. How grateful to the eye in their varied forms and colors, hanging from the vine, pendent on the tree, half hid in the leafy shrub, cluster, berry, pulp, juice; red, golden, russet, scarlet, and all the shades between, as if all the colors of the sky and all the sweetness of the earth had agreed together to fashion something which could tell the child of God how much his Father delighted to please him.

Plainly enough the ear was constructed most curiously for the transmission of sound; and it might have subserved all the necessities of life without ever having caught one of those strains of music, one of those sobs of the sea, one of those plaintive cadences of the wind, which now diffuse through the sensitive frame the delicious sense of melody. The conformation of the organ, its cells and tubes and drum, would have attested the skill of our Maker as well, if it had served only to report those dull sounds which relate to needful work; but we begin to think of something more than skill, even of goodness playing in its own exuberance, when, as Milton writes in style suited to the theme, we are

> Lapped in soft Lydian airs
> Married to immortal verse,
> Such as the meeting soul may pierce,
> In notes, with many a winding bout
> Of linked sweetness long drawn out,
> With wanton heed and giddy cunning
> The melting voice thro' mazes running,
> Untwisting all the chains that tie
> The hidden soul of harmony.

He who can sing, or he who can feel the thrill of song, as Milton did at the organ, has an argument for God's superabundant goodness before which infidelity should flee away.

"Beasts and all cattle, creeping things and flying fowl," objects introduced by name in one of the sacred lyrics, are invited to join in the chorus of universal praise. All these might have met the ends and offices of their existence, according to any scheme of utilitarianism, even if they had been made to plod or sleep through a joyless existence; while in truth, the gambols of the whole animal creation are forever expressing how much of pleasure belongs to their lot. It is a morning in the spring, warm and sunny; the air is all alive with insects, sporting in jocund life, whose existence seems to us nothing but pleasure; and the birds—those teachers whom Christ has placed beside the lilies, whose brilliant plumage and graceful shapes often remind us of the flowers, endowed with life and motion—fairly shriek out their delight, as they skim and sail and shoot about, as if making fun of all the laws of nature. "The poppies and the corn-blades," as we read in Sir Philip Sydney's Defence of Poesy, "might chide the lark for flying so high, striving and straining after mere air, losing its time, and bringing back nothing but weary wings and an empty stomach," but her sweet voice and soaring wings belong to God, and she goes up circling higher and higher to pour out her jubilant song at the very gate of heaven ; and the " Bobolink," that jolly favorite of boyhood, would have performed its office as well in clearing the ground and trees of noxious grubs, if it had been unfurnished with those liquid notes which come trilling out of its throbbing throat, when seated on that slender top bough which is even now "tilting up and down with his effort in that last joyous cadenza."* See the lambs on the hill-side, walking up together so soberly, like a company of children making a business of play, and then of a sudden wheeling short about and scampering down so full of glee ; they would have supplied joints for your table, and fleeces for your coat, without that exuberant joy. The trout in the stream would subserve the use of man for food just as well if it had been made stiff and shapeless as a stick, instead of springing through the sparkling stream, in the fulness of elastic life ; and the brook itself could have turned a mill-wheel or watered a meadow, if it ran more straight and grave like an artificial canal, instead of winding about at its own sweet will, falling every now-and-then over the rocks, and, like a child, laughing at its own tumble, composing itself to a more decorous deportment, and tripping away among the grass with so many musical

* See L'Abri, by N. P. Willis.

murmurs. The clover might have been just as succulent for pasturage, if it had not been half so fair and fragrant as it now is ; and the sky might have served as well for a canopy, if it had been one cold, melancholy blue instead of an ever-shifting panorama of royal colors, with sun-rising and sun-setting of imperial splendors, and sparkling by night with all the glory of the stars. We begin now to comprehend why, in one of the Psalms, the sun and the moon, the waters and the stars of light, snow and hail, and wind and vapor, hills and trees, heights and depths, are summoned to the act of praising their Maker, for they all are but different expressions of God's exuberant delight.

He who discerns with a well-trained eye what abundance of beauty is in all the works of God, will acknowledge the method by which we may cultivate the art of being happy. *Playfulness of spirit* is an expression very likely to be misunderstood, because we put an ill sense into good words ; but the true idea denoted by this expression is grand and holy. The life of God is one of delight ; and man, with all his culture and attainments, falls short of his proper nature if he does not reach a positive pleasure. A disposition to find delight in all things is akin to high-toned religion. The beauty which pervades the works of God is but an image of the higher beauty of His moral kingdom, the harmonies and ravishments of that Redemption which reconciles man to a lost felicity. Man reaches the true life of the soul when, emerging from the necessary conditions of penitence, discipline, restraint, his heart plays freely and joyfully in the midst of all that is fair, and generous, and noble, and good. Humor is a gift of nature: it should be controlled and used, not destroyed. It is the oil of the machinery which otherwise would grate and wear. To be thoroughly trained and remain thoroughly natural, like a child, is the rare greatness of a man. He who knows how to enjoy, will find so much pleasure in the simplest and the commonest objects, that he will never feel the need of an artificial stimulus.

One argument against theatrical entertainments is, that they are *elaborate* imitations of nature. They are called the *play*, but in fact they are a toil. Of pomps and masquerades Goldsmith has well said that

> —— toiling pleasure sickens into pain,
> And e'en while fashion's brightest arts decoy,
> The heart, distrusting, asks if this be joy?

There is something incongruous in the idea of playing to fulfil a contract; of working up the spirits by an artificial process for which one must pay as for services rendered. Play must be simple and natural, and if we paid more attention to those innocent instincts with which Creative Wisdom has endowed us; if tastes were simpler and pleasures less artificial, and our senses were quicker to catch the beauties which God has created so profusely, there would be far less difficulty than has been imagined in the attempt to reconcile true pleasure and religious obligations.

Home is the proper centre of all innocent delights; and that man is vastly to be pitied who has any pleasures greater than those which meet him in his own dwelling—that play-ground of the affections. What a power has she who presides over the abode, the minister of its beautiful tastes, whose office it is to make us good by means of our pleasures! What profound wisdom, dressed in poetic form, in the advice of old Roger Ascham to Lady Jane Grey, concerning her husband—"Do thou talk with him, ride with him, play with him, be his fairy, his page, his every thing that love and poetry have invented; but watch him well, sport with his fancies, turn them about like the ringlets on his cheeks, and if he ever meditate on power or ambition, go toss thy baby to his brow, and bring back his thoughts into his heart by the music of thy discourse."

The Puritans—it would be hard to discuss such a subject without lugging them in—have been accused of being unnaturally severe and stern, and implacably hostile to all that was playful and beautiful. Those who make this charge invariably overlook the one main fact of their history. The struggle in which they were engaged, being for the right of personal liberty, they were compelled, by the necessities of their case, to suppress and crucify many an innocent and educated taste, for the very purpose of showing their proud defiance of despotism. When that lubberly fellow, King James, issued his royal commands, requiring Christian men to frequent Bear Gardens on the Sabbath, and obey the "Book of Sports," be not so shallow as to impute it to hypocrisy, when such men drew their faces into extraordinary length and gravity, and with a good will and purpose gave a nasal twang to conventicle hymns; for their object was, by the boldest contrast, to express their resolute antagonism to tyranny. You would have done the same, even if you, like some of them, had been bred in the best universities, in the finest culture.   You would have sacrificed your best tastes, as Jephtha did his own daughter, had it been necessary to defy the enemies of liberty.   If despotic power prescribed something else, you too would do as did they —offensive as it was to taste—call your own fair daughters by the uncouth names of PATIENCE, PERSEVERANCE, EFFECTUAL CALLING, and GREAT TRIBULATION—your purpose, like theirs, being to show in the face of courts and cavalier frivolity, and royal enactments, that they gave no secondary place to religious liberty.   The struggle ended, it was needful that nature should have its way, and reassert its rights.   The sun will shine on the snows of winter, and throw its rays into the densest forests.   Even so the long suppressed tastes for the playful and beautiful, which belong to our nature, gleam every now-and-then through the rigid severity of Puritan character.

A good part of those feats which were ascribed to witchcraft in Massachusetts can be accounted for without the necessity of imagining any supernatural agency.   It would be nothing extraordinary if aged men and women, of uncommon gravity, should complain of the sensation of pins sticking into their flesh, and unaccountable noises rumbling in the chimneys, if boyish spirits were again put under the pressure of a forced and unnatural seriousness. The fountains of nature, repressed in one place, will break out in another.   Instead of destroying by violence, or exciting by toilsome stimulants, it is better to guide our impulses into the channels of a more quiet and simple, yet real enjoyment.

When we have recalled what God has given us in excess of all necessity, for the purpose of pleasing us, let us remember that we have taken but the first and lowest step leading up to a vast and glorious subject. If God has done so much for us here on the earth, what will he not do for us hereafter in heaven? If God is so generous now, what will he be in the world to come? The eye looks forth upon the streams and meadows and trees, and up to the skies, all so full of beauty, and reports that these material images are employed to describe that better country which is reserved as our eternal home. That heavenly world is not described in the dull lines of didactic prose. All the pleasant things in the universe are made to complete the promise of that ultimate enjoyment. Now is it a landscape—green pastures, still waters, the tree of life with leaf and fruit—every image of contentment and delight. Now rises an imperial city—its gates of pearl, its foundations of precious stones, its streets of gold, and all the nations pouring their glory into it. Now is it our Father's house with many mansions; a festive board, with unmeasured plenty; with songs of joy, and garlands of gladness upon the head. The true end of existence is "FULNESS OF JOY," and "RIVERS OF PLEASURE" at the right hand of God.

HOME.

For there is a yearly sacrifice there for all the family.

1 Sam. 20 : 6

III.

H O M E .

ABSENT, on a certain occasion, from the table of Saul, and knowing that his absence would be noticed and misrepresented by the jealous king, David directed his friend Jonathan to say, when inquiry was made for him, that he had gone down to Bethlehem to a family gathering. " For there is a yearly sacrifice there for all the family."

It would appear from this that there existed in the family of Jesse a time-honored custom of observing a yearly festival, when all the children met in their father's house. Though mention is not made of the fact, we are led to infer that at this time Jesse, the father, was dead ; for it is recorded of him, in a previous chapter, that he went among men for an old man in the days of Saul ; and subsequently, when Saul saw that David's place was empty, and passionately demanded the reason of his absence, Jonathan answered, " David earnestly asked leave of me to go to Bethlehem, and he said—Let me go, I pray thee, for our family hath a sacrifice in the city, and my *brother* (he saith not his father), he hath commanded me to be there ; and now, if I have found favor in thine eyes, let me get away, I pray thee, and see my brother."

3*

Though their father and mother were in the grave, yet so long-established was this usage of an annual gathering, that the scattered children were summoned by the eldest son to meet at the accustomed time, in the old cottage in which they were born, to celebrate their domestic festival.

Among the many associations connected with the day of Thanksgiving, none are more vivid or delightful than those which are attached to it as a season for gathering together family connections, and drawing closer again the many hearts which the separate interests of life are continually tending to divide. Such occasions exert a most beneficial effect upon the character, and are indeed absolutely necessary to counteract the chilling influences of a frosty world. It is a beautiful coincidence, which, by insensible affinities, from remote generations, has led those with whom this day has been most generally observed, to make the season of joyful Thanksgiving to the common Father of us all the occasion of uniting friends and kindred, quickening every fond association, and kindling every affectionate sympathy.

So it has occurred that the very season of the year which has invariably been consecrated to this observance, has its appropriate influences to deepen the flow of domestic delights. When the earth is decked in its embroidered robes of green and gold—when the trees are decorated with blossoms or richer fruits—when the birds are blithesome, and the air is all balmy and serene—then are we attracted abroad. But when the birds have fled to a warmer clime, and the frost has locked up the streams, and the trees are bare of their foliage, and the harvests are garnered, and the fields are shrouded with the snows of winter—then the affections come home for food and shelter, and from the nakedness and cold of the world without, we seek a covert at our own altars, and find our delights in the warm sympathies of domestic life.

> " O Winter ! ruler of the inverted year,
>   I love thee, all unlovely as thou seem'st,
>   And dreaded as thou art.
>   I crown thee king of intimate delights,
>   Fireside enjoyments, home-born happiness,
>   And all other comforts that the lowly roof
>   Of undisturbed retirement ever knew."

In quiet times we drop upon a quiet theme—home and its many blessings—as the occasion of devout thanksgivings to Almighty God.   But what shall I say?   When our hearts are full of joy and good-will at the remembrance of home ; when we reflect upon the nature of our enjoyments abroad, and cast them up and find them so few, and then turn home again, and see that its pleasures are countless, it may be thought that we could speak and write of them without ceasing. But it is not so. " Though the feeling of home never wearies, because kind offices, and the thousand little ways in which home attachments are always uttering themselves keep it fresh and full in its course ; yet the feeling itself, and that which feeds it, have a simplicity and unity of character of which little is to be told, though they are always with us." *   Like the light and air of Heaven are these domestic influences : so accustomed are we to their daily presence, that we pause not to pronounce upon their vital necessity.

* Richard H. Dana.

"Truly, the light is sweet, and a pleasant thing it is for the eyes to behold the sun"—but so constant and invariable are those cheering influences of day, that the most of men would first be reminded of their value by the consternation which would follow their total withdrawal. Born amid the affections of a Christian home, nurtured under its gentle dews and blessings, we go out and come in, lie down and rise up, but seldom recounting in distinct reflection our unspeakable obligations for such a grateful retreat. We say a Christian home; for it is Christianity alone which enriches home, with its virtues and endearments. Home is something more than a house in which to live, a place in which to be lodged and sheltered and fed; it is the sanctuary and seminary of the affections; and nowhere on earth can you find a place which deserves the name, or the praise we give it, save where the religion of Christ, by its direct or indirect influence, has nurtured into life those affections which give to home all its substantial value. The heathen are "without natural affection," and surely it is no small occasion for thanksgiving to God, that the lot of life has fallen to us in a place wherein those kindly instincts and feelings of our nature, to which Paganism does rude violence, are protected, fostered, and strengthened by the gentle spirit of a pure religion.

There is a great variety in our household affections. Each has its separate beauty, all harmonizing in simple unity, as the primary colors, each distinct, blend together to form the brilliant light of heaven. We must apply the prism to the heart, and discover of what curious sympathies it is compounded.

The love of a father for a child—what singular com-
binations enter into its composition !   Analyze, if you can,
his great emotions, when, for the first time, he feels his
first-born's breath.   Gladness he had felt before ; but
new joys play through his soul like a sparkling sea, and
" the concealed treasures of the deep " are not so great as
the comforts that unfold themselves in this new affection.
Scarcely is the first emotion of gratitude expressed, when
sadness gives a tinge to his love, for he is full of awe,
beholding how he stands related to an immortal spirit.
Reverence is not a quality of filial love only ; it belongs
also to the descending affection of a parent for a child,
who, strong man that he is, trembles at the thought
that the shadow of his own earthly self must pass over
the pure mirror of that unclouded mind.   Pity, too, is an
ingredient in the novel compound, for there is an uneasy
sense that the being so weak and dependent will be exposed to a thousand ills from which it can be protected
by no human arm.   Pride, too—shall I call it ? yes, if we
can conceive of a permitted feeling under this name
which has no alliance with the meanness of sin. Name it
rather the high pleasure which a parent feels, either in
anticipating or beholding the success or goodness of a
son, on whom concentrate all his hopes—the reduplication of himself, for whom and in whom he lives ; all this
enters as another element into that strong love which imparts an impulse and a glow to his whole life.   " Call
not that man wretched," says Mr. Coleridge, " who, whatever he suffers as to pain inflicted, pleasures denied, has
a child for whom he hopes, and on whom he dotes.
Poverty may grind him to the dust, obscurity may cast

its darkest mantle over him, the song of the gay may be far from his own dwelling, his face may be unknown to his neighbors, and his voice may be unheard by those among whom he dwells—even pain may rack his joints, and sleep may flee from his pillow; but he has a gem with which he would not part for wealth defying computation, for fame filling a world's ear, for the luxury of the highest health, or the sweetest sleep that ever sat upon a mortal's eye."

In the love of a father for his children there is some measure of reserve, as if the full expression of it all were allied to weakness. There is, withal, too much of the world about it. It is subject to great ebbings, impatient and indignant at the misconduct of its objects. But the love of a mother for her offspring knows no such exceptions. First of all, she gives her own life in proffered exchange for the life of her child—going within the precincts of death to purchase the priceless treasure, and ever after holding her own life as nothing in comparison with the welfare of her offspring. The full and vehement expression of her love, instead of being counted in her a weakness, is her very life and glory. Blind to every defect of the person, to her eye there is a beauty in her own child which works like a spell, and, fully apprised of each defect of the character, there is a fulness of affection which survives it all. That child may be wayward and incorrigible; he may practise every crime, so that the world may justly count him a pest and a nuisance, and by all this he may even break the heart of her who bare him; but, oh! he cannot, even then, destroy the love which that fond heart contained.

The perfume of partial affection will forever linger among the scattered pieces of the shattered vessel. What the world casts out as worthless, she will pity and love to the last—forgiving when the world only censures, and when the grave hides from her sight the miserable victim of vice, she shall sigh and weep, refusing to be comforted because he is not. " Can a woman forget her child, that she should not have compassion on the son of her womb ? " Oh, what were this world to us, in the absence of her love, who has been more than all the world to us—so gentle, so hopeful, so constant, so changeless !

Then the love of children for their parents has its own separate qualities. As parents are not dependent upon their infant children, but children upon their parents, the economy of nature makes it necessary that the love which descends to the helpless should be stronger than the love which ascends to the helper. Filial affection, beyond the simple impulses of instinct, is of slow growth. There are many weeds of waywardness, and heedlessness, and wilfulness, which hide its early beauty, and it does not attain its full development till later years. It is an affection which increases the older we grow. Never can we appreciate our parents' love for us till we become parents ourselves; and one of the first impulses which we feel on arriving at this relation is to hasten home, if our parents still survive, to make some new expression of our gratitude and love for them ; and the longer we live the more the feeling grows upon us, as if we wished to atone for our youthful impatience by a more just and grateful conduct. But even in childhood, what a simple grace do we see in filial love—the compound of gratitude, reverence, and trust. The confidence of others may be won by slow degrees, but an affectionate child knows that its own parents are to be trusted with all the heart. They, as it were, put in the place of God, are the first objects of love, the first of faith. The first deep thought sealed on the infant's mind, when most susceptible and all untouched by other impressions, is the idea of parental care ; the image of two faces, beaming with benignity, grows into the very texture of the soul , and when other and more superficial impressions fade away, and the outward accretions about the heart fall off, the first deep picture becomes more distinct, so that we incline to think and speak the more of our parents' virtues, twining the image of those revered forms with garlands of graces and beauties and excellences, rehearsing them to our children and children's children as our highest boast and glory.

The relation between brothers and sisters has also its own distinct characteristics. Independent existences, yet similarly related to the same stock ; nourished at the same fountain of life, sleeping on the same pillow, fed at the same table—their sympathies and affections become all intertwined and inseparable, like the branches of the vine on the side of their dwelling. One peculiarity is there in this relation—that it never can be thought of without calling to mind the common home and parentage in which it originated ; and this becomes the guarantee of its continued warmth and vigor. But for this common centre, it would inevitably happen that, as the independent relations of each multiplied and extended, the several branches in course of time would be

pushed off into entire estrangement. As there is a quality of manliness in the love of a brother, so there is a
gentle beauty in the affection of a sister. Cast in a finer
mould, endowed with a nicer sense of the proper and the
delicate, her influence begins, over her associates of the
rougher sex, even in the nursery. Entering into a complete companionship of feeling, she speaks with such a
soothing voice, and moves about with such a quiet grace,
that she insensibly assimilates to herself the future man,
who is now her constant associate ; and blessed is he
who has been favored by such gentle sympathies. Pity a
man who has no sister.

So much has been written in sonnets and romances
of the love between husband and wife, that many are
tempted to think that the affection exists only as a poetical fiction or fancy. It is indeed a mystery, that two
beings, born and bred at remote points, in entire ignorance of each other's existence, should, in after-years, be
brought into such a close companionship, and should
attain to such absolute confidence, such an identity of
interests, so completely harmonizing into one life, as to
be the symbol which the Son of God has chosen to shadow forth his own love for his espoused Church. Infidelity may scoff at the tie, and vice stand abashed before its sanctity; but every heart that is right and true
will be thankful to God for that relic of Paradise, which,
surviving the general wreck and ruin of the apostasy, has
secured to us the sacred companionship which, softening
the asperities of life, helps our better purposes by means
of our domestic pleasures.

There is a special beauty in the relation between

grandparents and their descendants.   The young of ani
mals, so soon as they cease to be dependent on their
dam, forgetful of all affection, mix and mingle with the
common herd.   But the love of a human parent for his
offspring, instead of fading away, travels down and spreads
out with a peculiar tenderness on children's children.
Those far advanced in years would not fear, as they
often do, that they have survived their usefulness, if
they reflected how much of good they accomplish by
being the object of respect, reverence, and love, to the
young.   The thrifty vine is never so beautiful as when it
twines itself around the old oak, as if it would bind up
its shattered branches and tenderly conceal the ravages
of time.

These are the affections which combine to form the
glowing lights of home.   And shall we not be thankful
to God for these transcendent delights of domestic life ;
for the happiness of parents and children, husbands and
wives, brethren and sisters?   This is a source of pleasure
which depends not at all on adventitious distinctions.   It
belongs to the humble poor, as well as to the more ele-
vated in fortune, in equal, and oftentimes in larger, measure.   Adversity has no power to extinguish these home-
bred comforts ; for its roughest blasts, while they put
out all the lesser lights which flicker around us, serve
always to blow the larger affections to a brighter flame.
This serene satisfaction cheers the cottages of the poor—
lightening the weary burden of toilsome iife, while it or-
naments the mansions of the rich above all the costly
fabrics of art.   In many an unpretending abode of rural
contentment, sheltered among the hills, may you find the

reality of the peaceful picture which Inspiration has sketched for our admiration—" whose sons are as plants grown up in their youth ; whose daughters are as cornerstones, polished after the similitude of a palace ; whose garners are full, affording all manner of store, where there is no breaking in, nor going out; within whose walls there is no complaining "—and from our hearts do we join in the exclamation, "Happy, yea, happy is that people that is in such a case."

To the beneficent influence of Christianity are we indebted, not only for the refinement and enlivenment of our domestic affections, but also for the security of the abode in which they grow. Home is neither an open bower nor a barricaded castle, yet it is our own vine and fig-tree, beneath which we repose, with none to molest us or make us afraid. Here is nurtured that sense of independence in the individual man, which, but for this safe retreat, would be trampled down by the huge herds of a crowded world. Each native peculiarity of character has here its space and quiet in which to grow. There is a sense of security which we feel when young, within the enclosure of home, which never comes back again to us in its full force. All this is needful to the development of a healthful mind and body. The tender child is spared the shock of care and apprehension. Its parents, invested to his eye with the perfections of divinity, seem to have the power of protecting him from harm. To such, death itself presents but little dread, for they feel as if their parents could shield them even from this ; and so, sheltered from anxiety and danger, in that secure retreat in which God hath planted them, they quietly grow up into life.   Though the illusions of childhood pass away, yet there is much of this very feeling which we retain with us to the last.   We go forth to toil and come home for rest; we could not survive the steady pressure of burdensome cares always, nor safely give up ourselves to the agitating passions of life ; so there has been provided for us a still and retired abode, in which we may throw off the weight, and by the play of gentler affections renew our jaded strength.   However the world may go with us, here is one pleasure always in reserve.   Whatever misfortunes may befall us elsewhere, here are those who share them with us.   Here the aching head is soothed, the broken heart bound up, and here it is, when life wanes, that we retire to die.   The heathen parent is buried alive by his own children, to rid themselves of the care of decrepit age, and the mother, unblessed by the Gospel, casts her infant child to the flood or the jackals.   But God has given us a home, not only to live in, but where we may die.   Here, surrounded by weeping children, the beloved parent breathes his last ; and here the child is attended by all the care and love which was the first influence it felt when born, and the very latest also when it dies, hovering with noiseless steps around the bed of unconscious suffering.   "May you die among your kindred," is the common form of Oriental salutation.

The thought has been variously expressed, as not the least among the high praises of a Christian home, that it is the place for forming a good character.   It is true in more senses than one.   We call ourselves the instructors of our children ; with less pretensions, they are our instructors also.   The nursery is the best school for men as well as for infants. Its playful inmates more than repay their teachers, by many an unconscious lesson. Jesus Christ took a little child, and placed him in the midst of his disciples, and said unto them, " Except ye become as little children, ye cannot see the kingdom of God." Would you learn simplicity of character—that great virtue—look in the " open face " of your child, and study the lesson. From the same sunny look, read the beauty of unaffected humility. Steal softly up to the corner where that busy child is employed in mock labor, erecting, out of his blocks or corn-cobs, a church, or barn, or schoolhouse, and listen to his sage talk, investing with life whatever he touches ; then mark the crimson which mantles his cheek on finding himself detected, and the confusion with which each fairy thought will hasten to its cover on being observed, and learn there that fine lesson of delicate and modest reserve, which you can learn nowhere else half so well. Go in the stillness of night into the chamber where your infant children lie in softest slumber, and there call to mind the innumerable forms of evil which beset them ; the sickness from which no care of yours can protect them ; the temptations from which no vigilance of yours can shield them ; then listen to the voice which comes from your own heart, as well as from heaven, " Commit thyself and thine helpless offspring unto the Watchman who never sleeps ;" and then kneel down in thanks to God, for the bestowal of a gift and a charge, which have involuntarily taught you how to pray.

" A family of children, walking amidst a thousand dangers and often escaping, is one of the most striking proofs of a particular Providence that ever met my mind. To talk about the general laws of nature, immutable and unbendable to the interposing will of Deity—away with such metaphysical trash! It is just fit for old bachelors to write. It is very unfortunate that some of the great geniuses who have undertaken to enlighten the world by their infidelity were not married men. It would have done more to help them to digest the venom of their spleen than all the long volumes of rejoinders which have been written by metaphysical theologians. It is generally to be noticed that infidelity and misanthropy have an affinity for each other, and are often combined in the same heart. But how is a man to avoid misanthropy? No man ever became a misanthrope under the smiles of an affectionate wife, and surrounded by a family of ruddy children. These are tender chains which connect us with the universe; they bind us in harmony with our species; they lead us to feel our need of a higher protector—to see the glory and the goodness, and therefore to believe in the existence, of God. God, when he built the world, designed to pack men together in families; and it is the only way in which you can throw the human species together, without impairing their principles and endangering their virtue. A man goes into a splendid city; he becomes too licentious, or too lazy, or too proud, to establish a family. He passes his time among the rubicund inmates of a fashionable boarding-house. He spends his evenings at the theatre or billiard-table. He rails at women, and hates children, because he only knows the vilest of the sex, and has never seen a child which was his own. His affections become warped, his heart is insulated; and because he has lost his humanity, he has never found his religion." *

A year rolls round, and it is fit that a family should meet together and recount their manifold blessings. Changes not a few may occur in a twelvemonth. Grateful acknowledgments should be made for God's protection and God's bounty. Are parents yet spared to bless you? they in the sear and yellow leaf of age, and you in your maturity? Count it a special favor that they are continued to you, at that period of your life when you are both able and disposed to appreciate the blessing. Now the pleasure is yours of honoring the hoary head, and ministering to those who lived only to minister to you. Remember that, however high and honored you may be before the world as men and women, to your parents you are nothing but children still; and bring to your yearly festival a heart thankful to them and to God. Have your children been spared to you for another year? It is wonderful, when you consider how thick about them are the dangers which threaten their life. Fail not to be thankful to Him who keeps the sparrow's children and yours.

It was a beautiful custom among the ancients to throw the gall of the nuptial sacrifices far behind the altar, as a sign and pledge that every bitterness should be excluded from the relation which was then consummated. Approaching the household altars, with an oblation of united thanks for personal and family blessings, let every bitter thought be banished from the sweet and sunny charities of the domestic sacrifice; and let every occasion—alas! but too few and infrequent are they—be improved to ce-

* Withington.

ment the relations we sustain to one another by means of a warm and special gratitude to our Father in heaven.

So it may be that the day, which to most is one of peculiar pleasure, to some is one of irresistible sadness; and the very words here written, instead of cheering, have only pierced their hearts with many a poignant pang. They remind them of happy scenes which have gone, never to be renewed. The old homestead, whither they were wont to go, has passed into the hands of strangers, and its former inmates are now in that narrow house where there are no greetings—and no welcomings. "The delights of which you have spoken," say these, "once were ours; but ours they are no longer." Recall the word. Scenes like these never fade—pleasure of this description can never die. What you have already felt and enjoyed can never be taken from you. It is yours still, and will be yours forever. You have an invisible property in these remembered delights which death itself cannot steal from you. The forms of your beloved parents may have mouldered back to dust; but their memory and their love can never decay. You cannot rid yourself of their influence; no wave of oblivion can wash out the fond recollection of all they were, and all they did. You are rich in these priceless memories and affections. You have treasures garnered up in the past which gold could not buy. The spiritual can never perish. It was the vir-tue, the affection of those remembered but now departed relatives alone which you loved; but death never can touch these immortal qualities of their life. Desolate, in-deed, would your heart be, if despoiled of all these cher-ished recollections. The mould may be broken up and thrown away, but the spiritual fabric which was cast therein never can be marred nor stolen ; and the product of those scenes and relations whose loss you so bitterly regret, lives in these grateful memories and kindly affections, which neither time nor bereavement can ever touch; and which, even now, are exerting their influence to make you better and happier. Count yourself, then, no more solitary ; for the dead still live—their voices, their smiles, their examples, their virtues, are still yours beyond the reach of vicissitude : and with them you will hold close sympathy until your own hearts crumble to dust.

Perhaps the shadow of a more recent bereavement is on you. Some seat at your table is vacant ; some bright and darling head, on which you were wont to put your hand with a blessing, is pillowed beneath the winter's snow. Surely, you will be thankful that religion has taught us how many mercies are mingled with our bereavements. When night comes, the different members of a family go to their separate apartments for sleep ; the morning soon unites them—and waking or sleeping they are one household still. So is your family separated for a season—a part are here, and a part are in the chambers of the tomb ; but the bond is not broken ; and soon the morning will come, when you shall meet again, face to face. The most important thing of all would have been omitted, had I failed to say that the best and greatest blessing which religion has conferred on a Christian home, is, in making the affections immortal. If we were all thrown together fortuitously, the companions of a brief moment, our true wisdom would be in moderating or even destroying those affections which would expose us to sorrow from the violence of their rupture. Far different is it when Christianity assures us that, beyond the narrow pass of death, our present fellowships are to be perpetuated in endless harmony. We meet around the home-hearth at the yearly sacrifice—and then plunge anew into life's dangers and cares; but hereafter we shall meet in our Father's house in Heaven, with welcomings and rejoicings that never shall cease. Who of us will not be thankful with such a prospect gilding his skies, and such a promise shining on his path?

We cannot close our chapter with any thing more fitting than the lines of Charles Sprague, on

THE FAMILY MEETING.

We are all here !
Father, mother,
Sister, brother,
All who hold each other dear.
Each chair is filled, we're all *at home*.
To-night, let no cold stranger come.
It is not often thus around
Our old familiar hearth we're found.
Bless then the meeting and the spot—
For once be every care forgot;
Let gentle peace assert her power,
And kind affection rule the hour ;
We're all, all here.

We're *not* all here !
Some are away—the dead ones dear,
Who thronged with us this ancient hearth,
And gave the hour of guiltless mirth.
Death, with a stern, relentless hand,
Looked in, and thinned our little band.

Some like a night-flash passed away—
And some sank, lingering, day by day.
The quiet grave-yard—some lie there,
And cruel ocean has his share.
　　　We're *not* all here !

　　　We *are* all here !
Even they—the dead—though dead, so dear.
Fond memory, to her duty true,
Brings back their faded forms to view.
How life-like through the mist of years
Each well-remembered face appears !
We see them as in times long past ;
From each to each kind looks are cast ;
We hear their words, their smiles behold—
They're round us as they were of old.
　　　We *are* all here.

　　　We are all here !
　　　Father, mother,
　　　Sister, brother,
You that I love with love so dear.
This may not long of us be said,
Soon must we join the gathered dead,
And by the hearth we now sit round
Some other circle will be found.
O then, that wisdom may we know,
That yields a life of peace below :
So, in the world to follow this,
May each repeat, in words of bliss,
　　　We're all, all *here.*

A CHEERFUL TEMPER.

He that is of a merry heart hath a continual feast.

PROV. 15 : 15.

A merry heart doeth good like a medicine.

PROV. 17 : 22.

IV.

A CHEERFUL TEMPER.

THE greatest boon of Providence is a disposition to
enjoy all things. Mr. Addison closes one of his essays
in the *Spectator* with these lines, adopted now into our
Sabbath hymns, and familiar to all who read the English
tongue :

> "Ten thousand thousand precious gifts
> My daily thanks employ;
> Nor is the least a cheerful heart,
> That tastes those gifts with joy."

Not the least! It is the whole. It is the mind itself
which colors all outward conditions ; and affluence of gifts
would leave one in misery if there were no interior disposition to cheerfulness. "He that is of a merry heart
hath a continual feast." Some nicety of discrimination
is necessary, if we could hit the exact meaning of the expression. Changes have occurred in the significancy of
words since our English version was made, which might
mislead the unthinking. Merriment most readily suggests the idea of conviviality and jollity. A "Merry
Andrew" excites boisterous laughter. We naturally as-

sociate with merriment the absence of the higher qualities, and, except in the case of children, with whom animal spirits arc an exuberant fountain of gaiety, we more generally connect it with artificial stimulants—the sparkling cup and the shout of high-sounding festivity. Instead of commending hilarity like this as a medicine, we have an impression that the Scriptures compare it to something else, which begins with an M—madness. Milton's *L'Allegro* was written when he was in the flush and buoyancy of youth, before the dark shadows of serious ills had passed over his eye and heart. It will always be admired as a proof of the sweet rhythm of the English tongue, while many of the images it embalms, of the morning lark, the cheery crowing of the cock, the ploughman whistling in the furrow, the mower whetting his scythe, the sweet-scented haycock, always give a sense of refreshment to a jaded spirit. But the nymph which he invokes, with

> Jest and youthful jollity,
> Quips and cranks and wanton wiles,
> Nods and becks and wreathed smiles,
> Such as hang on Hebe's cheek,
> And love to live in dimple sleek ;
> Sport that wrinkled care derides,
> And laughter holding both her sides,

was a Pagan goddess of mythological pedigree. There is a species of mirth which the highest authority has likened to the crackling of thorns under a pot—a light, flashing blaze, which produces a bubbling and boiling of waters, soon to subside into insipidity.

Collating the several passages in the Old and New Testaments, in which the word translated "merry" is used, we find no difficulty in ascertaining the precise intention of the word. "Is any among you merry? let him sing psalms," says the Apostle James. The word used is the very same which Paul employed when addressing the ship's company in danger of wreck—"Be of good cheer;"—circumstances suggesting the pertinency of bravery and hope, but forbidding any approach to hilarity. The Hebrew word used by Solomon is translated in the Septuagint by a synonym which is used elsewhere in the New Testament (1 Thess. iv. 11) to express quiet content; the same which Plutarch frequently employs in his essay on *Mental Tranquillity*. So that we are fortified by usage, scriptural and classical, in adopting this as the exact shade of thought—" A *cheerful* heart doeth good, like a medicine." The etymology of the word εὐθυμέω, be of good cheer, conveys a lesson—*well-minded, well-disposed*—for cheerfulness always has in it an element of goodness, while merriment may co-exist with folly and crime. When Milton describes the fallen angels, after the Stygian Council was dissolved, dispersing in various directions, some indulging in feats of strength and speed, with uproarious mirth; and when Death himself is represented by the same author as "grinning horribly a ghastly smile," it does not shock the taste; but had he described either as *cheerful*, radiant with smiling tranquillity, we should have felt the incongruity, for he is describing the dark forms of guilt and woe.

Let us mention a few more distinctions separating cheerfulness from other things with which it is often con-

4*

founded. It is not the same as wit; though a cheerful temper may show its play through wit, if this intellectual quality exist. "Foolish jesting" is condemned alike by good manners, taste, and Scripture. The quick associations of wit are of the intellect and not of the heart, and too frequently have they been associated with cruelty of disposition. Endeavoring to be witty is always weak and pitiable. That was sage advice which Dean Swift gave to a young clergyman: "I cannot forbear warning you," says he, "in the most earnest manner, against endeavoring at wit in your sermons, because, by the strictest computation, it is very near a million to one that you have none, and because too many of your profession have made themselves everlastingly ridiculous by attempting it." To which may be added, if the pulpit is ever the place for wit, never is it the place for levity. Though this intellectual gladiatorship of wit is often employed in the service of cruel satire and stinging sarcasm, yet it may be associated with more genial and kindly qualities. Should I say that there were a few cases in which the Apostle Paul has used the rapier-thrust of wit, I should not be understood by those who do not comprehend, through a translation, the sharp point of certain Greek words. The principle advocated by Shaftesbury, that "ridicule is a test of truth," cannot be conceded ; but if ever there was a book mighty in its wit, it is Bunyan's *Pilgrim's Progress.* The names of the streets in Vanity Fair ; of the judges, jury, and counsel in the trial of Faithful, excite a smile at the witty adroitness ; but it is a wit like the smooth beauty of the lightning, which demolishes what it hits.

So, again, cheerfulness is distinct from the sense of

the humorous, however acute it may be.   Humor is a sign of sensibility, of pathos, a deep, rich fount of feeling, even though it be sad; the very word signifies moisture, and, like April-weather, smiles and tears are mingled together in its composition.   The most grotesque images may be suggested and enjoyed by a sense of the humorous, when bodily and mental disease will not allow cheerfulness; of which Cowper was a remarkable instance.   The amusing description of John Gilpin, which the most sedate cannot read without laughing, was written, it is said, during one of the longest and gloomiest of those seasons of melancholy to which his sad life was subject—a streak of crimson and gold on the edge of the thunder-cloud.   Instances are well authenticated, in which actors on the stage, with the keenest perception of the humorous, by which they have convulsed houses in obstreperous mirth, have consulted physicians and clergymen for relief from a settled melancholy which was wasting their life.

Cheerfulness is not intellectual ability; it is not mere animal spirit; it is not the excitement of artificial stimulants; very distinct is it from jocularity and uproarious laughter.   It is the tranquil, hopeful, benign, blessed mood, which is rightly described as well-mindedness.   It is not a talent, but a disposition.   Making all allowance for diversities of constitution, it is a temper which is to be carefully and wisely cultivated.

The things affirmed of this cheerful heart, thus defined, are, that he who has it, has a continual feast, and that it doeth good like a medicine.   He who has a feast only on the last Thursday in November has a sad life. There is a daily festivity, which depends not on the quality of the fare with which the table is spread, whether it be a dinner of herbs or stalled ox, but always on those genial qualities of the heart which incline us, as we say, to look on the bright side, and to make the best of every thing. Strange that this disposition is not universal. But we come in contact with a most singular fact, which at first is not so easy of analysis, that people are intent on playing the miserable, as if there were a virtue in it. The real solution is, that it is an exhibition of selfishness ; for no one is habitually cheerful who does not think more of others than of himself. Multitudes appear to be studious of something which makes them unhappy ; for unhappiness excites attention, and attention is supposed to inspire interest, and interest compassion. You have seen a person of very robust and corpulent habit, so robust as ought to excite perpetual gratitude for joyous health, sometimes putting on the airs of an invalid, for no reason in the world but to draw out toward him some expression of affectionate concern, and so gratify his self-conceit. That very mood which in children is called naughtiness, in young people is dignified with the name of " low spirits," for which they are to be petted and pitied ; while in elderly people it is known as " nervousness," for which it is expected they should be humored to the full tension of mortal patience.

The first place for the festal and medicinal play of cheerfulness is home. The parent who does not practise it, loosens the strongest bond which draws children to virtue. Once make the impression that goodness is austere, and it has lost its charms for those who reach conclusions, not through reasoning, but the feelings.

Perhaps you can recall persons with whom you have been thrown into contact when you were young, who, in your present judgment, were good, very good, but in every way repulsive. You never associated them with sunshine. You felt that goodness had a strange tendency to make one unhappy. Some of the best men the world has seen have lived to regret just this thing—the want of habitual cheerfulness in the presence of their children. It may be taken as a postulate of the social system, that home should always be the most cheerful and attractive place on earth ; and whatever is expended to make it such, is expended wisely and economically. No man is qualified for the first offices of an educator, at home or elsewhere, who is not habitually cheerful. Reverence is an essential quality of character, but it is a mistake to exact it by gruff austerity. Nothing can be more grotesque, for example, than the enactments for respect which prevailed in some of our American colleges during the last century, when the wearing of a hat in the college-yard by a Freshman was interdicted by statute ; and the exact measure in rods was specified at which obeisance was to be made to that specimen of the *multum in parvo*—a college-officer. Respect, reverence, are not to be compelled by big wigs and elongated faces and assumed dignities ; they must be given to cheerful worth, as flowers open themselves to the sun. Grave mistakes were made in his home by that great metaphysician—of whom any family or any country might be proud —Jonathan Edwards. His biographer informs us that his children were not expected to keep their seats in his presence ; that he ate from a silver bowl, as one set apart for special reverence, and that his features seldom relaxed from the one expression of grave austerity. There is one, and, so far as I know, only one, passage in all his voluminous writings in which he dropped into a mirthful vein of argument in refuting an opponent. He is arguing that the doctrine of the Arminians concerning the will is an absurdity, and he writes as follows : " If some learned philosopher who had been abroad, in giving an account of the various observations he had made in his travels, should say he had been in Terra del Fuego, and there had seen an animal which he calls by a certain name, that begat and brought forth itself, and yet had a sire and a dam distinct from itself ; that it had an appetite, and was hungry before it had a being ; that his master, who led and governed him at his pleasure, was always govern-ed by him and driven by him wherever he pleased ; that when he moved, he always took a step before the first step ; that he went with his head first, and yet always went tail foremost, and this, though he had neither head nor tail, it would be no impudence to tell such a traveller that he himself had no idea of such an animal as he gave an account of, and never had, nor could have." I have often imagined what sort of an expression must have stolen across the thin, pale face of Jonathan Edwards when he wrote that most grotesque paragraph. It must have been somewhat like a sun-gleam in the solemn pine-woods of a New England winter.

If we speak of the mistakes of good and pious men, what shall we say by way of commending that sweet cheerfulness by which a good and sensible woman dif-fuses the oil of gladness in the proper sphere of home.

The best specimens of heroism in the world were never gazetted. They play their *rôle* in common life, and their reward is not in the admiration of spectators, but in the deep joy of their own conscious thoughts. It is easy for a housewife to make arrangements for an occasional feast. But let me tell you what is greater and better. Amid the weariness and cares of life ; the troubles, real and imaginary, of a family ; the many thoughts and toils which are requisite to make the family the home of thrift, order, and comfort ; the varieties of temper and cross-lines of tastes and inclination which are to be found in a large household—to maintain a heart full of good-nature, and a face always bright with cheerfulness, this is a perpetual festivity. I do not mean a mere superficial simper, which has no more character in it than the flow of a brook, but that exhaustless patience, and self-control, and kindness, and tact, which spring from good sense and brave purposes. Neither is it the mere reflection of prosperity—for cheerfulness then is no virtue. Its best exhibition is in the dark background of real adversity. Affairs assume a gloomy aspect—poverty is hovering about the door—sickness has already entered —days of hardship and nights of watching go slowly by, and now you see the triumphs of which I speak. When the strong man has bowed himself, and his brow is knit and creased, you will see how the whole life of a household seems to hang on the frailer form, which, with solicitudes of her own, passing, it may be, under the " sacred primal sorrow of her sex," has an eye and an ear for every one but herself ; suggestive of expedients, hopeful in extremities, helpful in kind words and affectionate smiles, morning, noon, and night, the medicine, the light, the heart, of a whole household. God bless that bright, sunny face, says many a heart, as he recalls the features of mother, wife, sister, daughter, which has been to him all that these words have described. Mr. Dickens has not been very fortunate in his portraiture of clergymen. If Mr. Chadband must stand as representative of the profession, we must say that the author has not been very happy in his circle of acquaintances. But as for his portraiture of kind-hearted, cheerful, brave women in humble life, he has certainly done the world a service ; for when the more stately forms of Shakspeare's imagination and the rollicksome or thoughtful heroines of Walter Scott are forgotten, lowly homes will be cheered with the picture of " Little Dot," diffusing an atmosphere of kindness so long as there is a cricket to sing on the hearth.

The first object of an intelligent physician is to inspire cheerful hope in his patient. This is better than drugs. And so the medicinal effect of cheerfulness is most apparent in times of peril and calamity. There are some who have an eye for nothing but evil, whose office it is to croak, till at length the mischief apprehended comes to pass. Indifference to danger is no sign of a Christian or a patriot. The very love we bear to the Church and to our country, renders us sensitive to any thing which threatens their peace and prosperity. But we ought never to despair of the fortunes of either. The best medicine in the worst times is a cheerful heart. Authentic records inform us, that in the seventeenth century our Puritan fathers enacted a law, requiring that any person who should thereafter be elected to the office of Governor, and would not serve, should pay a fine of twenty pounds sterling. What would the modest shades of Winslow and Bradford say to the habits of our times, when men scramble for office with an unconcealed ambition for spoils? Can any one doubt that one of our greatest perils is the greed of personal ambition? In Middleton's *Life of Cicero*, we have an account of the mirth which was occasioned at Rome, by the spectacle of a few Britons, dressed in their savage attire, led along in the military ovation decreed to their returning conqueror. What changes since then in Britain and Italy, as to the relations of barbarism and civilization! Wealth and power lead to luxury and enervation. This is the one lesson of history; and the most fatal influence which threatens our strength, is that increase of opulence which excites admiration, and fosters pride, while it may insidiously sap the foundations of our true life. Magnify and multiply all these occasions for alarm, as much as you will. What then? Shall we give up the ship? Shall we let every thing go by the board, and sit down in blank despair? Let us rather imitate that noble class of men who show the best qualities of our nature, on the deck of the ship, when the storm is at its worst, whose bravery, when driven from one expedient to another, inspires the timid with hope. Excitements do not imperil, provided the temper be right. When the temperature of an individual or a community is raised, every thing which belongs thereto comes out with the greater force; and the peril is always and only from that which is evil. Let there be nothing but what is humane and kind and good in our nature, and danger is not to be apprehended, even if we

be excited to a white heat. Reformers who have suc
ceeded the best in Church and State, were of a most
hearty cheerfulness.   In Luther it amounted very often to
jollity.   Old Samuel Adams, of Boston, was renowned as
much for his sonorous singing of hymns as for his patriotism.   Suppose that affairs should wax worse and
worse, never will they be mended by impatience, irritabil-
ity, and petulance.   " Fret not thyself," is an inspired
counsel for troublous times.   Have a good heart, and
do the best you can.   Trust in the Lord, and mischief
will be averted.   Reformations which cannot be accomplished by good temper, will not be brought about by ob-
jurgations and wrath.

How can a cheerful temper be acquired ?   Is not the
world evil, and are not occasions for uneasy fears innumerable ?   Differences in constitutional temperament are
very obvious.   Let all allowance be made for them.   We
speak of what pertains to personal culture, and here we
claim that cheerfulness must have a religious basis ; and
the first thing religion teaches is, the immensity of mercy
which has supervened upon demerit. True, sin has strick-
en the world, and a curse has followed upon sin. But this
is not the whole. God has dealt with us incomparably
above our deserts. As an old writer has expressed it :
" It was a rare mercy that we were allowed to live at all,
or that the anger of God did punish us so gently ; but
when the rack is changed for the axe, and the axe for
imprisonment, and the imprisonment changed into an enlargement, and the enlargement into an entertainment,
and the entertainment passes into an adoption, these are
steps of a mighty favor and perfect redemption from our

sin. And thus it was that God punished us. He threatened we should die, and so we do, but *not so as we deserved ;* we wait for death, and stand sentenced, and every day is a new reprieve, and brings new favors ; and at last, when we must die, by the irreversible decree, that death is changed into a sleep, and that sleep is in the bosom of Christ, and there dwells all peace and security, and this passes into glory and felicity. We looked for a Judge, and behold a Saviour ! We feared an accuser, and behold an advocate ! We sat down in sorrow, and rise in joy. We leaned upon rhubarb and aloes, and our aprons were made of the sharp leaves of the Indian fig-tree. And so we fed, and so were clothed. But the rhubarb proved medicinal, and the rough leaf of the tree brought its fruit wrapped up in its foldings, and round about our dwellings was planted a hedge of thorns and bundles of thistles, the nightshade, and the poppy ; and at the root of these grew the healing plantain, which, rising up into a tallness by the friendly invitation of heavenly influence, twined about the tree of the cross, and cured the wounds of the thorns, and the curse of the thistles, and the maledictions of man, and the wrath of God. *Si sic irascitur, quo modo convivatur ?* If God be so kind when he is angry, what must he be when he feasts us with caresses of the most tender kindness ?* Every thing we receive above the line of deserts should foster a spirit of cheerful gratitude.

Next to this reflection, the specific we would prescribe for a cheerful habit is activity in well-doing. Yes, there is evil enough in the world, and we must strive to make

* Jeremy Taylor.

it less. How can we be cheerful in such a suffering world? Strive to make it better. Despair sulks, and pampered indolence is a prey to *ennui;* but he who works for a good object keeps the enemy at bay, and good works leave no place for moodiness. Excepting such cases of bodily infirmity as incapacitate for all motion, in which patience and submission may enact their own cheerfulness—for those flowers are sweetest which bloom by night—I cannot conceive of one having a cheerful temper, who is not accustomed to healthful bodily exercise.   If there was oddity in the common prescription of the late Dr. Abernethy, of London, to his rich patients, there was much sound wisdom—"Live on sixpence a day, and earn it."   Half the melancholy which invades the domain of religion, has its origin in laziness.   Doubts and difficulties in spiritual concerns, and despondencies in prayer, quite as often arise from the want of bodily exercise as from a discriminating conscience. Never pity the man who swings a sledge, or holds the plough, or works the ship, or prosecutes a trade. Give your compassion to the poor, shriveled form, that has nothing to do. Cheerfulness is the first-born child of daily work.

He who is the busiest, out of regard to duty, is the happiest of all men. Matthew Henry says, in his quaint style, of Adam required to dress the garden in which he was put, "if either a high extraction, or a great estate, or a large dominion, or perfect innocency, or a genius for pure contemplation, or a small family, could have given man a writ of ease, Adam had not been set to work." As God is full of blessedness, because he is full of benevolent activity, so we find the true zest and sparkle of life in the constant exercise of all our faculties, in the way of well-doing.

> Come, Brother, turn with me from pining thought,
> And all the inward ills that sin has wrought;
> Come, send abroad a love for all who live,
> And feel the deep content in turn they give.
> Kind wishes and good deeds—they make not poor;
> They'll home again, full laden, to thy door.
> The streams of love flow back where they begin;
> For springs of outward joys lie deep within.

There is a subject suggested in this connection which deserves ampler discussion, and the best consideration of the best men : the necessity of some kind of recreation, which, being innocent in its nature, and incapable of perversion, shall give to body and mind a needed stimulus and refreshment. It is, of course, in city life, that the problem is of the most difficult solution. No one who began life in the country, can forget its simple recreations, its healthful sports. Who does not feel his spirits rise as he recalls the amusements of a northern winter, when sun and stars looked down on the smooth and brilliant ice, tempting the skater to his joyous speed, and turning the horse from the dirt and flint of the road to the crystal path, where, with merry music of bell and laugh, he coursed over the surface of water without wetting a hair of his fetlock.

Sidney Smith has shown an uncommon amount of sound English sense in this one direction, to all who would attain an habitual cheerfulness : "Take short views." His meaning would not be comprehended, if we did not remember how many are prone to distress themselves by the fear of remote possibilities. "Borrowing trouble" is the common expression which describes the habit. It is not the actual occurrence of to-day which grieves and afflicts; but it is the imagination of what is likely to occur in some contingency of the future. "Take short views," says our adviser. Look at what you have already—this present day, this present hour. What is this but a paraphrase of our Lord's own direction— "Take no thought for the morrow; for the morrow shall take thought for the things of itself." Travelling on some of the railroads of the country—such, for example, as that which winds through the Alleghanies, or the Water-Gap of the Delaware—looking far in advance, it would seem that huge mountains were dropped directly upon your road, obstructing all progress, and bringing you to a pause. But when you advance to the spot, you find that there is a way along which the road may wind, narrow and circuitous, perhaps, but smooth, and safe, and level as elsewhere, working itself free from all impediments, and emerging at length again into the open and extended plain-country. Just so is it in the journey of life. We anticipate formidable obstructions, and imagine that an end has come to all farther advances, by the towering mountains which stretch away across the distant horizon. Shorter views would make us content with the road which is ready for this day's journey; and past experience should satisfy us that there are no hills so high, no valleys so precipitous, no passes so rugged, but that a road runs through them all, when the time has actually arrived for the march. Every man gets through the world without coming to a halt.

Another thing for which Sidney Smith deserves admiration was, amid all his honorable aspirations, the absence of mean jealousies. He had a brother who was titled and wealthy, but toward him was nothing exacting or envious. He occupied his own sphere, and was very brave and contented in managing his own affairs, and the very cattle in his inclosures had occasion to be thankful for his kindness. Here was regulation of desire within proper limits. This also is conducive to cheerfulness. The conditions of contentment are put at a very low figure in the Scriptures—" having food and raiment." It is the intrusion of envy and jealousy which destroys cheerfulness.

The bee sucks honey out of wormwood ; and the wasp secretes venom from the juice of the ripest plum which it stings. The habit of cheerful gratitude depends on our minds, not on the events of our times. Some are so unfortunate in disposition and ways of thinking, that they detect nothing but evil even in that which is good ; while others make it their rule and their habit to discern good even in that which is felt to be evil. Theophrastus, the favorite pupil of Aristotle, to whom we are indebted for the preservation of his master's writings, has left us a book entitled " Characters," or Portraits, in which we find the following description of a " Discontented Man." Though the portrait was drawn more than two thousand years ago, it will serve for the likeness of men now living on the earth. " A discontented temper," writes he, " is a frame of mind which sets a man upon complaining without reason. When one of his neighbors, who makes an entertainment, sends a servant to him with a plate of any thing that is nice—'What!' says he, 'your master did not think me good enough to dine with him?' In a dry season, he grumbles for want of rain; and when a shower falls, mutters to himself, 'Why could not this have come sooner?' If he happens to find a piece of money—'Had it been a pot of gold,' says he, 'it would have been worth stooping for.' He takes a great deal of pains to beat down the price of a slave; and after he has paid his money for him, 'I am sure,' he says, 'thou art good for nothing, or I should not have got thee so cheap.' When a messenger comes with great joy to acquaint him with the birth of a son and heir, he replies, 'That is as much as to say, my friend, I am poorer by half to-day than I was yesterday.' Though he has gained a cause with full costs and damages, he complains that his counsel did not insist upon the most material points. If, after any misfortune has befallen him, his friends raise a voluntary contribution for him, and desire him to be merry— 'How is that possible,' says he, 'when I am to pay every one of you the money again, and be obliged to you into the bargain?'"*

Were I to string together a few brief hints additional as to the manner in which this bright virtue may be cultivated, they would be on this wise: As every man has a will of his own, you must expect every day that your own will be crossed; when this is done, you must bear it as meekly as when you cross the will of another. Expect not too much of others, then they will be more tolerant of you. Esteem others more highly than yourself, and

* Addison's Works, vol. iv. p. 336.

watch for the opportunities in which you can say a kind word and confer a small pleasure. Be studious to see what is good and hopeful to be applauded in another, rather than what is evil to be reproved ; and amid all the trivial annoyances of life, measure those substantial blessings which come to you every hour from the open hand of Christ ; and if the practice of these rules does not cure a clouded brow and an irritable manner, then it is because you need, and most probably will have, some other medicine besides that of a merry heart.

Chief of all, if you would be cheerful in such a world as this, you must exercise a constant trust in an all-wise Providence. We mean the recognition of that Divine Supremacy which directs the revolutions of time and events with a wisdom and love and power superior to our own, and an obedient deference to His will. If we will consider it honestly, we shall be convinced of the fact, that the occasions for individual and national gratitude which are owing to our own power and achievement are very few, while those are boundless which spring from Him who watches alike the sparrow and the empire. In the worst times let this be our joyous confidence, "The Lord God omnipotent reigneth." " Although the fig-tree shall not blossom, neither shall fruit be in the vines ; the labor of the olive shall fail, and the fields shall yield no meat ; the flock shall be cut off from the fold, and there shall be no herd in the stalls : yet I will rejoice in the Lord, I will joy in the God of my salvation."

Mirth to the sorrowful might be the occasion of affliction and pain, by the intrusion of contrary qualities. But

5

as to cheerfulness, what heart knows so much of it as that which has been mellowed by affliction ? Not he who has been elated by long-continued prosperity knows the secret of true serenity, but meek-eyed sorrow speaks with a low and gentle voice of the goodness of God; and the best incentives to gratitude are those which memory brings up from the shadows of the past. If your young child is no longer with you, thank God for its better home, and the warm and better love you bear it, now that the heavens have received it.

If there are tears and clouds, there is also a bow. Be still ; be cheerful ; be thankful.

HAPPY MEDIOCRITY.

Two things have I required of thee ; deny me them not before I
die ; remove far from me vanity and lies ; *give me neither poverty nor
riches ;* feed me with food convenient for me, lest I be full and deny
thee, and say, who is the Lord ? or lest I be poor and steal, and take
the name of my God in vain.

PROV. 30 : 7-9.

—— Auream quisquis mediocritatem diligit.

HOR., *Od.*, 2. 10. 5.

V.

HAPPY MEDIOCRITY.

THE Scotch have an old proverb : " That an ounce of mother is worth more than a pound of clergy." If it be true, according to the best criticism, that Agur and Lemuel were brothers, their mother, judging from the words she taught them, must have been a person of remarkable endowments. Singularly fortunate were Ithiel and Ucal in their preceptor. Very little do we know of Agur, but he has hit the true philosophy of life better than all the sages of classic fame. For aught that appears, his sententious wisdom may have often delighted listening disciples ; but these few words, " *give me neither poverty nor riches,*" assigned a place among inspired aphorisms, have reached the good fortune of the one insect in a swarm, which a drop of amber has embalmed imperishably.

In the estimation of this Idumean teacher, character was the object of chief concern ; and outward conditions were to be regarded by their tendency to affect this favorably or unfavorably. Character does not depend upon the outward estate ; though we are prone to judge otherwise. As that shrewd observer, our great English dramatist, has said : "We make the sun, moon, and stars guilty of our disaster ; as if we were ignorant of necessity ; knaves by compulsion ; and all that we are evil in by a divine thrusting on."   "Burden not," says old Sir Thomas Brown, " the back of Aries, Leo, or Taurus, with thy faults ; nor make Saturn, Mars, and Venus, guilty of thy follies.   Think not to fasten thy imperfections on the stars, and so despairingly conceive thyself under a fatality of evil.   Calculate thyself within, seek not thyself in the moon, but in thine own orb."   Nevertheless, it must not be forgotten that each and every condition in life has its own tendencies or influences for good or evil, and if we are wise we shall be most thankful for that conjunction which is most favorable to virtue and happiness.

The prayer of Agur deprecates for himself the two extremes of great wealth and severe poverty, as being both conducive to evils ; while he asks for himself the happy medium, which is alike removed from pride and sensuality on the one hand, and discontent and dishonesty on the other.

Perhaps it may be found difficult to define, with precision, the condition here intended.   Riches and poverty are relative terms.   We are all rich, we are all poor, according to the standard of comparison which we adopt. In some parts of the world he would be counted rich who possesses the means of securing for himself a sufficiency of food and raiment, warmth and shelter ; while, in other phases of society, one might attain to the possession of all comforts and many luxuries, and yet fall short of the common measurement of wealth.   In fact, the standard of judgment is in the mind, and not in the estate. He is a rich man who has the means of gratifying his wants, be they few or many, great or small, ambitious or humble; and he is a poor man, even though his title-deeds and securities certify to the largest investments, whose greed outgrows his ability to supply it. The legislation of God, accordingly, in reference to this subject, addresses the heart, teaching us to moderate and control *desire*, so bringing the conditions of contentment, and gratitude, and peace within the reach of all. Though this be true, both Scripture and observation instruct us that there are extremes of condition—wealth, enormous wealth, hereditary or acquired ; and poverty—real, pinching, pining poverty ; while between these polar extremes lies that temperate zone, that table-land of happy mediocrity, which requires the exercise of our best qualities—industry, exertion, economy, self-reliance—and where, by virtue of such practices, all our real necessities, as physical, intellectual, social, and religious beings, are honestly and honorably supplied. The leprosy of a most miserable error has already cankered our hearts, if we are indisposed to appreciate the blessedness of such a condition for ourselves and our children.

A traveller from the United States, visiting the Old World—especially those parts in which feudal institutions have been longest entailed—is painfully struck with the inequalities which exist in the condition of different classes, reminding him of the results of our winter-storms; here, immense drifts of snow, and there, the ground entirely bare. The laws of primogeniture, by which property is accumulated and entailed in one line of descent, are the support and perpetuity of an aristocratical order.

Here is an estate, extending five, ten, or thirty miles, including farms, villages, churches, towns, the property of a single owner.   In some favorite spot, where Nature, in her happiest combination of hill and vale, wood and water, has done her utmost to delight the eye, rises the baronial hall or castle, covering, with its various offices, some acres of ground.   Sums incalculable have been expended in rearing and ornamenting it.   Within, the walls are decorated with costliest art—pictures and statues and books, the behests of ages; while gold and silver and tapestries of hereditary value dazzle the un-practised eye.   Without and around are the grounds which rejoice in the perfect cultivation of hundreds of years.   The grass grows on the smooth lawn as if each blade knew the exact measure of the velvet texture. Miles of parks are filled—most beautiful of all natural growths—with trees, with their " sylvan honors of feudal bark," whose massive trunks and wide-spreading tops are the copies which nature gives to art, in all kinds of archi-tecture—pillar, arch, and roof.   Horticulture, with its exotic fruits and flowers, is here carried to its perfection, while artificial lakes and rivers and cascades are called into existence at the summons of affluence.   The very animals rejoice in sleek abundance; horses and hounds luxuriating in stalls and kennels, which, for cost and com-fort and elegance, exceed the largest ambition of an ad-jacent peasantry.

Remote from this is another extreme.   An iron hand grasps the poor as soon as he is born, and holds him down.   " A cottage" sounds pleasantly in verse and tale, and picturesque is it in a rural landscape, or in the cort-

folio of a tourist, and within many are as good and noble and happy hearts, winter and summer, as the world contains. But, in many parts, the cottages of the poor are the abodes of heart-rending distress. The thatch which strikes the eye of a summer-traveller so green and pleasant, in winter black, sour, and mouldy, drops continual moisture on the puddly floor of clay or stone, stiffening the rheumatic limbs which know no better shelter. Poverty here is no romantic imagination, but a grim, gaunt, and ghastly foe, against which the over-worked fight hard for very life. Comforts are not dreamed of ; the struggle is whether they shall barely live. It is all hard, downright, back-breaking labor. The choice is not as to the wholesomeness and nutritiousness of food ; enough if a little of the coarsest, obtained at the hardest, can keep off starvation. Excessive toil, and meagre diet, and unsuitable dwellings, bring on premature age ; and when exhaustion produces sickness, disabling from work, which cannot afford a respite, there is no hope for thousands, even in a parish poor-house—only in a pauper's grave.

> "Over the stones
> Rattle his bones."
> " Oh, God ! that bread should be so dear
> And flesh and blood so cheap ! "

Would you know what real poverty is, you must go far away among a foreign peasantry. You must look upon the men who from their birth are so familiar with the load of heavy penury, that their very bodies are bent, and they go along cringing, as if in apology for presuming to live. You must visit foreign manufactories, and

5*

mark young children creeping out of their miserable houses, while it is yet dark, roused from insufficient sleep by the stroke of the workhouse-clock—fed on thin potations of gruel—pattering along the wet and snowy streets with naked feet, deformed in head and limbs, and sitting down to their work so solemn, that it cuts you to the heart to see children that do not, and cannot smile. You must visit yet other lands, where no sort of charity pretends to help the helpless ; where no amount of toil promises compensation. You must suffer yourself to be assailed by a Swiss or Italian beggary, so deformed, so diseased, so wan, so importunate, that their forms will haunt you in your dreams, touching your very soul with the sad cry for pity. Still further eastward must we go, for the more despotic kings and sultans are in the land of " barbaric pearl and gold," the more miserable are the poor. Here is the Great Sahara of human life. The victims of famine are computed, every year, by thousands. The body suffers so much, that the whole man is brutalized ; loathsomest things—vermin, insects, reptiles —are counted as lucky food for greedy hunger ; and when death comes, the human body obtains not the poor respect of decent interment, but is thrown into the sea, or left exposed as a prey to the vulture and the jackal. Thank God, if we have not overgrown and aristocratic wealth, we have nothing which deserves the name of poverty. And if there are any among us who doubt whether we, as a people, have occasion to be thankful, even amid judgments which our own sins and follies have provoked, they ought to vacate these fields, which the Lord has blessed, and exchange places with the peasantry of Ireland, the

Lazzaroni of Naples, the Arabs of Syria, the Digger Indian—who would be glad and grateful enough if they might only take the crumbs which now fall from our groaning tables.

Inequalities of social condition will always exist. We have no faith in theories which are wiser than Providence, or better than the Bible. We do not look for the introduction of any atheistical-political millennium, in which property is to become a common stock, from which each is to draw the same amount of rations—a state in which there will be no superiority to occasion pride, and no inferiority tempting to envy, but "one great plain, without protuberance or indentation, over which the whole team of human animals, equally yoked, may move on to annihilation in blessed equanimity"; and we do well to beware that no devils' bridges touch our houses, on which infidel notions like these may travel, in seemly garb, to the overthrow of our social organization. The poor we expect to have always with us, and those who are rich above their fellows will not be wanting on the earth.

The perils of the extreme poor are many, and their trials severe. Agur prayed most wisely that he might be delivered from a state which endangered his honesty. Many there are who have battled bravely against adversity, sternly keeping faith, in extremest penury, with God and with themselves. The brightest jewels of truth, honor, patience, and meekness, have been found imbedded in the rocks and shells and mire of the most abject poverty. The lily which floats on the surface of the water, pure and fragrant, has its root in the oose and slime. Men there are, poorer than any we know, whose hands are hard as horn ; whose hearts are meek and gentle as a child ; who, poor beyond all our experience or conception, would not tamper with a dishonest thought for all the wealth of the world ; who fight against want with a brave heart to the very last, trampling on the sharp thorns in their path with a firm foot; hanging the burdens which are too heavy to bear, about the wing of faith ; trusting, as did Lazarus at the gate of precarious charity, in an invisible and almighty Friend, to soothe and glorify the soul at last. Nevertheless, it cannot be questioned, that the tendency of extreme poverty is to mischief. Political statistics prove that crime waits on the footsteps of poverty. Districts remarkable for penury, are equally remarkable for violence and vice. As Cowley said in another case, " It is hard for a man to keep a steady eye upon truth and right, who is always in a battle." The fiercest perils of a great and crowded municipality are from the vicious poor. The transition from absolute necessity to crime is very easy. The poorest man feels that he is a man, and that he has a right, like others, to live upon the earth ; and once, not having before his eye the fear of Mr. Malthus or Mr. McCullough, or any other political economist, he had the audacity to marry—and how can he see wife and children shivering with cold and starving for want of food, when a little taken from the superfluous wealth of the affluent, would minister such substantial relief? Then come wild musings about the injustice of Providence, and these break forth into unconcealed murmurings, impatience, and wrath ; ripening quick in the bitter fruit of dishonesty, fraud, robbery, and murder. Well may we deprecate a condition which exposes to such temptations

"Give me not poverty, lest I steal, and take the name of God in vain." It is certainly an occasion of gratitude that we are not reduced to that degree, which tempts us to doing hard and dishonest things, under the pressure of necessity.

In the opposite extreme are the perils of the rich. These, it is to be observed, are seldom feared. We should all probably regard ourselves as proof against them, and readily would venture upon the encounter with this brilliant and flattering enemy, rather than that other foe,—rough and implacable want. Riches, an enemy! Many speak of them as if in themselves they were an evil. Quite the contrary. They are a blessing, if rightly used. That surplus of possession which is in excess of physical wants, is the power of social progress, the material of civilization ; it is not only the instrument of benevolence, bread to the hungry, clothing to the naked, but knowledge to the ignorant, the support of the liberal arts, the means of all social culture ; and so strews this life with blessings, and builds "everlasting habitations" in the life to come. Still farther, to guard this part of our subject from perversion, we must admit that some of the rarest specimens of meekness, condescension, and humanity that ever blessed the world, have been in the mansions of the opulent. Nevertheless, it is true, that the extremely rich stand on a perilous pinnacle, and the highest virtues of our nature are put to the severest test, when one's tent is pitched on the enchanted ground of boundless affluence. I have nothing now to say of care increasing with riches, and which so deranges and distracts the mind, that enjoyment is limited in proportion as means are multiplied—the lust of wealth growing with what it feeds on; nothing of that common experience —satiety of every sense, *ennui*, weariness, and disgust of life, out-living the simplicity of Nature, and the skill of art; for these consequences of perverted wealth have been the theme of satire in all ages and in all languages, and have been condensed into familiar proverbs—those portable results of universal experience.

Who can doubt that extreme affluence, with its tendencies to indolence, vanity, self-indulgence, and display, puts one beyond the use of many virtues, and exposes one to mischief not less perilous, because it is not considered vulgar? "Give me not riches," said Agur, "lest I be full and deny thee, and say, Who is the Lord?" This is the portraiture of one who, inflated with wealth, regards himself as absolutely independent of God and man; who is rich to the extreme of arrogance, full to wantonness, proud to the disdain of all control, and self-indulgent, knowing no law but the capacity of pleasure. Is it not true that national opulence has, almost invariably, been followed by national luxury, impatience of restraint, corruption of morals, effeminacy of manners, enervation of body and mind, and a general deterioration of the race, "rotting from sire to son"? It was overgrown wealth, with its necessary consequences, unredeemed and uncontrolled by self-preserving virtue, which ruined the successive dynasties of ancient empire, and prostrated the glory of kingdoms before the lusty strength of barbaric invasion. We have need to be reminded of these tendencies, because every thing around us stimulates the lust for possession. National thought and legislation and enterprise all converge on the increase of national opulence. Our tendencies as a people are to extravagance ; and extravagance is always a crime. The passion for acquisition is so intense that it gives an expression, it is said, to the national features and the carriage of the person. Advertisers, wishing to give the greatest publicity, whether to a political nomination or the sale of their wares, have ascertained that the best place for posting them is upon the pavement, and along the very edge of the gutter, as if in the city all were the worshippers and followers of him whom Milton has immortalized in his epic :

> " Mammon, the least erected spirit that fell
> From heaven ; for e'en in heaven his looks and thoughts
> Were always *downwards* bent, admiring more
> The riches of heaven's pavement—trodden gold—
> Than aught divine or holy else enjoyed
> In vision beatific."

There is, then, such a thing as a wise preference in regard to condition. There is an intermediate state equally removed from great poverty and great riches, most favorable to virtue, most conducive to happiness, the safest and most blessed of all earthly allotments ; and though even this has many diversities and gradations, it is an occasion of thankfulness to God that the lines have fallen to us within these goodly limitations.

I have already hinted that it may not be easy to define with precision what is intended by this happy mediocrity. Perhaps we shall not stray far from the truth if we fix the boundaries at the point where work is required and

work is adequately rewarded.   Surely, that condition in
life which demands and develops self-exertion, and which
compensates that exertion with a competency, is rich
enough in all substantial blessings.   I have chosen the
word *work*, and that other word, self-exertion, rather than
labor, because we are accustomed to associate with the
latter more of intensity and drudgery and severity than
we might like.   Mr. Thomas Hood has rendered a most
kindly service, in the interest of humanity, in those
poems, the " Song of the Shirt," the " Workhouse Clock,"
and the " Lay of the Laborer," in which he has so skil-
fully depicted the sufferings of those who are doomed to
severe labor, but are denied an adequate compensation.
It is in the last of these that he describes one asking for
nothing but honest work and honest remuneration :

> " A spade, a rake, a hoe !
>   A pickaxe, or a bill !
>   A hook to reap, or a scythe to mow,
>   A flail, or what you will—
>   And here's a ready hand
>   To ply the needful tool,
>   And skill'd enough, by lessons rough
>   In labor's rugged school.
>
> " Aye, only give me work,
>   And then you need not fear
>   That I shall snare his Worship's hare,
>   Or kill his Grace's deer ;
>   Break into his Lordship's house
>   To steal the plate so rich ;
>   Or leave the yeoman that had a purse
>   To welter in a ditch.

" Wherever Nature needs,
Wherever Labor calls,
No job I'll shirk, of the hardest work,
To shun the workhouse walls.
My only claim is this,
With labor stiff and stark,
By lawful turn my living to earn,
Between the light and dark.

" No parish money, or loaf,
No pauper badges for me,—
A son of the soil, by right of toil
Entitled to my fee.
No alms I ask ; give me my task :
Here are the arms, the leg,
The strength, the sinews of a man,
To work, and not to beg.

" Still one of Adam's heirs,
Though doom'd by chance of birth
To dress so mean, and to eat the lean,
Instead of the fat of the earth ;
To make such humble meals
As honest labor can,
A bone and a crust, with a grace to God,
And little thanks to man."

Now just this is the description of our social state. There is work enough for all ; all are required to work ; and, saving painful exceptions, work is sufficiently rewarded. We hear sometimes slang phrases in regard to the " laboring class," when, in truth, we all belong to it. We have no strata of society separable one from the other, by a necessity of work imposed upon one from which others are exempt. This word *work* does not define the occupation ; as if he only was a workman who employs the muscles of the arm and the back. Where estates are not entailed-in one line of accumulation, the whole population is placed under this necessity,—let us change the word under the *privilege* of self-exertion. He is a workman who employs his brain, as much as he who wields a sledge or plies a spade. In such a state of society we should expect the utmost expansion of the inventive faculties, and an illimitable variety of methods by which to earn an honest living. A studious lawyer, a learned physician, a good teacher, a sagacious merchant, and a good minister, work no less than those addicted to manual labor. No less? The clock strikes six, the shop is shut, and the tired mechanic finds that sleep is sweet ; but he whose work is with that finer organ, the brain, knows no such ready suspension. Thought cannot be recalled so quickly, and a sleepless night often follows the work of the day. Those will always be found who are expert in devising methods of shirking this law of work ; and these are busy-bodies, meddling with other men's matters. In a country where government patronage is so immense as in ours, and where this is dispensed by such a frequent rotation in office, by popular elections, there is no kind of genteel idleness from which we have more to apprehend than that which makes politics a profession, foregoing all regular and honest work, and expecting to clutch some spoils from the revolving wheel. Dr. Parr, being asked on one occasion, by a young man who wished to draw him into a discussion, "What he thought of the introduction of evil into the world," simply replied, " that in his

opinion, we could have got along very well without it."
Politics belong to all good patriots ; but these, of course,
are incidental, and correlative to other personal pursuits ; and oftentimes we are inclined to think the affairs
of State would go along most swimmingly, if there were
not so many who, too lazy or maladroit to take care of
themselves by working with their own hands, spend their
whole life in an immodest and meddlesome taking care
of the State. There may be times when we are all disposed to wish the rigor of work were somewhat relaxed,
and that its sternness were somewhat more indulgent of
repose. Sometimes her brow is knit with care, and soil-
ed with dirt, and her voice imperative and harsh ; but,
next to religion, she is the best friend we have in the
world.

To say of any possession that it was well-earned, is
the quality which gives it its chief value. To enjoy the
fruits of our own industry, is the richest pleasure. To
be able, with God's blessing, to provide for ourselves
and our children, is the very luxury of life—personal
independence. This is better than to be fed passively
by angels.

There is an invisible wealth in possessions acquired
by personal industry and economy, which cannot be computed by the numeration table. The fancy strikes an
affluent nobleman or a king, that he will erect a palace.
With a sort of creative fiat, he says, " Let it be built," and
it is built. With no farther care on the part of the
lordly proprietor, the " fabric huge rises like an exhala-
tion," and when complete, my lord chamberlain's order,
or a banker's check, covers all the disbursements. A man

in circumstances of mediocrity undertakes to build a house for his personal use. First of all is any amount of contriving and planning. Long before the first stone is laid, he has studied out every convenience, and imagination has invested every apartment with a wealth of domestic delights. Already he sees the fireside where he will seek repose, when weary ; already he hears the winter's hail and rain beating upon the roof, which gives to content-ment so sweet a shelter. He overhears the voices of happy children, and watches all the pleasant offices of cheerful housewifery. Then industry puts to her hand. Economy is brought into play, and at length the grateful proprietor takes possession of what, under God, is his own—all his own—earned by his own honest hand. Think you not, there is here more of real pleasure and *comfort*—I like much that good old English word—than in all the sumptuousness of royal palaces?

Walking sometimes along the thoroughfares of the city, I have detected myself in the national habit of guess-ing at the condition and thoughts of strangers, so easily recognized as they pass. Here is a plain and most worthy couple from the country, accompanied by their son and daughter. They have just purchased that com-fortable coat for the one, and that nice muff for the other, upon which both are looking with such entire complacency. That purchase has been the theme of many a domestic conversation. Those parents have anticipated the need of it, wondered whether they could accomplish it, denied themselves a little here and there, and now, in obtaining their wish, they have purchased a pleasure for themselves for the whole season, of which the millionaire never dreamed when despatching an order to a draper for his fastidious children.

If there be such a gratification in expending for one's self whatever is honorably earned, who shall compute the value of that which, industriously acquired, has been well husbanded and well spent for the benefit of another? Gifts which have no self-denial in them, lose half their worth. See that small treasure in the hands of frugal industry. It is not a part of a large dividend or legacy. Every coin of it has in it days and nights of work. Against how many temptations has it been kept! One would like to retain it. How many conveniences it would purchase for one's self. But it has been saved for another—an indigent parent, an unfortunate brother, a widowed sister, a dependent child. Tearful blessings are in that money, for him who gives and him who receives. Call not that unrighteous mammon. Count not that as common pelf, or as the unmissed donation of the opulent. It is the coinage of love, and God's blessing is with it wherever it goes. That condition of life which affords no place for self-denial, robs life of the noblest virtue.

Am I at fault, when asserting that this condition of mediocrity is the proper domain of the affections? Extreme penury produces insensibility, as drowning men lose regard for others in the impulse of self-preservation; while the opposite extreme of affluence makes one independent both of love and hate. Disappointed expectations or alleged injustice in the disposal of great estates, have alienated many opulent families; while the affections of those in humble life are more closely cemented by the trials which they share in common. Those who are allied, not merely by consanguinity, but the common necessity of exertion, must be moved by the liveliest sympathy in each other's success. The self-denying effort which a parent expends on his children, deepens his own love for them ; and children, observing with what an amount of tender care they are clothed and educated, will be prompt to repay the act with more than ordinary gratitude and affection. So it is, that those who walk along the middle course of life, will generally be found most distinguished for love and sympathy and domestic happiness.

> Tell me on what holy ground
> May domestic peace be found :
> Halcyon daughter of the skies,
> Far, on fearful wing, she flies,
> From the pomp of sceptered state,
> From the rebel's noisy hate.
>
> In a humble home she dwells,
> Listening to the Sabbath-bells ;
> Still around her steps are seen
> Spotless honor's meeker mien ;
> Love, the fire of pleasing years,
> Sorrow, smiling through her tears,
> And, conscious of the past employ,
> Memory, bosom-spring of joy.

All have observed that familiar phenomenon, the reflection of objects from the surface of still waters. In hours of grateful recollection, when there is no ripple on the placid surface of the heart, we gaze at the pictures which are so faithfully mirrored therein. With us it is not the Lake of Avernus, shadowed with gloomy woods, of which Homer and Virgil both have sung; nor that Thessalian Fount which reflected the image of Narcissus; nor the Italian Como, rendering back cultivated terraces and classic architecture. Look at the scenes pictured in our own " chambers of imagery." There are houses in the landscape of various styles and dimensions. They are unlike any you have seen elsewhere. They have no resemblance to the Swiss chalet, the French chateau, the English hall or cottage, the Irish hovel, or the slave's cabin. Here is one of goodly size and shape, painted of cleanly white, with green blinds; it is approached by the " front yard" and a straight gravel-walk; and around it are cherry trees and lilac bushes and sweet roses, and hard by the great barn, and the meadow with cattle that would charm the eye of Paul Potter and Rosa Bonheur; and within are the evidences of inexpensive tastes and refinement and plenty.

Not far distant is another of still humbler pretensions, built in defiance of all orders of architecture : for preservation, and not for ornament, it is painted red; the long steep roof on one side descends nearly to the ground; and banks of tanbark are laid against the underpinning to keep out the frost from the cellar. We enter; it is neither the home of affluence nor the dwelling-place of penury; but the home of happy mediocrity. There are no sumptuous carpets of foreign looms to be faded by the warm and bright sun which shines in with no obstruction; the floor is sanded by the hand of cleanliness; in the fire-place, if it be summer, you will see sprigs of feathery asparagus so arranged as to hide the jambs, smoked and blackened by the winter's generous fire,* by the side of which many a group has listened to the stories of the Indian wars and the Revolution, and where many a prayer has been offered up, precisely when the town-bell was rung for nine o'clock in the evening, the whole household, in snug contentment, going to honest sleep before the time when the jaded votaries of fashion in the city are beginning to dress for luxurious dissipation. It is the home of simplicity and truth and love; and every thing within and without wears the aspect of decency, and healthiness of body and mind as far removed from the excitements, revulsions, temptations, and disgusts of the town, as the soft pictures of Claude from the wild and terrific creations of Salvator Rosa.

Somewhere in the landscape you are sure to find a certain building, bearing no resemblance to the Academies or Lyceums of classic Greece; yet prolific of all things good and great—the country school-house. What memories come thronging back at the mention of the place—

> We ne'er forget—though there we are forgot—

the low, square, red school-house, with its hard seats, straight backs, and narrow desks; the mistress' chair; the entrance of the noisy group at the tap of thimbled finger on the window; the act of "manners" at the door, the low-dropped courtesy, the head-long bow; the sports of changing seasons, the nut-tree, the "huckleberry" pasture, the squirrel-trap, the skating-pond; the long winter

---

* "Yea, he warmeth himself, and saith, Aha! I am warm; *I have seen the fire.*" Is. 44 : 16.

evenings with books and slate and household games;
examination day, when, in the presence of committee-
men, deacons, and minister, were paraded out those

> "—— bright and ordered files
> Like spring flowers, in their best array,
>   All silence and all smiles,
> Save that each little voice in turn
>   Some glorious truth proclaims,
> What sages would have died to learn,
>   Now taught by cottage dames."
>
> KEBLE.

The Puritan School, strictly so called, is now an
obsolete institution. No one expects that it ever can be
revived. The New England Primer cannot again be
used in the District School. We cannot say much in
praise of the poetry or the fine arts of that remarkable
book. We laugh at some of its rhyming alliterations
and uncouth pictures. But the jingle of its rhyme carried a truth, and the woodcut made an impression. It
contained the portrait of " the Honorable John Hancock,
Esq., President of the *American* CONGRESS ; " " the young
Infant's morning and evening prayers, from Dr. Watts ; "
" the Lord's Prayer ; " " the Apostles' Creed ; " " the
Golden Rule ; " " Agur's Prayer ; " the picture of Mr.
" John Rogers dying courageously for the Gospel of JESUS
CHRIST ; " and " the Shorter Catechism." Hard would it
be to find any thing better to be wrought into the brain
and bones of those who, in a free republic, are expected
to illustrate the virtues and blessings of the happiest social condition.

More conspicuous still is another object in the scene—

the house of God, with its silent finger pointing ever to the sky, and hard by the grave-yard,

Where the rude forefathers of the hamlet sleep.

No architectural pretensions are there; no storied window, few contrivances for convenience, and none for luxury and cushioned indulgence. But beneath that old sounding-board stands a man who, for a moderate stipend, faithfully did all the preaching and public praying for the town; who, oft as the Sabbath came, with a steady hand, and a calm voice, gave forth the word of God, whether men would hear or whether they did forbear; and who, on the memorable days of Fasting and Thanksgiving, exercised his liberty, so as it was never done before or since, in uttering his mind round and full about the political affairs of the country. Burns has given us an incomparable description of the Cotter's Saturday night in Scotland; but the most poetical image we can recall, is that of a New England Sabbath morning, in the olden time; so bright, so calm; so fragrant with odors of roses and clover; so profoundly still that you could hear the buzzing of a fly in the sun, and the crowing of the cock echoed on from one end of the village to the other, and well-clad, honest, and happy people left their unfastened and unmolested homes, and went up together to worship the God of their fathers.

THE BLESSEDNESS OF TEARS.

They that sow in tears shall reap in joy.

Ps. 126 : 5.

VI.

THE BLESSEDNESS OF TEARS.

THE Proclamations appointing the annual Thanksgiving, invariably make mention of an abundant harvest as one of the objects which ought to excite our gratitude to Almighty God. How many pleasing images are suggested by that one word—harvest! Fields covered with grain, ripe for the reaper's sickle ; the corn, whose silken banners a little while ago were playing with the west-wind, now ready for the garner ; wains loaded with fragrant spoils ; barns bursting with abundance ; the harvest-moon standing still for a week, prolonging the farmer's opportunity, as once it stood for another kind of harvest in the valley of Ajalon ; the animals stalled in the midst of comfort and plenty ; the homestead, where cheerfulness laughs at want : wonder not that poetry has gathered up these associations and set them to blithesome music, in every age, and in every tongue, to celebrate the rich and jocund autumn.

For all this abundant and joyful reaping, there was an earlier season of toilsome sowing. The ground was prepared by great painstaking to receive its trust. The heavy plough was dragged along its surface, ripping open the sod, tearing up the very roots of the grass, disembowelling the earth, exposing its quiet secrets to the winds and storms and suns; it was overturned and harrowed as by instruments of torture ; and if this were the first time in which it was subjected to the process, the trees and shrubs which had grown there unmolested were cut down by the sharp ax, and burned with fire. All these amputations, and severities, and seeming cruelties, all this toil in making ready the ground for its office, and then the actual burial of the seed out of sight, in the bosom of the earth—sad symbol of the disposal of the human body, amid tears and mournings, where it is to see corruption—all these were the necessary antecedents of the joy and plenty, the gladness and wealth, of the golden harvest.

There is a harvest of contentment, and cheerfulness, and plenty, and peace, and joy, in every true life, and there is a preparatory sowing for the same, in toil, trouble, and tears.

Young readers will not comprehend my meaning at first, since they have always associated tears with misery ; but I am greatly mistaken if adult experience does not catch a glimpse of the sentiment even before it is unfolded as an occasion of gratitude. "They that sow in tears shall reap in joy." Tears are the seed of a joyful harvest.

Let us understand one another at the beginning. I am no enemy to laughter, if it be of the right quality— the offspring of good nature, and not of pride. Philosophers have defined laughter to be the property of rational beings ; animals weep, but do not laugh. So long as it is the expression of cheerfulness, and not of folly ; of humor, and not fantastic levity; of true wit, and not of cruel ridicule, let us hope that we may never be too wise to indulge in it.

An old monk of the Papal Church, preaching from the text, "I said of laughter, it is mad; and of mirth, what doeth it?" lays down the doctrine that "laughter was the effect of original sin, and that Adam could not laugh before the fall." Our first impulse pronounces that a falsehood; but the more you revolve it, the more will you be convinced that the point furnishes ampler material for discussion than many others which have employed monastic wit. Probably there is no metaphor which is so common in all languages as that of laughing applied to nature, when the fields are covered with verdure and flowers, and the trees with blossoms, and the streams are running and leaping in their playful freedom; so that we must interpret the term as an expression of innocent joy. Nevertheless, are we not disposed to regard the happiness of the first pair, made in the image of God, as too deep and serene to express itself in mirthful convulsions? We never think of the angels—whose joy is as perfect as their holiness—as inclined to laughter, though it does not strike us as incongruous when poetic conception describes them in tears, as the expression of a benevolent sensibility—a kind and blessed pity. Was it not a most philosophical accuracy which led Milton to connect the only act of laughter to be found in his immortal epic, not with the sinless angels winging their joyful ministries through the realms of God, but with the fallen spirits inventing and discharging their artillery, rallying their opponents in a string of diabolic puns on the effects pro-

duced by their curious enginery?   We do not associate
frivolous laughter with what is grand and heroic.   It was
exquisitely natural and human for Virgil, in that episode
of the Æneid which describes the games and diversions
of the Trojans, to relax into a laugh—the only one in the
book—when Menœtes was thrown overboard from his
boat, and left to dry himself upon a rock.   After all that
may be said in defence or advocacy of laughter, it is not
the expression of the highest and best qualities of our
nature.   It has its uses, it has its place, it has its time ;
but the best sensibilities of the soul, like deep waters,
flow smooth and still.   The most wearisome person in
the world is a perpetual laugher.   Like shallow water
running along a rocky bottom, the noisiest of all streams,
he betrays his want of depth by a constant cachinnation.
There is too much that is pleasing, too much that is grotesque, in this world, for us never to laugh at all ; there is
too much which is serious and earnest and great, to allow
us to laugh always.

It was necessary to say so much on this subject, that
I might not be misunderstood when I come to speak of
another.   It was needful that I should confess that I believed—after a certain way—in laughter, that the reader
might not be repelled by the assertion that I believe
also in tears.

Tears ! an occasion for thanksgiving.   'Perhaps you
intend to adduce them in proof of the divine benignity,
after the manner of Paley.   Perhaps you intend to give
us a physiological argument for the goodness of God
from the structure of the eye.   Tears ! why, I can describe
them and their uses very quickly,' says the anatomist.

They are a limpid fluid, of a saltish taste, secreted by the lachrymal glands, somewhat heavier than water, con·taining pure soda, also muriate, carbonate, and phosphate of soda, and phosphate of lime. Their use is to prevent the pellucid cornea from becoming dry and opaque; they prevent the pain which would otherwise arise from the friction of the eyelids against the bulb of the eye, and they wash away the dirt and every thing acrid that has fallen into the eye. In a natural state, the quantity is just sufficient for these uses; but when stimulated by sorrow or any thing pungent, they are secreted so fast, that, unable to be discharged through the proper conduit, they overflow from the internal angle of the eyelids, in the form of copious drops, upon the cheek, and so relieve the head from congestion!' That sounds very good, very wise; but that is not what I wish to say.

Tears—perhaps you intend to entertain us with all the conceits which the poets have associated with the name. Have they not been likened a thousand times to pearls and diamonds? Did not Rogers give us a fine thought when he wrote—

> " That very law which moulds a tear,
>   And bids it trickle from its source,
>   That law preserves the earth a sphere,
>   And guides the planets in their course."

Has not the author of Lalla Rookh elaborated an Oriental romance, " Paradise and the Peri," out of the value of a tear, caught from the cheek of Penitence, and made the passport through those celestial gates which will be opened to no other bribe? Aye, but this is trenching fast upon the very truth and sobriety of my theme, and I must desist a while.   It is nothing learned, nothing philosophical, nothing poetic, nothing curious, nothing extraordinary, which I propose in the theme already announced. I take tears as the symbols of grief and affliction; real, bitter, scalding tears, the signs and consequences of actual sorrow.   When we dwell, on festal occasions, upon those mercies which lend brightness to life, there are those who feel that they cannot sympathize with the strain, inasmuch as they are conversant with keenest suffering. Many cannot be excited to cheerfulness and gratitude by the description of those objects which are the occasion of joy to others, because many of those objects have been withdrawn from themselves, and in their place are losses and bereavements.   We must not blink the case of such.   No man will ever be cheated into a sense of gratitude by any attempt to render him oblivious to his griefs.   Whatever cheerfulness you succeed in imparting to sorrow, must be administered in that sorrow, and through it, and by means of it, rather than by any attempts to obstruct its flow.   What empiricism, what ignorance of our nature, are implied in all attempts to cheer and comfort a real grief by the action of contrasts !   Mirth to a heavy heart is like vinegar upon nitre.   Sorrow hugs to itself the very memory which haunts it, and never will it consent to have it torn away by violence.   We must meet afflictions just as they are, and inquire whether there be not a goodness in them for which we should be thankful.*

* How profound the philosophy of Mr. Coleridge on this subject.   *As he that taketh away a garment in cold weather and as vinegar upon nitre, so is he that singeth songs to a heavy heart,* Prov. 25 : 2o.

Tears there are in many an eye ; we are quite content to retain them if there be a method by which they can be shown to be the very instruments of cheerfulness—as the rain-drops on a summer's afternoon bring out to view

Worldly mirth is so far from curing spiritual grief, that even worldly grief, where it is great and takes deep root, is not allayed but increased by it. A man who is full of inward heaviness, the more he is encompassed about with mirth, it exasperates and enrages his grief the more ; like ineffectual weak physic, which removes not the humor, but stirs it and makes it more unquiet. But spiritual joy is seasonable for all estates : in prosperity, it is pertinent to crown and sanctify all other enjoyments, with this which so far surpasses them ; and in distress, it is the only *Nepenthe*, the cordial of fainting spirits : so, Psal. 4 : 7, *He hath put joy into my heart.* This mirth makes way for itself, which other mirth cannot do. These songs are sweetest in the night of distress.

There is something exquisitely beautiful and touching in the first of these similes : and the second, though less pleasing to the imagination, has the charm of propriety, and expresses the transition with equal force and liveliness. A grief of recent birth is a sick infant that must have its medicine administered in its milk, and sad thoughts are the sorrowful heart's natural food. This is a complaint that is not to be cured by opposites, which for the most part only reverse the symptoms while they exasperate the disease—or like a rock in the mid-channel of a river, swoln by a sudden rain-flush from the mountain, which only detains the excess of waters from their proper outlet, and make them foam, roar, and eddy. The soul, in her desolation, hugs the sorrow close to her, as her sole remaining garment : and this must be drawn off so gradually, and the garment to be put in its stead so gradually slipt on, and feel so like the former, that the sufferer shall be sensible of the change only by the refreshment. The true spirit of consolation is well content to detain the tear in the eye, and finds a surer pledge of its success in the smile of resignation that dawns through that, than in the liveliest shows of a forced and alien exhilaration.—*Aids to Reflection*, p. 54.

the splendid bow of God.　When the Scripture tells us
that sorrow is better than laughter, that it is good to be
afflicted, rely upon it, such expressions are not a pretence
or mockery—

> " Which keep the word of promise to the ear,
> And break it to our hope."

There is a profound truth in these sayings which it is
wise for us to comprehend.　Having been cheered into
smiles by those forms and expressions of Divine goodness
which we call blessings, let us now inquire whether there
be not a power to produce the same effect in what we are
accustomed to regard as evils—even the griefs, wrongs,
and troubles which extort the bitterest tears.

" In the account which Plato gives us of the conversation and behavior of Socrates, the morning he was to
die, he tells the following circumstance.　Socrates, whose
fetters were knocked off (as was usual to be done on the
day that the condemned person was to be executed),
being seated in the midst of his disciples, and laying one
of his legs on the other, in a very unconcerned posture,
began to rub it where it had been galled by the iron ;
and whether it was to show the indifference with which
he entertained the thoughts of his approaching death, or
(after his usual manner) to take every occasion of philos-
ophizing upon some useful subject, he observed the pleasure of that sensation which now arose in those very parts
of his leg that just before had been so much pained by
the fetter.　Upon this he reflected on the nature of pleasure and pain in general, and how constantly they succeed

one another. To this he added, that if a man of a good genius for a fable were to represent the nature of pleasure and pain in that way of writing, he would probably join them together after such a manner, that it would be impossible for the one to come into any place without being followed by the other." *

Acting upon this suggestion, Mr. Addison has constructed a fable, the substance of which is this: That Pleasure and Pain, two beings of a very different pedigree, belonging to two families always at variance, came into this world of ours, the one to take possession of the virtuous, the other of the vicious ; but, after many experiments, they discovered that they often laid claim to the same individual—that in this intermediate planet of ours there was no person so vicious who had not some good in him, nor any person so virtuous who had not in him some evil. To avoid dispute, and come to some accommodation, a marriage was proposed between them, and at length concluded ; by which means it is that we find Pleasure and Pain are such constant yoke-fellows, and that they either make their visits together, or are never far asunder. If Pain comes into a heart, he is quickly followed by Pleasure ; and if Pleasure enters, you may be sure Pain is not far off.

Do we mean by all this, nothing more than the commonplace sentiment that our pleasures are heightened by contrast? that the most direct method of promoting a cheerful contentment, is to recall the troubles from which we have been delivered, and the sorrows through which

* *Spectator*, No. 183.

we have passed? By no means. This would be but a small part of the truth. Nevertheless, this decimal part of the truth is too important to be overlooked. One of the inspired lyrics (Ps. 126) is set to this very sentiment. It was the outburst of joy and gratitude, in view of a great national deliverance. Reinstated amid the freedom and blessings of the Holy City, the Church enhanced its gladness by looking back to the shame and loneliness of heathen bondage—and thus she sang : " When the Lord turned again the captivity of Zion, we were like them that dream. Then was our mouth filled with laughter, and our tongue with singing. The Lord hath done great things for us, whereof we are glad. They that sow in tears shall reap in joy. He that goeth forth and weepeth, bearing precious seed, shall doubtless come again with rejoicing, bringing his sheaves with him."

Following this idea, how many are filled with gratitude when contrasting their present condition with what it was in former days of bitterness and trouble. Seated by his cheerful fire-side, or resting on his quiet pillow, one remembers the nights of tempest and gloom when he confronted death on a wreck at sea, and the louder the storm howls around his dwelling, the deeper is the sense of happy security and contentment. The man now in possession of a competency looks back to days of penury, when he began life alone, and struggled hard with many a grim and defiant trouble—to other days, when property was wrecked and credit low ; and recalling what God has done for him since, in giving him abundance, he is moved by the contrast to lively pleasure. In the enjoyment of health we remember the days of debility, when food had lost its relish, and the nights when pain held our eyes waking, and the memory becomes the fount of gratitude. The conception of ancient mythology, which represented departed spirits as drinking of Lethean waters, and thereby becoming oblivious to all the sufferings of life, is most heathen and cruel. Far different is the wisdom of the Scriptures, which, by every appliance, would quicken memory and never benumb it ; which would counsel us to look back from every eminence in our advancing journey upon the way in which God has led us, and which has promised us at the last, as the inspiration to an immortal song, a vision of all the woes and miseries and perils of life, from that world of blessedness where we shall drink of another and sweeter river than Lethe—

> " Which flows through a land where they do not forget—
> Which sheds over memory only repose,
> And takes from it only regret."

The great body of those odes which compose our inspired hymnology, are set to this very key-note—gratitude to God, in memory of personal and national troubles, from which he has wrought our deliverance. This is the philosophy of Christian joy—the harvest-reaping coming after the sowing of tears. Nor can I think of a surer method of promoting rational cheerfulness, when families are assembled at their domestic festival, than conversing together about earlier struggles and depressions ; how they wrestled with difficulties in getting a start in life ; of the self-denials which parents practised to give a son an education ; of the brave trust with which they battled with many a trouble—days of gloom and of bitterness, which have been succeeded by brighter skies and a truer sweetness.

While all this is true, it is not the pith of my subject. We must advance most decidedly, and say that tears have a blessing of their own. Without equivocation or reserve, I mean that tears and joys are immediately related, as sowing and reaping, as means and ends, as beginnings and issues. It is no poetic conceit concerning the "luxury of grief," devised by those who never knew the touch of actual sorrow, as one of the ancients wrote on the advantages of poverty when he had two millions out at usury ; it is no notion of Pagan stoicism, denying the existence of evil, and counselling insensibility under that which is so called ; it is nothing like either that I would employ to delude the sorrowful into a better bearing of their grief; but the sober, honest truth, that sorrow, like the rains and plowing of the Spring, does us good. He is only half-educated who is conversant with prosperity only. There cannot be the richest harvest in the soul and life of that man who has not passed through the preparatory process of sowing in tears.

Seneca, discoursing on a kindred subject, puts into the mouth of Demetrius this remarkable saying : " Nothing would be more unhappy than a man who had never known affliction." A notable saying, most certainly ! It is something more than the truism that prosperity may prove an injury by pampering our passions with over-fond and mistaken indulgences. Mark the word : " Nothing would be more unhappy"—the Latin, *infelix*, does not mean unfortunate merely, but unblessed—nothing would be more unhappy and unblessed than one who had never known affliction. Just what the ax, and plough, and harrow, and storm and rain, do for the mould, developing its latent properties, tearful afflictions accomplish in our own conscious being. It is a phenomenon familiar to those who are engaged in clearing new countries, that oftentimes, as the ax levels the forest, fountains of waters, till then concealed, spring to the surface. That illustrates what takes place in the human heart when sharp afflictions prostrate the pride and the strength which have overshadowed affections deep-seated and unknown. Paradoxical as it may sound to the inexperienced, we are enriched by losses ; and many a man has emerged from sorrow wiser, happier than before. The rod has struck the rock, and from the hard and flinty bosom has gushed forth a sensibility which brings a blessing. Sympathy with others, gentleness, patience, love, forgiveness, meekness,—are they not all qualities of a benign mood ?—are nurtured always and only amid real tears. Let a man be subject all his life to the hot glare of prosperity, and the same effect is produced on his sensibilities as on a clayey soil by the summer solstice—it is baked hard and dry. Mr. Dombey stands as the pattern of the class—hard, cold, stiff, iron ; the world made for him, and his proud will the central power. He needs to be softened, and affliction must do it. To make a man of him, something must touch the hidden fountain of tears. To make him thankful, cheerful, and serenely happy, he must suffer. To make one blessed, the iron stiffness must come out from pride and stateliness ; before one can weep for joy, he must weep for sorrow ; before one can become conscious of the deep power and blessedness of his own being, he must bow his head to stormy sorrows, and become a little child.   Goethe has hit a noble truth :

> " He who ne'er eats his bread with sighs,
>   Or through the live-long night
> Ne'er weeping on his pillow lies,
>   Knows not divine delight." *

In the Sketch-Book of Mr. Irving there is one piece, entitled " The Wife," which is the general favorite of young gentlemen of a certain age, and it is much to their credit and honor that it is so. It represents a city-merchant unexpectedly and irretrievably embarrassed in affairs, and brought down from affluence to bankruptcy. Vacating his opulent mansion, and taking a modest cottage in the rural suburbs, he is just about to go to his new home, to join his young wife—and he is tortured with the apprehension of finding her weary, dejected, and disconsolate. Instead of this, a new chapter in life, before unread, is opened to his eye. She comes tripping forth to the gate to meet him, full of cheerfulness and delight ; and to his astonishment he discovers that his dreaded disasters have given birth to a novel contentment and enjoyment. Has not that experience been reduplicated many times in seasons of commercial distress ? When gallant fortunes are wrecked, a minister of religicn

---

* " Wer nie sein Brod mit Thränen ass,
    Wer nie durch lange Mitternächte
    Aul seinem Bette weinend sass,
    Der kennt euch nicht, ihr hohen Mächte."

moves about endeavoring to cheer those who are afflicted by the loss of their estate, with the best sympathy and cordials he can administer. A year passes, and what is the result? You were forced to reduce and retrench your expenses to a very low degree; you dispensed with familiar luxuries; you made many sacrifices; you have practised sharp denials; but I should not be surprised to hear you say that this was the happiest portion of your life. You and your family have been united in a closer and gentler sympathy; you have found in one true and warm heart a love which was purer and stronger than ever; your children have shown a considerate affection and care for you under your new burdens, which has made you proud and happy; they have all tasted the novel pleasure of foregoing personal preferences for the sake of comforting and aiding you; you have preserved a good name—an untarnished honor; and should you rise again to wealth and splendor, I am not sure but you will always look back to this season of trial as the one in which you gathered the richest harvest of love and sympathy and cheerfulness and contentment that ever you knew.

If Hume and Voltaire, and Rousseau and Bentham— unmarried as they all were—had each been the father of a family; if they had ever gone in person to summon the family-physician in some exigency of intense anxiety, we should never have heard of those frosty and infidel philosophies from their pens by which so many hearts have been chilled and cursed. As you entered the family-chamber, and bent over the couch hallowed by the " great mystery of birth," and the tears of high-wrought sensibility could not be restrained as you caught the breath of your first-born, you discovered all at once that a new well had begun to spring up in your soul, deep and living beyond the reach of drouth.   .

Sickness has come, and the time for watching, weariness, and prayer.   That child, who had lived long enough to be the music and the light of your dwelling, twining itself around your living self, and associated with every hope and happiness of your life, is now in fearful peril. Its hot and hectic cheek lies against your own, as you pace the room in the dead of night, bearing it to and fro in its suffering and patience.   In those hours of suspense and pain the seed is dropping fast for a future harvesting—if your child should live, in love and tenderness and sympathy ; should it die, a bosom full of gentle memories and great thoughts, too great for words, clustering about this one belief, that, should you act your part aright, you will meet in heaven a bright spirit who will call you father.   I see in your dwelling a little coffin, and within it a form exquisitely moulded, the ringlets parted on its white and rounded forehead ; an unopened bud lies on its bosom, and were it not for that marble coldness, you might take it for a sleeping angel.   And there you stand, the tears falling down your cheek, as the rain-drops drip from the boughs after a shower. Tell us, now, does the thought ever occur to you to wish that your child had never been given you ?   Would you purchase exemption from all this grief at the price of forgetfulness? Would you, if you could, overstep all this anguish, and be again as you were before that child had an existence ? Never.   That brief scene of compressed sorrow is more fruitful in all which belongs to a soul-harvest than a score of years passed in cold and polished prosperity ; and from that small grave you will reap many a sheaf of blended memories and hopes and gentle affections, every year, till you are yourself laid by its side.

> " The good are better made by ill,
> As odors crushed are sweeter still."

It is said that one of the most distinguished senators of our country, who was bereaved of a little child, when his eye rested, months afterwards, on a small worsted shoe —recalling, as few things can more vividly, the bright vision which had fled—put it into his bosom, where, as was known, he carried it long next to his large and manly heart. That heart had a calmer pulse, a gentler sympathy, a richer sensibility, a truer greatness, because of contact with that small memorial of a domestic sorrow.

There is an incident in the life of Edmund Burke, which is familiar to all who cherish his great fame. In the evening of public life he lost his only son, at the age of twenty-one, of the rarest genius and varied accomplishments. The favorite horse of this young man, after the death of his master, was turned into the park and treated with the utmost tenderness. On a certain day long afterwards, when Mr. Burke himself was walking in the fields, this petted animal came up to the stile, and, as if in expression of his mute sympathy, put his head over the shoulder of the bereaved father. Struck with the singularity of the act, and overpowered with the memories which it awakened, he flung his arms around the neck of

the horse and burst into a flood of tears. The incident
was observed by one passing by, and gave rise to the
rumor that Mr. Burke had been smitten with sudden in-
sanity.   But never did the mind of that great statesman
display a manlier quality ; and when that sudden tear-
flush had subsided into a calmer recollection, had you
asked England's most philosophical orator for an analysis
of that experience, and to give you the balance of sorrows
and joys, he would have answered you in the words of
England's laureate :

> " Better to have loved and lost,
>   Than never to have loved at all."

There are some persons who think it unkind to speak
to the bereaved of their losses.   Their mistaken art it is
to console, by diverting the thoughts from all memory of
that which occasioned pain. Judged by this policy, every
allusion to a deceased friend would be an unwelcome
intruder.   What sciolists in the treatment of the human
heart, are they who prescribe oblivion for its cure ! From
such a sowing can come only a harvest of nettles and
rankest weeds.   Dam up the flow of tears by violent obstruction, and the back-water will drown and desolate the
soul.   Let departed friends be welcomed back to your
thoughts, for you cannot be happy unless you remember
them ; and let your love for the lost make you more
gentle, more tender, more affectionate, towards the living.

I alluded, a short time back, to the poetic conceit of
Mr. Moore, which represents a Peri gaining admission to

heaven, by bringing some gift esteemed by heaven most dear. And what was that?

First, she tried the sigh of expiring love, sacrificing itself for the good of another; but the crystal bars moved not yet. Next she brought the last life-drop of a hero's blood, dying for freedom and his country; but this did not avail. At last she spies a man, hard and haggard in sin. Crime had crimsoned his soul, and he had no hope, no joy. Across his path there passes a little child, innocent and glad; and at evening it kneels before his eyes in simple prayer.

> " And how felt he, that wretched man
>   Reclining there—while memory ran
>   O'er many a year of guilt and strife ?
> ' There was a time,' he said, in mild,
>   Heart-humbled tears—' thou blessed child,
>   When, young and happy, pure as thou,
>   I looked and prayed like thee : but now '—
>   He hung his head : each nobler aim
>   And hope and feeling which had slept
>   From boyhood-hour, that instant came
>   Fresh o'er him, and he wept—he wept !
>   Blest tears of soul-felt penitence !
>   In whose benign, redeeming flow,
>   Is felt the first, the only sense
>   Of guiltless joy that guilt can know.

Heaven's choicest gift at last was found. Divest the rhythm of all that is fanciful and scenic in form, what is the residuum but that substantial truth which fell from the lips of the Son of God? " Blessed are the poor in spirit, for theirs is the kingdom of heaven ! " Let this evangelic lesson be learned and practised by all, and we shall better comprehend on earth and in heaven these words of the Spirit : " They that sow in tears, shall reap in joy." Through the grace of our Lord Jesus Christ, penitential sensibility gives birth to peace, to the gladness of hope, joy unspeakable, and everlasting songs.

CHEAP CONTENTMENT.

He hath made every thing beautiful in his time.

ECCL. 3 : 11.

7

VII.

CHEAP CONTENTMENT.

HAPPINESS depends more upon those things which are common to all than upon those which are the rare and signal property of the few. Those matters in which men differ from one another on the scale of social condition, are not half so important and valuable as those in which they agree. In regard to all which is substantial and needful for our good, it is certainly true, " the same Lord over all is rich unto all."

Take the two extremes of life—infancy and age. It might strike the ear of some as a very questionable truth when we say, that it is altogether unnecessary to do any thing by way of making a little child happy. But careful observation will fully confirm the remark. Our beneficent Maker has abundantly provided for the happiness of children, and of all children alike ; and all that is needful on our part is to be careful to put no obstructions in their way. The brook needs no artificial aid to give motion and music to its waters ; throw no dam across it, and it will take care of itself, delighted with the freeness and swiftness of its running. No more does a young child need any expensive and solicitous thought for its happiness.   The first pleasures of the human infant are physical altogether, such as accompany the gratification of its animal appetites.   Next to these, are the pleasures of the imagination, when the young child has attained sufficient growth to hold its toys, and dispose around it the materials of amusement, investing them with life, conversing with them, or soliloquizing among them, as if they were living personages.   Always excepting those rare cases of extreme penury, happily so rare with us, when infant and adult life pine away in desperate famine, what possible difference can there be between one child and another, in palace or cottage, as to the amount of their physical enjoyment?   Parental fondness takes pride and pleasure in surrounding the occupants of a nursery with every object which itself may imagine to be necessary; and so pleases itself by fancying that it is pleasing the object of its needless affluence.   But what matters it to a child, of what rank in life, and of what quality of clay may be the person from whom it draws its sustenance, provided it find enough to satisfy its appetite?   Adult vanity may feel the difference to itself; but what difference does it make to an infant-child, whether it be dressed in costly lace or linsey-woolsey, or is without any dress at all, if its tender surface feels that degree of warmth or coolness which is most agreeable?   If it be permitted to fall asleep just when it feels inclined, and sleep as long and soundly as it will, what does it care whether it swing on "a tree-top," heedless of a fall, or is rocked in a nautilus-shaped cradle, inlaid with pearl, with artistic forms of angels spreading their wings over its satin canopy?   The delight of motion, the pleasure of exercis·

ing their own limbs and organs, is an enjoyment which childhood shares with lambs scampering down the hill-side ; with birds, now mounting aloft, and now shooting downwards. If this motion be only allowed them free and unmolested, of what concern is it to children whether they romp in a garret, a corn-barn, or on a velvet carpet, and within tapestried walls? At a very early age, children take delight in matings and companionships. Who ever observed among them any regard for the distinctions of rank and wealth, if left to themselves, unpoisoned by the suggestions of older pride ? In their overweening care of their first-born, parents do not discover—but discover it at length they do when observation has grown calmer and wiser—that it is altogether superfluous to purchase expensive toys, and take pains to invent amusement for young children. The only value of a toy is to help that earliest of the faculties, the imagination, in its pleasant and playful creations. For the pleasure of infantine architecture, a few corn-cobs, and as many small blocks, which never cost a penny, will do as good a service, and confer as much real satisfaction, as costly devices of ivory and sandal-wood ; and for all the play and pleasure of imaginary maternity, while, as yet, the young child is in the honest simplicity of nature, untouched by the artificial lessons of pride, a doll constructed of rags and charcoal will excite every whit as much of happy prattle, and accomplish as kindly a service, on the bare boards of the poor man's cottage, as the costlier fabric of wax and porcelain in the carpeted nursery of the rich ; and a country-boy, nestling down on the warm side of a shed, " digging his Lilliputian well, and fencing in his six-inch barn-yard," will find a serener delight than his metropolitan contemporary, whom affluent indulgence is overburdening with the entertainments and pastimes of expensive art.   Never was there a vainer, a more useless thing, than to labor to make a young child happy.   Kind nature has provided for all alike at that period, if you will not unnecessarily obstruct their innocent freedom, nor throw your shadow in the way of their sunshine.   Study to supply them with means of happiness, and in manifold instances you will only defeat your own intention, kindling up an unnatural craving, a querulousness, and dissatisfaction, which is the greatest of curses which wealth can inflict on the tender nature of childhood.

Pass now to the opposite extreme of life—to *old age*—and you will observe that what is most essential to its comfort is common to all who have reached its dignified tranquillity.   In the words of Dr. Paley, "it is not for youth alone that the great Parent of creation hath provided. Happiness is found with the purring cat, no less than with the playful kitten ; in the arm-chair of dozing age as well as in the sprightliness and animation of youthful re-creations.   To novelty, to acuteness of sensation, to hope, to ardor of pursuit, succeeds what is, in no inconsiderable degree, an equivalent for them all, 'perception of ease.'   Herein is the exact difference between the young and the old : the young are happy when enjoying pleasure ; the old are happy when free from pain.   The vigor of youth is stimulated to action by impatience of rest ; whilst to the imbecility of age, quietness and repose become positive gratifications.   In one important respect the advantage is with the old. A state of ease is, generally speaking, more attainable than a state of pleasure. A constitution, therefore, which can enjoy ease, is preferable to that which can taste only pleasure. This same perception of ease oftentimes renders old age a condition of great comfort, especially when riding at its anchor after a busy and tempestuous life. It is well described by Rousseau to be the interval of repose and enjoyment between the hurry and the end of life." Do not imagine that wealth ministers to the happiness of age, by putting at its disposal excitements and luxuries. It needs not brilliancy, but prefers the softer shade. Noisy mirth, the revel, and the dance, are distasteful to one who asks for nothing but tranquil rest. Expensive journeyings, voyages, and spectacles, so attractive to the young, have no charms for those who desire only to be still. Desires have failed, the daughters of music are brought low; and could your affluence command all the sources of delight which were the ambition of younger life, when the passions were impetuous and the pulses strong, you could not give one moment's happiness to those who have reached the period of life when they need nothing for their happiness but to be freed from all physical and mental pain, and left to their long-sought and undisturbed repose. An unspeakable pleasure and privilege it is when filial gratitude is permitted to minister to parental infirmity and age ; but expensive, over-careful and officious kindness to such, is far more pleasant to those who give, than it is necessary to those who receive it ; for their wants are few and simple, within the reach of the humble as the opulent ; and as it was with infancy, so is

it with age : if you will but avoid putting obstacles and
obstructions in its way, our Creator hath provided for its
cheap and common contentment.

I have spoken of a community of blessings at different ages of life.   Let us look at differences of condition.
The chief necessities of cur nature are very few, and
very soon and easily supplied.   The healthful appetites
of the body are common to all.   If these are satisfied,
wherein lies the advantage of affluence over mediocrity?
The true limit is in our nature, not in our means.   The
appetite demands a certain supply; if a poor man ac-
complishes this, what more than this can be accomplished by the rich?   If one's appetites were multiplied in proportion to his means of gratifying them ; if his capacity
for eating and drinking was enlarged, in some correspondence to his ability to provide viands and beverages ; if
his power to sleep, for the length of its indulgence or the
sweetness of its oblivion, were graduated by the number
and quality of the beds his wealth could purchase; if
his various organs and senses acquired sensibility just
as fast as he acquired the means of expending for their
gratification ; if the sense of comfort in the use of raiment were in any degree proportioned to his power of
buying every species of wearing apparel by the bale or
cargo ; if the retina of the eye were expanded, in equal
degree with the enlargement of one's ability to pay for
all objects of beauty, and the tympanum of the ear gathered to itself new faculties of perception and enjoyment
just as fast as its possessor accumulated around him the
wealth of music ; if all this were true, then might we see
the prodigious advantage of the rich over the poor, in the

materials of physical enjoyments. But there is nothing like this in the dispensations of Providence. The length of one's purse cannot add one inch to his stature, nor one capacity to his organs; the plethora of his check-book gives no enlargement to limb, sense, or faculty. In all but the imaginary appetites of our physical nature, there is an absolute equality among all. We cannot transcend the capacities of our constitution. Build and own as many palaces as did Solomon, by a law of your nature you can-not be in more than one place at a time ; purchase as many horses as ever stood in stalls of cedar, in the sta-bles of any monarch, so long as you are a man, and not a monster, you can bestride only one at once. Should as many cup-bearers as stood before Persian thrones of gold wait on your thirst, and as many oxen and sheep load your tables as were daily served in ancient palaces, and as many beds of ivory, with sounds of adjacent fountains lulling to repose, as ever were seen in Aladdin's Dream, and as many garments of silk and wool and needle-work as make up the wardrobe of an oriental prince, you could neither eat, nor drink, nor sleep, nor wear one whit more than the common faculties and appetites of our nature require for your comfort. Strive to exceed these, and punitive reaction will prove your folly. Strive to surpass the ordinary bounds of nature, and the keen relish of health departs, enjoyment is turned into loathing ; excess ex-acts its penalty, and you are thrown back upon the wise equalities of nature, convinced that with these you can never trifle without doing yourself a mischief. The sleep of the laboring man is sweet. Vigorous is the relish with which he eats the bread of industry. Fortunate are the affluent if they can boast as much. They can certainly boast of nothing more. Just here, on this cheap and common ground, the wisdom of Inspiration puts the limit of physical good. " Hast thou found honey? eat so much as is sufficient for thee." The experience of any child will tell you what will be the consequences of repletion beyond sufficiency.

Travellers in the deserts of the East are often deceived by the *mirage,* that singular reflection of earth and sky, which assumes the appearance of inviting waters. No sooner have they reached the place of that welcome vision, than they find it sand instead of water; and surprised are they, when turning round upon the path which they have already trodden, to see in the horizon they have left behind them the same illusive spectacle—the vision of water now, where, a short time before, they found nothing but sand. Just so it is in the pilgrimage of life. There is a mirage before us and another behind us; but all the water we shall find in the desert is that we carry along with us day by day. The place where we now are is the very one which was once overhung with the mirrored promise of satisfaction; we have reached the spot, the illusion changes, and we now are filled with regret because we did not see the streams and the lakes which lay along the path which we have already traversed. The enjoyments of life are to be found in our present condition and occupations; and the wells from which we drink must be dug day by day where we pitch our tabernacle. Taking life just as it is, at this our present time, we must extract the true elixir of contentment from its common realities. Vastly are we to be commiserated if we are always to be the sport of illusive hope and illusive regrets ; not having learned as yet how the very sands on which we tread may become grateful as the greensward to our feet, in the march of duty and the offices of affection. How much I should be privileged to do for the happiness of the reader, if I could succeed in fairly lodging the conviction in his mind, that this succession of work and rest, care and relaxation, duty and sorrow, which compose the substance of our every-day life, this is the material, the common sand, dirt and rubbish, out of which we must gather all the particles of true gold, which constitute the ordinary means of our enjoyment in this earthly life.

A young couple commence their married life in humble mediocrity. No wealthy parents have enriched them with dowry or inheritance. No influential friends furnish them with facility, or help, or promise. Self-reliant, they are to depend upon their own industry, judgment, and patience. Nothing have they but their own minds and hands, and they work on. Busy temptation may whisper in their ears, that theirs is a life of thankless and ignoble drudgery. The mirage begins to gleam in the false future. Drive away that serpent falsehood, which will poison your peace. Work is not your bane, but your blessing. You know not now how much you owe to the necessity of that daily toil which you are tempted to hate and despise. Work on, and find now in honest industry and frugal living, and your own earnings, cheerfulness, contentment, health of body and mind. Certain it is, should success crown your exertions, and affluence be your future lot, that from days of listless leisure and splendid tedium, you will look back to this early toil, and wonder why you were not more happy under its sober blessing.

A classical writer of our times, describing the population of ancient Rome, all its rank and fashion and pride assembled in the Flavian Amphitheatre, as spectators of imperial shows, has ventured to ask whether it was probable that the elegant Fulvia, then and there present, ever thought of telling the happy news to her friend Lucretia that her baby had that day actually cut a tooth ! The implication is, that mothers who took delight in the gladiatorial exhibitions of the Coliseum, had reached that degree of splendid misery in which they had entirely outlived all taste and pleasure for the simple humanities of home. Hope and memory both may stand aside awhile : all that is great and magnificent in the world may withdraw for a season from the visions of the humble pair whose fortunes we are following, for all the world to them is that first-born, which has filled their home with wonder and gladness. Smile not at their simple happiness. What new thoughts and affections spring into life ; what memories of the babe of Bethlehem form a halo of light around that small cradle, with which their home is honored ; what discoveries, what surprises, what pleasures, what imaginations, what delights, are associated with the common, every-day, and simple incidents of that first infant's life ; and the time, unhappily, may come in later years, when those very parents will admit that some discovery, some achievement, or good-fortune of theirs which the world admires, has actually caused less congratulation, led to less remark, and produced in them less of satisfaction, than when, in simpler days, they discovered that their first-born child had achieved the wondrous act of cutting a tooth. Be contented and happy now. Lay hold of the "fleet angel of opportunity" who has entered your dwelling, and suffer her not to go till she has filled your heart with blessings.

Now come days of trial and fear. Adversity throws her sombre shadow over that humble home. Sickness comes, and there are long and weary watchings at the bedside. Is not the mirage of remembrance or delusive hope a blessing now to the thirsty soul? Ah! you know not what deep wells of love are dug by the sharp tools of solicitude and pain. Draw water now, and drink. More blessed are ye in mutual trust, in mutual dependence, in all the ministries and offices of kindness, than if sickness had never been known; and times of what the world calls prosperity may yet ensue, when the only way in which the hard heart can be softened, and filled up with blessedness, will be to recall the very season through which you are now passing—the hours of watching you have had by one another, and by your children, when your whole soul was suffused with tenderness.

Then came disappointments and disasters; the little fortune was wrecked, and business was deranged, and means of subsistence were few and precarious. They have gone down hand in hand into a low valley, and sometimes they are ready to despond and fear, as un-looked-for shadows settle around them. But these are times of heroism and fortitude, when the brave spirit learns to dispense with what was once thought to be ne-cessary, and so it rejoices in its own independence : now is the time for self-denials, the foregoing of little pleasures for another's help, of manly strugglings together for a livelihood, of frugal spendings, of careful savings ; what you purchase, what you earn now, has a value which cannot be computed in coinage. Now is the harvest-time of patience and trust and courage ; be strong, and use your sickle well ; fill your bosom with the sheaves of cheap yet priceless enjoyments, for no plenty of the past or the future hath been, nor will be, so rich in dear and precious memories as this very season of trouble, in which folly might tempt you to be discontented.

I will not hesitate to advance into darker shades. We have reached that stage in the journey where death becomes a visitant in the dwelling. His cold shadow falls on that bright and happy child, and a whole household shivers under its chill. From that shadow they cannot pass as yet. It seems at first, when that darling head had drooped, and that fair face was overspread with pallor, and death had actually taken your child away, that your heart would burst from its prison to follow him. But meek blessings come in the train of sorrow. Be not afraid of the darkness—for the night shall be light about you. Springs of blessedness will come now to the surface, of whose existence you had never before dreamed. You are passing through an experience now in which you are laying up memories, hopes, and affections for all your future being. The child that died out of your bosom is lost to the world, as if it were no more than one blossom of the Spring. But it will never be lost to you. How often, in visions of day and night, is that bright and laughing countenance turned on you, as if it had been the face of an angel. What an unspeakable tenderness will that memory impart whenever you look upon living children, your own, or those who are poor and neglected. When your eye falls upon children who are happy, it will not be envious of their life, for the life of the one who was taken is safer and happier than theirs ; and when you see or hear of those who have fallen into suffering and shame, you will have a kindly and compassionate feeling for them ; for so might it have been with yours, but for the safety and glory of its translation. There were no giving of thanks with many, if there were not some way of being happy in sorrow. Blessed are they that mourn. Wait not for future healing, but be calm and blessed, as you are.

Count it not presumptuous if we should dare to speak of their separation, whose united life we have traced so far. The blow has fallen, and one of the twain is left alone. The future has no mirage now, nothing but embankments of cloud ; the past alone is bright. Shall the lonely pilgrim travel back, expecting to find and realize again the vision which has vanished? Not so. He must find a present and immediate good, or he will perish. He cannot be deluded by any thing before or behind him. His feet are planted by the grave-side, and his eyes are turned upward. Strength has come, and the bereaved can be cheerful still. The widow or the deserted one, in that widowhood which is worst of all, pressed by kindly necessity, is surprised at her own preternatural resolution and heroism. Powers and faculties are developed within her, whose existence never before had been suspected. Thrown off from the supports to which it had clung before, the frail vine has shot out into a strong and elastic stem. Sympathy, honor, admiration, and rewards around her, gratitude and peace are within her. Though she cannot anticipate the supply of her wants in the future journey of life, yet the rock affords its drink, and the dry sand is overspread with manna, and, as she journeys on, that heavy body of clouds which overhung the future begins to brighten, and because of trouble and anguish of spirit, the bereaved rejoices in hope, and the weary looks forward to her rest.

What a hard, cold, cheerless, hopeless thing the human heart would be, if bereft of all recollections of past losses, griefs, and sufferings. The philosophy of the world is quite the reverse of this. When it would prescribe for our happiness, it interdicts any allusion to past occurrences which are painful. But when religion would deepen and purify our blessedness, it bids us remember all, not excepting even wrong and outrage; for, if these be forgotten, where were forgiveness and tenderness and compassion? and if memory be absent, where can gratitude be found? Come back, ye visions of the past: childhood, removed now so far—our first and earliest home—ours no longer, save in remembrance; follies, mistakes, sicknesses, deliverances, struggles, losses, bereavements, come back, and help us to be meek, quiet, tender, and grateful. Come back, ye long-mourned, departed ones. Our homes and our hearts would be desolate enough, if there were no remembrance of you; father, mother, husband, wife, brother, sister, child, years have gone since you left us; we have never forgotten you, and the thought of what you were to us soothes us into a special tenderness and affectionateness towards friends who survive.

Tire not yourself with what the old philosopher has called the "histrionism of happiness." There is nothing more empty of rewards than affectation. How many are downright sick and weary with show, brilliancy, and splendor. It is grateful to the eye sometimes to look on what is plain and homely; to relieve that organ, strained, bleared, and blinded by long gazing on high-wrought colors, by turning it to the sober shades of common life. The problem given us to solve—nay, it has been solved for us—the lesson given us to practise, is: to be happy, TAKING LIFE JUST AS IT IS.

When we speak of the Gospel of Christ as the charm and coronation of all mercies, this is its highest glory—it is accessible and free to all alike. "Beloved," says the Apostle Jude, "I write to you of the COMMON SALVATION." So cheap are the conditions of its invaluable gifts, that they are absolutely "without money and without price." Jesus of Nazareth sat down to meat in the cottage at Bethany as well as at the table of Simon and Zaccheus, the rich men of their day. So kindly and impartial are His visits still.

BALANCINGS AND COMPENSATIONS.

Now Naaman was a great man with his master, and honourable : he was also a mighty man in valour, *but* he was a leper.

2 KINGS 5 : I.

VIII.

BALANCINGS AND COMPENSATIONS.

SAADI, the Persian Poet, whose words breathe a wisdom and kindliness not unlike those of Inspiration, informs us that he never complained of his condition but once—when his feet were bare, and he had no money to buy shoes; but, meeting with a man without feet, he instantly became contented with his lot.

The world is full of these strange balancings and compensations. It is essential to our happiness that we take them into account.

We enter the city of Damascus in its palmiest days of ancient splendor. Lying on the high-road, along which passed the caravans of India, distinguished for the beauty of its position, its natural advantages, begirt by gardens of the richest fertility, watered by sparkling streams flowing from Lebanon; there was a time when it deserved the title which it formerly bore among the Orientals—"a pearl set in emeralds." In the days of Benhadad, Damascus was the metropolis of a very powerful empire; for we read that "thirty and two kings"—pachas, as they would now be called—accompanied their monarch in one of the campaigns which he undertook against Samaria. Entering this city, the seat of arms, commerce, and wealth, walking along the principal street, full of the pride of life, our eye is arrested by an equipage of unusual pretensions.   The man whom it bears along attracts universal regard and admiration.   He is the "observed of all observers."   Inquiring who he can be, we learn that he is the chief favorite of the king, the captain of his armies, by whose valor the country had achieved splendid victories, and a proud deliverance from her enemies.   This is Naaman, a great man with his master, and honorable, and no man in the land can vie with him in rank, wealth, or honors.   How many envy him.   All eyes follow him, as prancing steeds bear him along, in a perpetual ovation.   "BUT he was a leper."   Under all that splendid show, which made him the admiration of a throng, beneath that embroidered tunic, eating into his flesh, was an incurable and loathsome disease, which, had it been known, would have prevented the meanest man in Syria from exchanging places with him.   Had he been in Israel, his leprosy would have disqualified him for all public appointments. Afflicted with no such civil disabilities in Syria, with all distinctions and honors, regarded, so far as office and rank and emolument were concerned, as the most favored of men, nevertheless he was subject to one of the sorest of all calamities, so that life was a burden to him.

The reader already catches the drift of my theme— perceiving that a small conjunction may serve as a nail on which to hang many important suggestions in regard to the estimate we should form of human condition. Most men are perpetually misled by appearances.   They conclude that he is the most blessed who is in possession of those things which they themselves desire and have not. They leave out of the calculation the counter-weight and the drawback, forgetting that he whom they envy is wanting in some other object which they possess, or is afflicted with some form of suffering from which they are altogether exempt. This is a fact too true and too weighty to be overlooked. The writer will not be suspected of any thing morbid or misanthropic if he gives this fact a more expanded statement. There is a " *but* " in every man's life. There is some subtraction to be made from the sum-total of his condition. There is some alloy in the metal, some one thing which he could wish were other than it is, and which is the secret weight that a wise Providence has attached to the clock-work of life, the index-finger of which revolves on a dial of enamel and figures of gold. You are deceived and made unhappy if you do not take into account, along with all which you admire and covet in the condition of another, just that one subtraction which is suggested by this little, surly, evasive conjunction, *but*. Here is a man of extensive business, of great prosperity, of abundant wealth, *but* cankering care has so corroded into his life, he can neither eat nor sleep in comfort. Here is a man-sion which attracts attention by its costliness and ele-gance, sumptuous furniture, works of art ; *but* some secret domestic sorrow throws all that splendor into shadow. Parents live, and are in possession of such means as enable them to give their children every thing ; *but* all that they could give them was a grave. Jacob survives ; *but* Joseph is not, and Benjamin is taken away ; so that his gray head droopeth with sorrow towards the ground. One retains his property, *but* his character is suspected. Another rejoices in a good name, which never suffered a lesion or a stain, *but* he is distressed as to the means of subsistence. After years of strugglings, care, and toil, one reaches the fullest success in his profession ; *but* those who had been the charm and the motive of life are gone, and he is alone. David ascends the throne of Israel amid regal honors and affluence ; *but* how many cares and distractions had he in his home and his kingdom. Abraham was honored with the friendship of God ; *but* he had Ishmael for a son, in whose behalf he wept and prayed without comfort. Abigail is included in the roll of the saints for her sweetness and affectionateness ; *but* she had Nabal, a churl, for her husband. Paul gleams high among the children of men, as the chief of the Christian apostles ; *but* he had a thorn in the flesh, which pierced him for years, and which he prayed might be taken away. George Herbert united in himself as many qualities of ancestral wealth, serene piety, placid disposition, and poetic genius, as were ever united in any Christian minister ; *but* he had an infidel brother, the leader of the English deists. The suffrages of the world, to-day, would place the name of John Milton, for the nobility of his soul, his love of liberty, his sublimity of genius, in the highest niche of human fame ; *but* Milton was blind— Milton was poor. The whole human race admires the boundless philanthropy of Howard, judging that the measure of his blessedness was full because he was full of pity and love ; *but* he had a dissolute son, who died in a mad-house. You would find it difficult to fix upon another name which gathers to itself more of honor, as time rolls on, for varied qualities in science, philosophy, and religion, than Blaize Pascal ; *but* all his life he waged incessant conflict with fiercest pain, which, at the early age of thirty-seven, mastered and ended his earthly life. Many listened to the magnificent eloquence of Robert Hall, and many now peruse his books with delight, who knew not that these were prepared amid sufferings of body and mind which twice deprived him of reason, and which for years rendered life well-nigh intolerable. The author of the Task presents as many claims to esteem and love, both for talent and virtue, as any man that could be named ; *but* William Cowper was subject to that most cruel of all calamities incident to humanity, insane melancholy. Look at William Pitt : a prodigy of success ; at twenty-three years of age the Prime Minister of England ; at twenty-eight, occupying a position in the honors of his country, in popular enthusiasm, because of his eloquence, his power, his acknowledged authority in administering the government of a great kingdom, without precedent or parallel ; *but* so annoyed by political rivalries and coalitions, and so alarmed because of new and terrible exigencies arising out of the revolutions of the Continent, that sleep and appetite forsook him, and a broken heart laid him in Westminster Abbey at the early age of forty-seven. A distinguished jurist in this country once wrote to William Wirt, when in the zenith of his fame, congratulating him on some particular honor or success which he had just acquired. He was surprised by the reply which he received from that fascinating man. " I have no taste for worldly business. I go to it reluctantly. I dread the world, the strife and emulation of the bar ; but I will do my duty ; that is my religion." The world had forgotten the event which had left an incurable sorrow in his heart,—the death, years before, of a daughter, whom he thus describes : " She was my companion, my office-companion, my librarian, my clerk. My papers now bear her indorsement. She pursued her studies in my office, by my side, sat with me, walked with me, was my inexpressibly sweet and inseparable companion. We knew all her intelligence, all her pure and delicate sensibility, the quickness and power of her perceptions, her seraphic love. She was all love, and loved all God's creation, even the animals, trees, and plants. She loved her God and Saviour with an angel-love, and died like a saint." The arrow which felled her passed also through a larger and nobler frame, which never rallied from the hurt.

It is needless to multiply examples. These are not extraordinary exceptions, but instances of a common experience. There never was one upon the earth, who, however prospered, had not his own weight and damper. You see those who are exempt from the afflictions which are the most severe in your own case, and therefore conclude that they are the most fortunate of men ; forgetting, meanwhile, that they are subject to some other form of trouble, of which, happily, you know nothing at all. It may be secret, as the leprosy which was hid beneath the sleeve of Naaman ; or as palpable as any calamity which ever invoked public commiseration.

A truthful estimate can be reached only by the balancing of advantages and disadvantages. On many accounts one is to be congratulated. In many respects you are prospered, BUT—*but*, . . "The heart knoweth its own bitterness." There is the recent grief, or, what is often forgotten by others, the memory and the scar of a former affliction, which never is forgotten by the heart itself. There is some secret solicitude, some deep-seated care, some painful apprehension, some invisible thorn, never suspected outside of the privacy of home, or rankling unconfessed in the silence of a troubled heart. Naaman was a great captain, high and honorable, *but* he was a leper.

Here is a fact in the arithmetic of life too important to be left out of the computation. We must not look at our own troubles through a magnifying glass. It is better to consider them as our own, suited, in their nature, to ourselves by a Power wiser than we. This, and not another, is to be construed as our own peculiar property. That which is a trial to one, would be regarded as no trial at all by another. Jacob wrestled with the angel most sturdily and manfully ; nor was it till the finger of his antagonist touched a particular sinew, that his strength faltered. Achilles was invulnerable in every part but *one*; that one was discovered, and wounded. Oftentimes men are so constituted that there is only one place in which a wound can be inflicted. The arrow finds it before the battle of life is over. Nothing else could ever have given them a pang. This may be deferred for a long time, but sooner or later it comes. And this must be considered as belonging to *us*, and so to be borne with equanimity and patience. It is this

thought which cures all envy of others, and every desire
to exchange conditions with them. If such a thing were
possible, we should be the first, most probably, to regret
it. This idea has been elaborated, with great force, by
several authors, ancient and modern. It was thought by
Socrates that if mankind could throw all their miseries
into a common stock, and then make a choice out of the
whole heap, each would go away with a larger amount of
suffering and discontent than now attend the inflictions
which are appointed to each by Supreme Power. The
same idea is expanded by Horace in one of the most
celebrated of his odes. Addison, in one of the numbers
of the *Spectator*, has constructed a very ingenious fable
out of the same conception, for which he confessed himself indebted to those writers of antiquity. The dream
took a form somewhat like this: A proclamation from
Jupiter, that mortals might lay down all their griefs and
calamities, and then each was to choose out of the heap,
that which he preferred as being lighter and comelier than
his own. A vast plain was selected for the purpose ; and,
as the whole race threw down their pains, their deformi-
ties, and their burdens, the mass grew to a prodigious
size, reaching like a mountain to the skies. What a
sense of relief, what an exuberant gladness, was there,
upon this singular occasion ; every one permitted to make
choice out of this immense heap of any trouble, which he
should exchange for his own. How soon that satisfaction gave place to a most bitter sorrow! Not one exchange was made for the better. A venerable, gray-
headed man, who had been greatly afflicted for want of
an heir to his estate, immediately seized as his choice a

son, who, because he was undutiful, had been thrown upon the mass by a disappointed and disconsolate father. The graceless fellow soon made such exhibition of his violent temper, his low and vulgar passions, that his new father would gladly have receded from his choice as a positive relief. In short, this futile attempt to exchange burdens and maladies was the occasion of so many murmurs and complaints, groans and lamentations, that the Throne was petitioned that the old order of things might be restored, even that mortals might be permitted, a second time, to lay down their loads, and each one to take up that which was his own again.

It was a touching answer given to the question, proposed at an exhibition of deaf mutes—"Which would you prefer—to be blind, or deaf and dumb?" The sylph-like form to whom the question, with doubtful delicacy, had been put, immediately wrote upon the slate these words : "Even so, Father, for so it seemeth good in Thy sight."

Before we can dream of exchanging conditions with any mortals, we must be sure that we know not only what we are to gain, but as well also what we shall lose. If life is justly described as a barter of objects, before we give way to envy of any man's possessions, we should ascertain the price at which he has purchased them. This idea was elaborated ages ago by Epictetus in an argument which Mrs. Barbauld has paraphrased in one of her admirable essays. "We should consider this world as a great mart of commerce where fortune exposes to our view various commodities, riches, ease, tranquillity, fame, integrity, knowledge. Every thing is marked at a settled price. Our time, our labor, our ingenuity, are so much

ready money which we are to lay out to the best advan
tage. Examine, compare, choose, reject; but stand to
your own judgment: and do not, like children, when you
have purchased one thing, repine that you do not possess
another which you did not purchase. Would you, for
instance, be rich? Do you think that single point worth
the sacrificing every thing else to? You may then be rich.
Thousands have become so from the lowest beginnings,
by toil, and patient diligence, and attention to the minutest
articles of expense and profit. But you must give up the
pleasures of leisure, of a vacant mind, of a free, unsuspi-
cious temper. If you preserve your integrity, it must
be a coarse-spun and vulgar honesty. Those high and
lofty notions of morals which you brought with you from
the schools must be considerably lowered and mixed
with the baser alloy of a jealous and worldly-minded
prudence. You must learn to do hard, if not unjust
things; and for the nice embarrassments of a delicate
and ingenuous spirit, it is necessary for you to get rid of
them as fast as possible. You must shut your heart
against the Muses, and be content to feed your understanding with plain household truths. In short, you must
not attempt to enlarge your ideas or polish your taste, or
refine your sentiments; but must keep on in one beaten
track, without turning aside either to the right hand or
to the left. ‘But I cannot submit to drudgery like this—
I feel a spirit above it.’ ’Tis well: be above it, then; only
do not repine that you are not rich. ‘But is it not some
reproach upon the economy of Providence that such a one,
who is a mean, ignorant fellow, should have amassed such
wealth?’ Not in the least. He has paid his health, his

conscience, his liberty, for it ; and will you envy him his bargain because he outshines you in equipage and show? Lift up your brow with a noble confidence, and say to yourself, 'I have not these things, it is true ; but it is because I possess something better. I have chosen my lot. I am content and satisfied.' The substance of this philosophy is well expressed by Pope in his *Essay on Man :*

> Bring, then, these blessings to a strict account ;
> Make fair deductions :—see to what they mount ;
> How much of other each is sure to cost ;
> How each for other oft is wholly lost ;
> How inconsistent greater goods with these ;
> How sometimes life is risked—and always ease.
> Think ; and if still the things thy envy call,
> Say—wouldst thou be the man to whom they fall ?

But this is only one aspect of a great subject. To be cured of envy is one thing. This may be accomplished by the process now described, and most portentous mistakes still be made in the estimate of life.

Sometimes the eye, glancing over a newspaper, is caught by a glaring and pretentious advertisement of an infallible medicine. Some one claims to have travelled in foreign parts—to have been initiated into some great secret of nature, which promises a certain relief for all the most formidable maladies incident to humanity. For a consideration, he will communicate it to others. Now there is one real panacea for all the griefs to which mortals are subject. It may be obtained without money and without price. It is a prescription which will never fail to impart a genial warmth and comfort to the most prostrate and exhausted spirit.

In an algebraic calculation, it is of great consequence where and how your signs and quantities are placed. It makes the greatest difference in the result whether certain figures are used as items of subtraction or items of addition. We have seen how this particle "*but*" may be used to denote the diversified amounts which are to be subtracted from the sum-total of individual happiness. Now the very same word may be used, after another method, to denote the several items of cheer and contentment, on the other side of the equation, which should be added to the estimate of our condition. All the difference in the world does it make whether your "*but*" be regarded as a plus or a minus quantity; whether you use it to denote the diminution or the increase of your possessions. Now, the cheap but invaluable prescription for personal happiness may be expressed in this laconic form. Let every one estimate himself at the very lowest stage of demerit, and then use his "*but*" to measure off his ascending and accumulating mercies. Instead of beginning at the top, the pinnacle of success and prosperity, and proceeding to lessen one's happiness by what you are forced to take away, begin at the opposite extreme, at the very nadir of one's demerits, and then let every item of God's goodness be a stepping-stone by which you shall rise into a joyful gratitude. The process might describe itself by soliloquizing after this method: 'I am without many things which I could desire, *but* I have a thousand mercies beyond what I deserve. I am the man that has seen afflictions, *but* I am alive, and am not delivered over to the pains of eternal death. Troubles are on every side, *but* I am not in despair. Many things come to pass otherwise than I could wish, *but* the Lord hath not dealt with me after my sins, nor rewarded me according to my iniquities. Am I in danger of discomposure and envy when I see the prosperity of such as are never in trouble as other men? *but*, God be thanked, I am not with those who have died in their sins, and made their bed in sorrow. I have been disappointed in many a hope and confidence ; *but*, in this will I rejoice, God is the strength of my heart and my portion forever. I have met with losses ; *but* there is a Gospel which promises me what never can be taken away. I am poor as Lazarus—as lonely, diseased, and forlorn as he ; *but* I have hope in the Redeemer. My body is infirm and racked with pain ; *but* my soul has life and strength and joy in God. I miss the society of many a friend who once was my solace and associate ; *but* I have many of increased kindness and tenderness who remain. Had troubles rolled over me like the waves of the sea, I could not complain ; *but* here I am—the mercies of heaven crowning my life, and the portals of the celestial city inviting my entrance. I am a widow ; *but* my Maker is my husband. I am an orphan ; *but* God is my father. I am childless, and my tabernacle is spoiled ; *but* how much better to have sons and daughters in the skies, than to have Ishmaels and Absaloms to pierce the heart with what is sharper than a serpent's tooth. I have lost many a noble opportunity ; *but* life is not yet ended, and occasions still remain. I am weak and worthless ; *but* Christ has promised that his grace shall be sufficient for me. I ought to be better

than I am ; *but*, thanks be to God for the promise of an.
ultimate perfection.   Many a pleasure, many a gratification, which others enjoy, are wholly denied to me ; *but*,
God be praised that he has not left me to seek all my
good things in this life.   I am tortured often by the fear
of death ; *but* I can go and sit down in the tomb of
Joseph, and think of Christ and the resurrection.   I have
not all the assurance of faith and hope that I could
desire ; *but*, how can I be sufficiently grateful for the
least glimmer of consolation, through the abundant
mercy of the Son of God?   Multiply thorns, burdens,
and grievances, as you will ; *but* these afflictions are only
for a moment.   Make my condition deplorable as you
can ; let the worst that can be conceived come to pass ;
strip me of friends, of property, of health, of all things ;
but, what an unspeakable honor and blessedness it is to
be a child of God, and the heir-expectant of an eternal
kingdom !'

This is the mode of computation which ought to
keep us in perpetual thankfulness.   It was this method
of calculation which prompted John Newton, when
making a pastoral visit to a pious lady who had met with
a severe calamity in the sudden loss of all her property,
to accost her with smiles, saying, to her surprise, that he
had come to *congratulate* her.   "Congratulate, Mr. Newton ! why not condole with me ?"   "Why should I not
congratulate you for possessing that good part which
never can be taken away from you?"

A heart disposed to find material for gratitude on
all occasions, will never be wanting in substantial happiness.

> O happiness! our being's end and aim!
> Good, pleasure, ease, content, whate'er thy name!
> That something still which prompts the eternal sigh!
> For which we bear to live, or dare to die!
> Which still so near us, yet beyond us lies;
> O'erlooked, seen double, by the fool and wise.
> Plant of celestial seed! if dropt below,
> Say in what mortal soil thou deign'st to grow.
> Where grows? Where grows it not? If vain our toil,
> We ought to blame the culture, not the soil.
> Fix'd to no spot is happiness sincere;
> 'Tis nowhere to be found, or *every where.*

Happiness is a temper of the soul, not a condition of the person. Its essential elements are gratitude, kindness, truth, honor, and unfaltering trust in God; a disposition to see good in all things, and when evil comes, to bear it with patience, and more than that, with joy, because it is the will of God. The will of God! It is a phrase slipped most volubly from the tongue, but what a world of meaning does it contain. All things appointed by infinite intelligence, infinite wisdom, and infinite love! Could any one wish to absolve himself from such a jurisdiction?

When the will of God becomes our own—when, through the spirit of true piety, the appointments of Providence and our own choice are brought into harmony, the ultimatum of our spiritual education is attained, and we are prepared for an immortal blessedness. "Thy will be done on earth—and done by us—as it is in heaven!" Such must be our daily prayer. Let others choose what they will, pursue what they will, grasp what they will; give me, for my paramount motive, a

desire to know and acquiesce in the will of God, and I
have come into possession of the true elixir of life.

My God, my Father, while I stray
Far from my home, in life's rough way,
Oh, teach me from my heart to say,
  " Thy will be done."

If thou shouldst call me to resign
What most I prize—it ne'er was mine—
I only yield thee what was thine ;
  Thy will be done.

E'en if again I ne'er should see
The friend more dear than life to me,
Ere long we both shall be with thee ;
  Thy will be done.

Should pining sickness waste away
My life in premature decay,
My Father, still I strive to say,
  Thy will be done.

If but my fainting heart be blest
With thy sweet spirit for its guest,
My God, to Thee I leave the rest ;
  Thy will be done.

Renew my will from day to day ;
Blend it with thine, and take away
All that now makes it hard to say,
  Thy will be done.

Then when on earth I breathe no more
The prayer, oft mixed with tears before,
I'll *sing* upon a happier shore,
  " Thy will be done."

THE ZEST OF LIFE.

My meat is to do the will of Him that sent me, and to finish His work.

JOHN 4 : 34.

IX.

THE ZEST OF LIFE.

JOHN HOWARD once gave this prescription for a heavy heart—" Take your hat, and walk off to visit the sick, the poor and afflicted."

What is this but a practical paraphrase of that teaching which our Lord has amplified and illustrated concerning the true *zest* of life? I use a word of peculiar significance. It will readily be understood by all, even if they know nothing of its Persian origin and history. It represents that which makes the flavor, the relish, the heartiness of life.

It was sultry noon when Jesus came to the well of Sychar. He was travelling on foot. He was wearied with his journey, and so sat down on the curb. All his disciples had gone into the adjacent city to buy food for him and for themselves. There comes a woman to draw water at the well, and Christ asks her to give him some water from her pitcher. This introduces a conversation of a most profound import, relative to living water and ever-lasting life and spiritual worship and his own mission as the promised Christ and Saviour of the world. His disciples return from their errand, and find him engaged in this spirited conversation. They do not presume to interrupt it. They listen, and they marvel. They see the woman drop her water-pot and run to the city, with her strange testimony, and already troops of her neighbors and fellow-citizens are on their way to see for themselves this extraordinary Prophet. Meantime, his disciples press him to take of the food which they had brought. Our Lord declines, saying that he had a meat to eat of which they knew not. Perceiving that he appeared vigorous and refreshed, they instantly inferred that, during their absence, some one had brought him food, of which he had partaken. But our Lord interprets his own words. No man had brought him bread. No one had given him to drink. " My meat is to do the will of Him that sent me, and to finish His work." He had been engaged, during their absence, in doing good to a benighted human soul. That occupation brought its own reward. He was thoroughly refreshed and invigorated, body and soul. He had been reaping, and had received his wages. He had been working in the spiritual harvest, and he was full of joy. He had gathered fruit, which was more than food for the body—even for the sustentation of spiritual life in himself and in another.

Nor does such a satisfaction belong to himself only. He has no monopoly of this peculiar delight. Immediately our Lord announces a law on this subject which concerns all his disciples, from that moment to the end of the world. The harvest is already ripe, waiting for the sickle. Wherever there is a man ready to do good, opportunities for doing good are ready to his hand. Whosoever " reapeth receiveth wages and gathereth fruit unto life eternal, that both he that soweth and he that reapeth may rejoice together." We have, then, in this incident, the Christian teaching concerning that which constitutes the only *true zest* of human life.

There are multitudes whose whole life passes without any *zest* at all. They endure life ; but never enjoy it. They breathe, they eat, they sleep, they move, and all because they must ; but life has in it for them no real satisfaction. Nor do we include in this class those only who drudge along in abject depression ; for those who are under the necessity of daily work undoubtedly have an advantage over those in the opposite extreme of society, who, released from such a necessity, are often a prey to listlessness, vacancy, and disgust. These are they who have many *excitements*, by which they are occupied and stimulated from day to day. But *excitement* is a very different thing from *zest*, though it is often confounded with it. One cannot live on stimulants. If one attempts it, he discovers that they must be diversified and increased ; and after all, re-action is sure to ensue when the stimulant loses its own power, and the exhausted subject falls flat into indifference and vacancy. Life has lost its savor, like insipid and worthless salt. There are multitudes, in all classes and conditions, with whom life has no sapidity.

Nor can we doubt that many, in a general way, purpose to lead a life of religion, who utterly fail of all correct notions as to what religion is, and what it confers. Their conceptions of a religious life are bounded by the ideas of necessity and policy and obligation and self-interest. Their highest notion concerning it is, that it will afford them a bridge over the river of death, and an acquittal and security in the eternal judgment.   So far as its influence in the present life is concerned, they regard it as a power of restraint, imposing self-denial, and the stern performance of duty, often unwelcome and painful. Was not our Great Exemplar a "man of sorrows"? Was not He, our Great Captain and leader in the *via dolorosa*, in which all his followers must walk down to the grave, made perfect through suffering?

All this may be true ; but it is not all the truth.   For Christ tells his disciples that there is an immediate reward in his service ; that we need not think only of what is to occur in the harvest at the end of the world, for there is a compensation now present : he that reapeth receiveth wages—receiveth them even while he worketh, the sower and the reaper rejoicing together ; and every one who is now engaged in doing the will of God, as Christ himself illustrated it at the well of Sychar, shall enjoy the true zest of life, its rich and sparkling flavor, its tonic, nutritious, and invigorating qualities, day by day.   If discipline is severe, if trials are manifold, if sufferings abound, all the more important, all the more valuable, is that habit which constitutes the joyous heartiness of life, whether we *do* or *endure* the will of God.   That is a sad life, though it passes under the name of religion, which has in it no real zest.   That is a pitiable family in which affairs are so conducted that life, however varied, has no hearty enjoyment.   That is a dead church, barren and unfruitful in the work of the Lord, whose members do not make it their meat and drink, instead of their constraint and compulsion, to be diligent in the whitened harvests of Christian usefulness.

What, now, is the true and only true *zest* of life? that which never is exhausted, never wears away, never loses its potency, never re-acts, and never ends; but, on the contrary, always continues, extends, deepens, and grows to the very last of our days on earth? In other words, how is it that we ourselves may all enter into sympathy with the Son of God, when he described those spiritual refreshments which to him were more than meat and drink, and which, as he assures us, are within the reach of all his disciples?

A general answer, obviously, is ready to our hand. Our satisfaction must be found in the same quarter with that which Christ himself describes as his own—" My meat is to do the will of Him that sent me, and to finish His work." Analysing this prescription, we find for its ingredients these several elements: a reference to the will of God in all things, as the supreme motive and law of life, and constant activity, on our part, in performing what is assigned as our proper work in the world ; or, to express both ideas in a more laconic form, *ceaseless occupation of our faculties in the service of God.*

The first thing essential to this vigorous and happy life is, that God should be recognized in all that we do. There is a vast deal of activity in the world, and not a little of pleasure and satisfaction in the free use and exercise of our faculties in the varied pursuits of life. But all this pleasurable activity is insufficient and defective if it has no recognition of God, and our dutiful service to Him. Take out of life the ideas of God's existence, His distribution of talent, His appointment of place and duty, and all regard to His will and approbation, as the end and reward of our existence, and you rob life instantly of its most dignified and pleasurable ingredients, reducing it to a blank, dreary, and infidel fatalism. On the other hand, the first thing which results from a direct recognition of the will of God is, that we may dispense at once, and throw out of our calculation, all regard to condition and possessions and kinds of occupation, of which the most is ordinarily made in human estimate, infusing into all alike this common charm, that God assigns our work, and the means of doing it. Here is a zest for the man of one talent, as well as for him with ten ; for one who toils in poverty, and for him who has largest estates ; for him who works in the field, the shop, the mine ; and for him who makes laws, who forges thoughts, who sways senates, and rules over nations. The busy housewife in the lowliest cabin, and the proudest queen in all the palaces of the world, in this regard are on a level. Their condition is appointed of God, and all alike are sanctified and dignified by the idea of DUTY. This, indeed, gives a zest to life, and constitutes its most spicy and tonic quality—that it is pervaded by a sense of obligation and obedience to Almighty God, whose approbation is the highest and largest good. A scholar, a king, can reach nothing better ; the cripple cobbler may have as much.

> Whoever I am, wherever my lot,
>   Whatever I happen to be,
> Contentment and duty shall hallow the spot
>   That Providence orders for me ;
> No covetous straining and striving to gain
>   One feverish step in advance ;

I know my own place, and you tempt me in vain
To hazard a change or a chance.

I care for no riches that are not my right,
No honor that is not my due ;
But stand in my station, by day or by night,
The will of my master to do.
He lent me my lot, be it humble or high,
And set me my business here,
And whether I live in his service or die,
My heart shall be found in my sphere.

The good that it pleases my God to bestow,
I gratefully gather and prize ;
The evil—it can be no evil, I know,
But only a good in disguise.
And whether my station be lowly or great,
No *duty* can ever be mean.
The factory-cripple is fixed in his fate,
As well as a king or a queen.

For *Duty's* bright livery glorifies all
With brotherhood equal and free—
Obeying, as children, the heavenly call
That places us where we should be.
Away, then, with " helpings " that humble and harm,
Though " bettering " trips from your tongue ;
Away ! for your folly would scatter the charm
That round my *proud poverty* hung.

I will not, I dare not, I cannot ! I stand
Where God has ordained me to be—
An honest mechanic—a lord in the land :
He fitted my calling for me.
Whatever my state, be it weak, be it strong,
With honor, or sweat on my face,
This, this is my glory, my strength, and my song,
I stand, like a star, IN MY PLACE.

Starting with this idea, duty as related to the will of God, we have next to combine with it the habit of constant activity in its performance, and our inquiry is answered ; the true zest of life is discovered. Sure we must be to start from this point, of obedient regard to the will of God ; for so certain as we take it for the purpose of life to do our own will, to please ourselves in the way of a selfish greed and ambition, we shall come into the experience of all those rivalries and disappointments and frictions and vexations, which are the inevitable consequences of a misdirected and godless life. The will of Him that sent us into the world, and appointed our birth, condition, occupation, being our point of departure, now let every faculty be brought into exercise, diligently and constantly, and the secret of all Christian refreshment is disclosed. Not enough to know God's will ; we must do it. " My meat," said Christ, " is to *do* the will of Him that sent me." To have a *work*, and to be diligent in finishing it, in God's name—this is the charm of life. *Doing* and *working* are here in antithesis to idleness and apathy. He who is the most active, from the best motives, is the happiest of his species. God himself is full of blessedness, because he is full of activity. A divinity asleep above the clouds is a heathen conception ; ours is the *living* God. With Him is no night and no sleep, but all is ceaseless and infinite activity. Jesus Christ was always intent on *doing* good ; and he who finds the most occupation for all his time and all his faculties, and this from a sense of duty, is the most blessed of men. Some who are incessantly employed, often to the verge of physical and mental fatigue, imagine what pleasure there would be in leisure and rest. But they know not what they say. They are cheated by a mirage. A thousand-fold happier is he who is occupied, even to this degree, than another who drawls through life with so much time at his disposal that he knows not what to do with it ; who sleeps away as much as he can, and who, when he wakes, yawns, and wonders as to the way in which he shall dispose of the remainder. What a *zest* there is in sleep, to a man who comes to it wearied in the discharge of duty, and with the consciousness that it belongs to him. What a *zest* there is in a day of recreation,—a season of relaxation—when it comes in the evident course of duty, as a gift and appointment of the best of Masters, and not as a largess to be squandered in our own indulgence. What a flavor is imparted to the whole of life, to be occupied all the time, and this because we are serving our God and master. What a tonic pleasure there is, when one awakes in the morning, to know what his work is—that there is enough of it, and that he has a heart to do it. There is nothing in abundant leisure, in elegant ease, in listless vacancy, ever to be compared with this enjoyment of constant occupation in doing the will of Him who appoints our condition and our work.

Far as we have advanced in our subject, we have not yet touched its core. The occupations of our Lord were of a peculiar sort. They all had reference to what is distinctively benevolent—of good to the bodies and souls of men. His divine pleasure was the reflection of the happiness he conferred on others. While it is true that all the occupations which Providence appoints are in a real sense

to be regarded as religious, even those which in our common language we call secular, it is certainly true that he
who is the most busy in devising and executing what is
for the good of others, comes nearest to the holy heart
and joy of Christ. We can conceive of one propelled in
ceaseless activity to that degree that he escapes all of
listlessness and inanition, and the sad weariness of nothing to do, while there is about his whole manner too
much of mere obligation in the discharge of duty. He
needs a larger infusion of Christian benevolence. He
lacks the very spirit which made Jesus Christ so alert
and so happy in his endeavors to instruct and bless.
The whole mechanism, though it is at work, needs a certain lubrication. It needs the oil of joy and gladness.
In a word, the zest of life is activity, with a *kindly* spirit
and intent. It is charity out of a pure heart. He who
is pervaded with the love which Christ illustrated and
Christ enjoins, and is active therein, has reached far
nearer the centre of life, than he who is only active in
obedience to Providence. That we hit the truth on this
subject, appears from the fact that Christ refers his disciples to the harvest which was then inviting their toil.
He speaks of a peculiar kind of sowing and of reaping,
and a peculiar kind of wages. What a serene joy was
in the soul of Christ when he saw those Samaritans believing in him, to their own salvation. We endeavor to
conceive the joy of the widow of Nain, when receiving
her dead son alive again by the miracle of our Lord ; we
imagine the gladness there was in the homes where the
sick were healed, the cripple, the blind, the deaf, restored
to the use of their faculties ; but what was all this com-

pared to the deep and ineffable delight in the heart of Christ because he had wrought so great relief. This is the species of reward to which he invites his disciples by his word and his example. The very activity which Christ employed for the good of the citizens of Sychar, we are to repeat, as the means of sustaining and invigorating our own spiritual life. What pleasure is felt by the reaper, strong and robust, in a harvest-field, swinging his sickle with vigorous stroke; what a sensation of joyous health is his; the currents of life run smoothly and briskly through all his veins, and he needs no physician to assure him that he is well; he knows it; he feels it; and if we were half as active and diligent in doing good, our refreshments and rewards would be so palpable that our faces would shine with religious delight. If there was a better comprehension and practise of this exercise and activity in Christian work, no one would need a magnifying glass to make his religion visible. Instead of directing a telescopic sight at a religious feeling the moment it shows its head, and running after it till it is scared away and hides itself in its burrow, we should be conscious, through and through, of the life by which we are made blessed. All this irrespective of the results of our Christian working. We may be defeated in our most kindly intentions: not all of the Samaritans believed on Christ. We may not be rewarded in all instances with seeing the fruit of our labors for others; but we are sure of fruit for the sustaining of our own life, as wheat is for the nourishment of the body. He that reapeth *receiveth* wages. Here is a present compensation. Here is an immediate delight. Here is the *zest* of life: *constant exercise of Christian benevolence.* There is no poverty in the soul that loves; every thought, every wish, every act, which looks to the good of others, comes back to the heart from which it issued, laden with a double blessing.

While this is so—while payment and work are inseparable—there is another reward which is for the future. We are instructed as to the satisfaction which Christ enjoyed in his earthly work; shall we not think of the peculiar delight which will be his when he looks upon the fruit of his toil, gathered into the garner, at the end of the world? We read that he will see of the travail of his soul and will be *satisfied.* When all who have believed on him, to the saving of their souls, shall come home at the last, filling the heavens with their glorified forms, and overflowing with gratitude and joy, all their gladness compounded together will not equal the joy of Christ, the infinite Fountain of all good, in the conscious blessedness of having conferred such boundless happiness. Shall we forget that he has promised to every faithful servant of his, that he shall be a partaker of the same satisfaction? The words are written which will be uttered to all who come home bearing their sheaves with them on that great day of disclosure and result: "Well done, good and faithful servant; enter thou into THE JOY OF THY LORD!"

Mr. Coleridge has said:

"Would I frame to myself the most inspiriting representation of future bliss which my mind is capable of comprehending, it would be embodied to me in the idea of Bell receiving, at some distant period, the appropriate reward of his earthly labors; when thousands and ten thousands of glorified spirits, whose reason and conscience had through *his* efforts been unfolded, shall sing the song of their own redemption, and, pouring forth praise to God and to their Saviour, shall repeat *his* 'new name' in heaven, give thanks for his earthly virtues, as the chosen instruments of divine mercy to themselves, and, not seldom perhaps, turn their eyes towards *him*, as from the sun to its image in the fountain, with secondary gratitude and the permitted utterance of a human love."

To save us from those temptations to despondency which spring from the thought that they only are to be honored and rewarded, on earth and in heaven, who accomplish signal services, our Lord has more than once instructed us that he regards dispositions rather than quantities; that the gift of a cup of cold water, in the spirit of Christian kindness, shall not be unnoticed and unrewarded; and that the true affinities of our nature are to be decided by those acts which are within the reach and capacity of all—visiting the sick, caring for the stranger, ministering to the hungry, the thirsty, and the naked.

POLITICS AND THE PULPIT.

I exhort therefore, that, first of all, supplications, prayers, intercessions, and giving of thanks, be made for all men ; for kings, and for all that are in authority ; that *we may lead a quiet and peaceable life* in all godliness and honesty.

I TIM. 2 : 1, 2.

X.

POLITICS AND THE PULPIT.

PUBLIC attention has been frequently directed to what is generally understood by "*preaching politics.*" Confused and inconsistent notions concerning this subject are entertained by many. Some are very jealous of any allusions from the pulpit to matters affecting the State. Others insist that the pulpit shall be out-spoken and explicit in the advocacy of their own favorite policy. So long as the ministry is a power in the world, its influence will be deprecated or invoked in aid of all objects where power is coveted. Few men have objections to the preaching of politics, so long as it is their own politics which are preached.

A clergyman preaches a discourse which he thinks is demanded by the perils of the country. The doctrine he advocates is distasteful to certain conductors of the political press, who forthwith censure him for transcending his proper vocation. He is accused of meddling with subjects which do not belong to his profession. He is distinctly informed that if he ventures to intrude into such an arena, his high and holy calling will be disgraced, and the white robes of his office will be sullied by the missiles with which he will certainly be pelted by excited men.

Ere long the pulpit speaks again, from another quarter and in another tone. It promulgates doctrines now which happen to be agreeable to the very men who before censured the clergy for presuming to speak at all on such subjects, but who now congratulate themselves, the country, and religion itself, for such wise, wholesome, and timely counsels. 'Now the ministry is doing its proper work. It does not stand aloof from those practical concerns which affect the well-being of society, but, as God's most beneficent agent, it is shedding the light and authority of heaven on the interests of time.'

Herein is a manifest inconsistency. Silence and speech at the same time, and in regard to the same subject, cannot both be right. That is no pendulum which swings only on one side. Surely there must be some fixed principles pertaining to this subject which ought to be ascertained, otherwise the Christian pulpit is destitute of all dignity, exposed by turns to flattery or contempt.

As to the *chief and distinctive object* of the Christian ministry, there can be no diversity of opinion. It is to announce these truths which affect man in his highest relations—to God and immortality. Unlike other teachers who, beginning with the lower ascend to the higher, the Christian ministry are appointed to proclaim those truths which relate to the *supreme* interests of our race. In the act of doing this, irrespective of all earthly distinctions, ignoring all those strata and conditions of society which the Apostle intends by "knowing man after the flesh," the teachers of religion are by an insensible and indirect process contributing most to that secular prosperity which others make their direct and exclusive pursuit. Elevating man in the scale of character, by introducing him to an immediate fellowship with his Maker, you are sure to confer importance on all which concerns his relations to his fellow-men and this present life. We need not expand this thought, that intelligence, freedom, law, order, enterprise, commerce, arts, industry, wealth, follow in the train of the Christian religion. Any tyro in history and geography will admit as much. He who preaches repentance towards God and faith towards our Lord Jesus Christ, employing himself with those distinctive and germinant truths which are his peculiar themes, is contributing more than he knows to the welfare of states and the true prosperity of nations. In this sense, political reforms are embosomed in the doctrine of Justification by Faith, and national progress is insured by Christian devotion.

True religion should pervade the whole of man's being. The Sabbath, the closet, the church, are not its exclusive sphere; his business and his politics belong to it as well. By politics we understand his relations to the State. It cannot be admitted that these and other secular interests, as they are called, are too common and unclean for contact with religion, since the broad requirement of the Scripture is that "whether we eat or drink, or whatever we do, we should do all to the glory of God:" and if political duties and relations are not to be pervaded by the spirit of religion, then are we involved in the practical solecism, that there is a large part of our existence which is necessarily irreligious; and still farther, the necessity is entailed of a sufficient number being detached, even in the millennium, to rig and work the ship of State, an un-

9*

godly crew, beyond the suspicion of all sanctity and piety. This common distinction between the secular and the religious is a convenience of speech for certain purposes, but it conveys a falsity; since in the better generalization of the New Testament religion covers the whole extent of our being, the countless variety of our interests and relations; just as the sea fills all the bays and inlets and creeks with its in-flowing waters.

From these general principles, in this form, there can be no dissent. The difficulty is in the application of the latter principle on the part of the ministry, in an official capacity, to *specific cases*.

Perhaps it will help us in reaching the truth on this subject, if we refresh our memories with a few historical facts. The time was, in our ancestral land, when, Church and State being combined in one organism, the clergy with few exceptions were little more than the tools of the throne. "Tuning the pulpit" was a very significant expression, as used by Queen Elizabeth, to describe the subserviency of courtly chaplains in advocating the royal will. We are conscious of pitiful regret for the times and the men, when it was not uncommon, if a preacher expatiated with any thing of freedom, for a gruff Tudor-voice from the royal pew to bid him return from his "ungodly digression and keep himself to his text."

Life cannot always be cramped and fettered, and at length there arose an order of men who claimed the right to declare the truth of God in utmost freedom, accountable only to its divine Author.* The assertion of religious

* What Jeremy Taylor has called the "liberty of prophesying" in his famous θεολογία ἐκλεκτική.

liberty necessarily prepared the way for personal and political liberty, and Hume himself, tory and sceptic as he was, was compelled to admit that English Puritanism was the root and life of all true English freedom.

The colonization of New England was a *religious* movement; and to subtract from it the direct and positive influence of church and ministry, would be like taking out the bones and soul from the human body. Those colonists have been often censured and ridiculed for the ecclesiastical requirements which they exacted in political relations and magistracies. The truth is, that at that time every nation in Christendom required religious conformities of those who officiated in affairs of State. That which was peculiar and novel on the part of the Puritan colonists was, that their ideas of the church and of religion went beyond the outward form, to a heart-renovation—a new test which repelled and disgusted the adventurers who had no sympathy with spiritual religion.

So the foundations of our national life were laid. There are two distinct periods in our national history when the agency of the clergy was very conspicuous, the object of reprehension or encomium by different parties. The first of these was at and during the Revolutionary war, and the formation of a new government, independent of Great Britain. The second was from the change of politics under President Jefferson, culminating in the war of 1812, and extending down, with a gradual diminution of prejudice and violence, to a time within the memory of most of our readers. Consulting these several periods, we shall find much to admire, and much to censure; many mistakes, many fidelities and proofs of wisdom.

When troubles arose between the American Colonies and the British Government, the whole structure of society was shaken, and men of all professions and pursuits were compelled to avow their sentiments and choose their position.   At this distance of time it is common to suppose that the action of the American people was unanimous in advocating independence from the British throne.   This was far from being true.   The people were divided among themselves.   The crown officers, and many of the leading and opulent citizens, were opposed to separation from Great Britain.   The result was invective, reproach, and violence—distracted counties, towns, and parishes.   The idea of multitudes was to resist what they held to be unjust and oppressive on the part of the British Crown ; to demand the sanctity of charters—the right of representation ; but not to sever themselves as integral parts of the British realm.   In this assertion of colonial right and justice, the clergy with wonderful unanimity sympathized ; but God intended more than they at first foresaw.   The rock once loosened from its bed was destined to roll on notwithstanding all obstructions.   The idea of national independence gained familiarity and force ; and at length the struggle began.   There was a necessity that the clergy, in common with all other citizens, should adopt one side or the other.   Some for a while hesitated to commit themselves to what appeared to be *irreligious* rebellion.   Their scruples were founded on religious grounds.   The Episcopal Church, with some notable exceptions, was particularly conspicuous in this position ; indeed, some of the early pamphlets relating to the Revolution inform us that the hostility to Great

Britain cherished by the Congregational and Presbyterian ministers, was imputed to a sectarian origin, as being moved by the fact that the Episcopal Church was sustained and established by the parent-country. The precise state of many among the American people, in the incipient stages of the Revolution, will better appear from a few examples.

Dr. Jonathan Mayhew, the pastor of the West Church in Boston, published a thanksgiving sermon in May, 1766, on the occasion of the repeal of the Stamp Act, from the text : "Our soul is escaped as a bird from the snare of the fowlers, the snare is broken and we are escaped." This discourse, full of patriotism, is pervaded with the idea that justice had been done, the wrong redressed, and the difficulty adjusted. It was dedicated to William Pitt. On the 22d of June, 1775, Dr. William Smith, Provost of the University of Pennsylvania, preached a sermon in Christ Church, Philadelphia, in which he " pants for the return of those halcyon days of harmony during which the two countries flourished together as the glory and wonder of the world "—and while demanding that Britain should do justly with her colonies, he affirms that the idea of independence from the parent-country is "utterly foreign to their thoughts, and that our rightful sovereign has nowhere more loyal subjects, or more zealously attached to those principles of government under which he inherited his throne." Another instance yet more to the point: Dr. Duché, of Philadelphia, is known as the divine who opened the Continental Congress, in 1774, with prayer. In 1776 he was appointed Chaplain to the Congress, but at an early stage of the war he manifested a decided opposition to independence, and in a long letter to General Washington endeavored to dissuade him from the cause to which he was pledged. Dr. Zubly, of Savannah, in 1775 a member of the first Provincial Congress of Georgia, preached a sermon in that year at the opening of that body, impregnated with the spirit of patriotism and liberty, but strongly discountenancing the independence of the colonies. These examples will suffice to show how great was the hesitation on the part of many, and this on ethical and religious grounds, to a severance of the body politic. As Christian men they dreaded schisms in Church and State. The discourses from which we have drawn our illustrations were delivered in the *beginning* of the war, when ethics were not yet classified and adjusted by facts. With a very few and notable exceptions—such as the witty and eccentric Dr. Byles of Boston, whose connection with his congregation was dissolved in 1776 because of his toryism—who was denounced in town-meeting as an enemy to his country, and afterwards tried before a special court on the charge of praying for the King, receiving visits from British officers, and remaining in the town during the siege—who, in his own words, was "guarded, re-guarded, and disregarded "*—the vast body

---

* On one occasion, when sentenced, under suspicion of toryism, to be confined to his own house, with a sentinel over him, he persuaded this sentinel to go on an errand for him, promising to take his place. The sentinel consented to the arrangement, and to the great amusement of all who passed, Dr. Byles was seen very gravely marching before his own door, the musket on his shoulder, keeping guard over himself.—*Encyc. Amer.*

of the unprelatical ministry of the country advocated the Revolution, in public and private, on Christian principles. They justified the war on religious grounds. They believed that human rights and liberties would gain by its success. They had the sagacity to foresee its issue. Among the most faithful of religious men, modest and pains-taking in their parishes, there was no concealment of their sympathies. Many of them went as chaplains into the army, among them Dwight—*clarum et venerabile nomen;* and he retains in his lyrical collections that paraphrase of the Psalms which is now dropped out of our books, as judged to be obsolete :

> " Lord, hast thou cast the nation off,
>   Must we forever mourn,
>   Wilt thou indulge immortal wrath,
>   Shall mercy ne'er return ?
>   Lift up a banner in the field
>   For those that fear thy name ;
>   Save thy beloved with thy shield,
>   And put our foes to shame.
>   Go with our armies to the fight
>   Like a confed'rate God :
>   In vain confed'rate foes unite
>   Against thy lifted rod.
>   Our troops shall gain a wide renown
>   By thine assisting hand :
>   'Tis God that treads the mighty down
>   And makes the feeble stand."

Scarcely was there a battle-field in the Revolutionary war where the clergy were not present, as chaplains or surgeons, to cheer and bless. Their patriotism was a thing of general admiration. They reasoned themselves and the country out of all hesitancy and scruples, as they knew how to reason. They abounded in what Sir John Hawkins calls "precatory eloquence"; calling down the blessings of the Almighty upon the country; and the depth and sway of their influence in achieving the independence of the colonies cannot be too highly extolled. Withal, it was with them a time of great personal privation and hardship. They shared in the largest measure the calamities of the country. They practised the extreme of frugality to eke out their scanty subsistence. They were exposed to violent opposition in their distracted parishes. But they were, as a body, brave, patient, meek, pious, patriotic, and learned — an honor to any land. Under God, we owe it to the ministry of that day that the morals of the country were not hopelessly wrecked in the convulsions of the Revolution. The profession emerged from the war with increased credit and honor, and with the confidence, respect, and gratitude of the people. The war over, they led the nation in song and thanksgiving on the shores of the sea they had crossed, and forthwith addressed themselves to their appropriate work, in conservation of the liberties which the Revolution had helped to secure. A few here and there were left in a most pitiful predicament. In tacking ship they had missed stays, and were stranded on a lee shore. In proof that no human ministry is infallible, some had misjudged the case, and were forced to suffer the consequences. What was the state of feeling in those parishes, where the minister retained either loyalty to the British Crown or a professed neutrality, may be inferred

from a single incident.   Rev. Dr. Burnet, of the Presby-
tery of New York, was settled in Jamaica, L. I., and at
the return of peace felt himself obliged to resign his
charge.   At the close of his farewell service, he gave out
the 120th Psalm.   Whether the muscles of the choir
were equal to its musical intonation, or the minds of the
people to its devout response, tradition does not inform
us :

> " Hard lot of mine ; my days are cast
>   Among the sons of strife,
>   Whose never-ceasing quarrels waste
>   My golden hours of life.
>
> " Oh ! might I fly to change my place,
>   How would I choose to dwell
>   In some wide, lonesome wilderness,
>   And leave these gates of hell.
>
> " Peace is the blessing that I seek :
>   How lovely are its charms !
>   I am for peace ; but when I speak,
>   They all declare for arms."

We come now to the second period referred to, when
the preaching of some of the clergy on political affairs
was of a most notorious character.   A change had taken
place in political parties, and it was so marked that the
clergy could not conceal their sentiments.   With few
exceptions, they had been on the side of Washington, and
bore the name of Federalists.   When this unanimity was
disturbed by the election of Mr. Jefferson to the Presi-
dency, they inveighed against it, in some instances, with a
tremendous emphasis.   It must be borne in mind that

party spirit was then at fever-heat.   Families and neigh-
borhoods were set at variance, church-members of different parties refused to pray together, and young people
from families of different political preferences would not
dance at the same assemblies.   Never before or since
did the spirit of party prove itself so ardent and violent.
It was a new experience for the country.   The clergy
thought that it portended worse than it proved.   The
people of New England, especially, looked with horror
upon French infidelity—French revolutions—which they
had associated with the new party in our own land.   The
French Republic had just before decreed the abolition
of all religion, and the enthronement of Human Reason.
All Christendom was convulsed with terror.   In 1798
President Adams appointed a day of national fasting.
Doubtless this association was in part the cause of the
hostility which the clergy manifested towards Mr. Jefferson
and his party.   They stood aghast, thinking that the
country was ruined.   They thought that they would be
unfaithful to a solemn trust, if they did not lift up their
voice in testimony.   It amuses us, at this distance of
time, to read what they said and did.   Some of the
sermons of that day have a historic renown.   Such, for
example, as what is known as the Jeroboam Sermon of
Dr. Emmons.   It was on the day preceding the annual
Fast-day in Massachusetts, in the year 1801, that the
acute metaphysician of Franklin sat in his study, greatly
perplexed what to preach on the ensuing day.   What he
did preach was never forgotten.   It was just after the
inauguration of Mr. Jefferson, and Jeroboam was made
that day to play a parallelism which would have astonish-

ed himself. The curious analogy is a rare specimen of long-drawn, solemn, and withering rebuke. After it had been extended through nearly two hours, it hardly needed at its close what, according to the phraseology of the day, was called an " improvement," which was given in these words: " It is more than possible that our nation may find themselves in the hand of a Jeroboam who will drive them from following the Lord; and whenever they do, they will rue the day and detest the folly, delusion, and intrigue, which raised him to the head of the United States."

We are referring now to facts which need some explanation; for which much may be said in apology, but nothing in justification as a model of duty for ourselves. The mistake was, that, in the intensity of feeling which then prevailed, there was no discrimination between what was ethical and what was partisan. Opposing the new administration, on one point, because of its supposed affinity with French atheism, some fought it at every point, *pugnis et calcibus*—embargo, gunboats, no matter what—wherever it showed its hand or head.

These political antipathies were long-lived. They culminated during the war with England in 1812. But they cropped out long after whenever they could claim a show of decency. Some of the sermons preached during that period were of a most extraordinary character. No dried orange-peel or caraway-seed were necessary to keep audiences awake under those pulpit deliverances. One denounces Napoleon Bonaparte as the " first-born of the devil," and Thomas Jefferson and James Madison his twin brothers. Another takes for his text the 8th verse

of the 109th Psalm: "Let his days be few; and let an·
other take his office." The "Bramble" sermon of Dr.
Osgood, of Medford, (founded on the parable of Jotham,
Judges 9 : 14: "Then said all the trees unto the bramble,
Come thou, and reign over us,") is as famous as the
Jeroboam sermon of Dr. Emmons. There was no circum-
locutory preaching in those days. Velvet phrases and
uncertain inferences were alike discarded. It is reported
of one minister, that for a considerable time he was accustomed to pray for the Chief Magistrate that God would
"gently and easily remove his servant by death."* It
will be remembered by many of our readers, that on a
certain year a worthy gentleman in Massachusetts, after
being a candidate of the Democratic party for Governor
for twenty years, was finally elected to the office by a
majority of one vote. It will also be recollected by all
whose early life was passed in that State, that the custom
prevailed, whenever the Governor issued his annual proclamation for thanksgiving, of sending by the sheriff of
the county a copy of the same, on a large hand-bill, to be
read from every pulpit, which document invariably closed,
after the signature of the Governor, with the pious ex-

---

* In one instance a child was presented in church, for baptism.
The father, having imbibed a preference for the new politics, whis·
pered to the clergyman, as the name to be given to his child—
THOMAS JEFFERSON. Horrified at the sound, the old minister dip-
ped his hand in the baptismal font, and, with a firm voice, announced
that the child's name was *John.* "Thomas—Thomas Jefferson,"
interrupted the father. But the old Federalist would not budge;
finishing the scene as he had begun. He would not profane the
House of God by repeating in Christian Baptism the name he so
resolutely abhorred.

clamation, "God save the Commonwealth of Massachusetts!" On the year referred to the newly-elected magistrate issued his proclamation in the usual form. It is said that a venerable clergyman, of the old party, laid the broad sheet over his reading-board, and after performing the professional duty of reciting it, with an ill-disguised aversion, actually announced the official signature with this significant intonation: "Marcus Morton, Governor? God save the Commonwealth of Massachusetts!"

It is for an important purpose that we have referred to a few of these notorious incidents which belong to the history of the American pulpit. Admit that such acts and expressions on the part of the ministry were mistakes, never to be imitated,—much should be said for their exculpation. In the first place, the instances of such distinctively political preaching were comparatively few. The very notoriety which these have attained is in proof that the great body of the ministry, whatever may have been their private sentiments, addicted themselves faithfully to the great concerns of their office. In many instances, those who had practised this method of political preaching lived to express their personal regret for the same. The late Rev. Dr. Lyman, of Hatfield, at the installation of his successor, used language truly pathetic in the acknowledgment of what he regarded as a great mistake in his own ministry. Another thing to be said in their vindication is, that such utterances were not on the Sabbath-day, but, perhaps without exception, on Fast-days, or Thanksgiving-days, or—what was always celebrated in New England by a sermon—Election-day. Still another thing should be said. The clergy of that period had been educated to regard themselves as the "moral police and constabulary of the country," and silence, sudden and complete, was more than could be expected of mortal man, when on the losing side, after a lifetime of explicit and applauded testimony. Nor must we forget to add that, in times of high political excitement, the words of a minister, in prayer or sermon, receive a construction from interested and jealous parties which they were never intended to bear. Minds surcharged with political partisanship will pervert, and exaggerate, and apply the simple utterances of a minister, in a way which might well astonish him. Rev. Dr. David Ely, of Huntington, Connecticut, is described as one of the most prudent, faithful, spiritual pastors of his times. In a season of great political excitement, it was reported by persons hostile to him, that he had preached on political subjects in a neighboring parish. It was thought proper to trace the report to its source. The neighboring parish was visited, and the inquiry made : "Did Dr. Ely preach politics when here? Yes. What did he say? Well, sir, if he did not preach politics, he prayed politics. What did he say? *Say?* he said, ' Though hand join in hand, yet the wicked shall not go unpunished.' " Seasons there are when auditors are so magnetized with partisan passion, that they put their own sense on the language of a preacher, exaggerating or misapplying it, so that in the presence of such a suspicious and watchful jealousy he stands no chance at all, unless he adopt the resolution of the Psalmist on a certain occasion : "I will keep my mouth with a bridle, while the wicked is before me."

This rapid survey of a very extended historic period,

with its motley assemblage of incidents, may help us in our undertaking to state some of the principles which should govern the Christian ministry in their official relations to political concerns. Starting from that which we hold to be the grand design of the Gospel and its appointed heralds—to save the souls of men—whatever their nationality or their politics, we hold that every thing pertaining to the sphere of *morals* belongs to the province of the Christian theologian and preacher. We emphasize the word which helps us to discriminate between what has been right and what wrong in the practice of the pulpit. What is distinctively *ethical* may be discussed in its proper time and place on Christian principles. There are ethical principles which should govern our conduct in political relations. There are many things pertaining to what are called politics which involve no special relation to morals, concerning which a minister may have his personal preference, but which it would be highly indecorous for him to introduce and urge officially. The relations of morality and immorality to political economy are many ; but we would hardly judge that theories of free trade, and taxation, and naval architecture, and embargoes, were the proper material for pulpit instruction. Are we required to give the rule which should govern a minister in his treatment of those political questions which are directly related to morals? None can be given, beyond this—they should be presented according to the *proportion of faith;* in the right season ; and in the right manner. The whole gradation must be left to the GOOD SENSE and ENLIGHTENED JUDGMENT of the preacher himself. If he is lacking in these qualities, no number of specific directions would be of any avail. Topics in the whole range of moral relations, from the highest to the lowest, belong to his sphere—but the order, frequency, and emphasis of their discussion must depend on seasons and necessities which cannot be defined in advance.

Some things, however, may be made more specific. Happily, we live in a country where there is no alliance between Church and State. No political power, organized or unorganized, may prescribe and dictate what a minister shall preach. This freedom, however, has two sides or aspects ; for neither may a preacher prescribe or dictate to his hearers what they shall think or do, except in those cases where he has the authority of the Supreme. We touch at once the secret of popular jealousy in regard to pulpit utterances. These have been made, sometimes, with arrogance and assumed authority. There was a time when the clergy wore big wigs and an imposing official dress ; and it was expected that their opinions would be received with deference by a reverential parish.

> " For still they gazed, and still the wonder grew
> That one small head could carry all he knew."

The time has come when opinions do not prevail because uttered *ex cathedra.* If an incumbent of the pulpit indulges in crude thoughts, immature judgments, ebullitions of feeling, and false reasoning, he must expect animadversion, correction, and refutation. Another cometh after him and searcheth him. No one would curtail the freedom of the ministry, but the ministry must remember that there is a freedom and right of judgment for the pews as well as the pulpit. We should not for a moment hold controversy with a man whether he ought or ought not to assert and promulgate the will of God, when *he knows it*—and to challenge the obedience of all men to that supreme authority. But when he assumes the same tone and manner of authority in reference to matters unwritten, involved, and debatable, we may surely ask him to exhibit his credentials. We will be the first to submit to his dictation when we have actually seen the seal of heaven in his hand, and are satisfied on the capital point of his divine legation.* The occult principle which has occasioned all the rancor and hostility excited by the interference of the pulpit, is this assumption of divine authority in behalf of what is nothing but an individual opinion. If the man who derives his opinion, simply, by his own confession, from the personal study of the Scriptures, and who has enjoyed none but ordinary aids, who can advance no pretensions which others may not also challenge, is entitled to speak in the tone and to exercise the authority of a prophet or apostle, then what was the necessity of the extraordinary powers wherewith prophets and apostles were endowed? A vast distinction is there between the prodigious pretensions of the zealot demagogue and the modest expression of an individual judgment.

Every minister of the Gospel is entitled to the same freedom of opinion and preference on all subjects as other men. Paraphrasing the language of Shylock, he may say : "I am a minister , hath not a minister eyes?

* Isaac Taylor.

10

hath he not hands, organs, dimensions, senses, affections, passions? fed with the same food, hurt with the same weapons, subject to the same diseases, healed by the same means, warmed and cooled by the same winter and summer, as other men? if you prick us, do we not bleed? if you tickle us, do we not laugh? if you poison us, do we not die? and if you wrong us "—we will not add with the Jew, "shall we not revenge?" but we will say, "shall we not show you how to bear it?" This freedom of judgment allowed him, no minister has the right to protrude officially his private opinions and preferences in regard to matters which do not affect the sublime moralities of his vocation. Especially to indulge in personalities, in partisan advocacy or military criticisms in the pulpit, whatever right or liberty he may claim elsewhere, is a public scandal and wrong. It would seem to be the doctrine of some preachers, because *they* had certain opinions in regard to men and measures, therefore, they are bound on all occasions to avow them, going through the world, like the iron man Talus in the drama, with his iron flail battering down whatever opposes their private sentiments. The meanest thing which crawls on the earth is a man who, for his private advantage, will follow and cringe and swallow his own opinions; but the noblest form of manhood is he who holds his personal opinions on things indifferent in reserve for the sublime end of another's advantage—as the Apostle himself has expressed it: "I become all things to all men, if by any means I might SAVE SOME"; that nobility and grandeur of Christian motives imparting versatility of address, and deportment in the use of his varied faculties and opinions, lest he should frustrate that object—the salvation of the soul, which was his disinterested and lofty intention.

A fortunate thing it is for our country that its clergy of all denominations, unlike the clerical party of Continental Europe, regarded with suspicion as enemies to liberty and progress, are known to be eminently patriotic, and as a body are possessed of the confidence and respect of the people. If the great events of our time, absorbing thought, and eliciting national energy ; events which are rapidly consuming hecatombs of lives and millions of treasure, and threatening to involve the peace of the world, do not afford an occasion for the teachers of religion to lift up their voice in the name of God and humanity, then must we confess ourselves utterly unable to conceive of any conjunction of earthly interests to which Christian truth and motive are applicable.*

To inaugurate war gratuitously ; to attempt to overthrow civil government, *without adequate reasons*, such as are sanctioned by God and man, as necessary and benevolent, is a crime, which, measured by its consequences, makes all other crimes insignificant. This admitted, there are wars which are justifiable to Christian ethics.

---

* The substance of this chapter, and of several which follow, was written during that tremendous civil war out of which we have so happily emerged. Believing that the principles here inculcated are of no ephemeral character, the writer retains every thing in its original and unaltered form, hoping that it may be of permanent service, as illustrating the manner in which the Christian ministry in the Loyal States, with few exceptions, were accustomed to instruct their congregations as to the religious rules to be observed in the several stages of this most eventful struggle.

" The magistrate," says the word of God, " beareth not the sword in vain." It is to be wielded in defence of what is good,—for the conservation of a well-ordered society. It is not an inference, but the explicit assertion of Scripture, that government is God's ordinance, and as such must be obeyed, and those who do it violence must be smitten. An army is only the instrument of magistracy, the reduplication of official weapons.

We are engaged in a contest for the conservation of our national existence, and in such a cause may appeal to something higher than honor—the aid and blessing of that religion which has given its sanction to lawful magistrates and constituted governments. So long as this one object is kept in mind, distinct and unalloyed by malignant passions, we may leave our appeal with the Almighty, going forth to battle, with faith and prayer, for justice and humanity. What greater evil could befall—we will not say our own land, but all lands—than the success of ambitious and wicked men, misleading communities, dragging States into the vortex of war at their own passionate will, without rebuke or punishment?

Our country stands not in the rear but in the van of the grand army of nations. Behind us are great historic forces; before us are great duties, great hopes, great destinies. The drama of History is not complete. We have our own peculiar work to achieve, and that work is related alike to the past and the future of the world. We are acting now, not merely for ourselves and our children, but in the interest of all contemporary nations, and in behalf of all the nations that ever shall be organized on the earth. The question now to be decided is—and there is not an aspirant for freedom, nor an agent of despotic and irresponsible power in any part of the world, who does not watch the issue on the very tiptoe of expectation —whether any people are capable of self-government; whether the passions of men can be so curbed and moderated, that of their own accord free citizens will subject their private will to the public welfare, preferring the order and sanctity of law and government to personal ambition and private resentments; whether a free, equitable, and benignant government shall spread its protection over all classes alike, or whether it shall be stricken, stabbed, revolutionized, and overthrown, for the pleasure and promotion of a few.

Nor can we, if we would, blink the fact that we carry explosive problems in our own bosom, especially relative to that unhappy race on whose ebon faces the sad experience of centuries has sculptured the cast of patient subjection. We know not a subject which has more points of contact and relationship with the proper province of the Christian ministry than the existing condition and prospects of the African race. First of all, he who questions the unity of the human race, by denying those bronzed in hue a place in the common brotherhood, aims a blow higher than he knows, at the very structure of Christianity. That there is one parentage, one race, one historic necessity, one and only one Redeemer for all mankind, is the very alphabet of our creed. Then, again, comes in the doctrine of the New Testament, that while there is something better than liberty, even a relationship to Christ which lifts a human soul so high that it may be oblivious to the ordinary distinctions of earthly condition, yet on the same authority we learn that freedom is better than slavery, and so is, if it may be, to be preferred and used. These things, we should say, are axioms in social and theological science. If it were our object to express ourselves in strongest terms on this subject, we would agree to confine ourselves to the language used by the fathers of the Republic, especially those who were personally related by birth and inheritance to a system which they pronounced and reprobated as a tremendous evil, social, political, and moral.*

---

* Henry Laurens, for two years President of the Continental Congress, and afterwards appointed Minister to Holland, wrote to his son from Charleston, S. C., 14th August, 1776: "You know, my dear son, I abhor slavery. I was born in a country where slavery had been established by British kings and parliaments, as well as by the laws of that country ages before my existence. I found the Christian religion and slavery growing under the same authority and cultivation. I nevertheless disliked it. In former days there was no combating the prejudices of men supported by interest; the day, I hope, is approaching, when, from principles of gratitude as well as justice, every man will strive to be foremost in showing his readiness to comply with the golden rule."—*Collection of the Zenger Club*, p. 20.

Mr. Jefferson, when in France in 1786, in a note to M. Demeunier, whom he had furnished with copious materials for his article on the United States, about to appear in the great *Encyclopédie Méthodique*, uses this language: "What a stupendous, what an incomprehensible machine is man, who can endure toil, famine, stripes, imprisonment, and death itself, in vindication of his own liberty, and the next moment be deaf to all those motives whose power supported him through his trial, and inflict on his fellow-men a bondage one hour of which is fraught with more misery than ages of that which he rose in rebellion to oppose ! But we must await with patience the workings of an over-ruling Providence, and hope that that is preparing

Whether the conservation and extension of slavery be merely the pretext or the cause of the war ; whether any who originated the war can plead provocation in the form of fanatical acerbities, is not now the question in debate, though we cannot but regret that the temper which governed our fathers, regarding this as a common concern, to be tolerated as a necessity for a season and removed as soon as it could be—a temper which was merged and blended in a blessed patriotism—was not continued and perpetuated ; though we often frame to ourselves a picture of what this country might and would have been if all its different sections could have looked and acted on this subject in the charitable spirit of a family community of interest and honor, and a small portion of the immense treasures now expended in war could have been fairly appropriated for the removal of the mischief ; yet so it was not to be. Our regrets cannot recall the past, and the issue is made and joined. This war is not, in our interpretation and intention, for the abolition of slavery, though that event is involved in its issue. The responsibility of such an issue is with those who inaugurated the war, not unwarned of its inevitable consequences. The contest on our part is for the conservation of the national

the deliverance of these our suffering brethren. When the measure of their tears shall be full ; when their groans shall have involved heaven itself in darkness—doubtless a God of justice will awaken to their distress, and, by diffusing light and liberty among their oppressors, or, at length, by *his exterminating thunder*, manifest his attention to the things of this world, and that they are not left to the guidance of a blind fatality."—*Jefferson's Writings*, vol. ix. pp. 278, 279.

life, and the preservation of that constitutional government which, under God, is the only barrier between us and universal chaos. We know of nothing between us and that object which should obstruct our end. We intend to love nothing, conserve nothing, consult nothing, occupying intermediate ground between us and the life, honor, and constitution of the country. Whatever interposes itself between us and that grand and sacred end which religion sanctions, must take care of itself.

Lift high the bright banner which symbolizes Unity, Constitutional law, National honor and integrity, dearer to us now that the blood of our citizenship has sanctified every fold and star. Avoid every suspicion of political jealousy and ambition. Weaken not the " red right arm " of magistracy by suffering party rivalries to invade our armies. The very animals in the time of a deluge, seeking refuge in the same caves, forgot their ancient antipathies. Common dangers, common sufferings, common necessities, ought to unite us at that point where unity is essential to the preservation of life.

Whatever comes to pass, let us hold ourselves firm in the faith that there is an essential difference between what is right and what is wrong, between good government and wild revolutions, and as God lives, that which is right will ultimately prosper. The future is hid from our inspection. No words of empty boast or defiance have we in regard to menaces from across the sea. We are neither over-sensitive nor indifferent. Willing or unwilling, all nations are related by manifold bonds which mountains and oceans cannot destroy. What is of real and permanent value to us as a nation, will prove the same to all other nations in the end. We are very calm and confident as to the *final* issue. Intermediate suffering there may be, perhaps beyond all which we have ever imagined. The fires may wax hotter which Heaven shall see to be needful to burn up our dross and weld us into a purer and firmer nationality.

Hilarity is not becoming the hour of suffering, but cheerfulness is, and patriotism, and hope and love and faith in God. What a day will that be, when prejudice, passion, and falsehood shall all disappear; when there shall be no more occasion for war, because there is no more of lawlessness and crime; when there shall be no breaking in nor going out; when there shall be no more complaining in the streets; when the deepest of all questions, underlying the relations of employers and employees, the question of races, shall be solved in the harmony and love of the latter day; when all the cities which gem the shores of the sea, and all the valleys and cottages which brighten the landscape of our beautiful country, shall be cheerful with the music of industrial freedom; when confidence and goodly fellowship shall displace suspicion, rivalry, and jealousy; when Peace, with her olive-boughs and dove-like tones, shall bless the land, and all the people shall go up to the temples of religion with their songs of melody, thanksgiving, and praise. The Lord grant it in His own time!

CHRISTIAN PATRIOTISM.

Pray for the peace of Jerusalem : they shall prosper that love thee. Peace be within thy walls, and prosperity within thy palaces. For my brethren and companions' sakes, I will now say, Peace be within thee. Because of the house of the Lord our God I will seek thy good.

Ps. 122 : 6–9.

XI.

CHRISTIAN PATRIOTISM.

I SEE not how any man of ordinary sensibility can read, intelligently, the 122d Psalm, known as a song of degrees—a chant for the going up to the Holy City—with a full comprehension of its origin, import, and use; recalling the scene as it was, on a bright Sabbath of the Spring or Summer, the tribes of Israel coming down from the slopes of the mountains round about Jerusalem, and coming up from the glens of the vine and the olive, flowing together in their multitudinous processions towards their sacred city and the House of God, singing aloud in the open air, fragrant with the scent of the rose, and musical with the hum of bees; joining in full-voiced chorus as the gates were passed—"Our feet are standing within thy gates, O Jerusalem—whither the tribes go up, the tribes of the Lord, to give thanks unto the name of the Lord,"—I cannot see how one can catch the full inspiration of such a scene, and such words, without having his eyes suffused, and his heart dilated with high and grand emotions. When we analyze the Psalm itself, we find it embodies two great sentiments—*Religion* and *Patriotism;* or, to express the truth more accurately, these sentiments which, under analysis, appear distinct and several, are here combined and blended into one great emotion of *religious patriotism ;* the love and worship of God promoted in the hearts of Israel's tribes by the memory of what God had wrought for their country ; and that country made a thousand-fold dearer to them all because it was the seat of the house of the Lord their God ; the abode chosen above all others upon the earth for the display of His majesty, and justice, and mercy.

This Psalm harmonizes so perfectly into one feeling the love of God and the love of country, that it has been preserved in the treasures of inspiration, not as a dead relic of a dead and forgotten generation, but as an incitement and an expression of those high-toned emotions which ought to characterize all *Christian Patriots.*

When I think that he who has determined to establish a kingdom of his own upon the earth—a kingdom whose brightest regalia are righteousness, and love, and joy—a kingdom for whose coming we are taught to pray every morning and evening of our lives ; when I remember that He who has ordained the end has also ordained the means and the instruments ; that if there is to be a church in the world then there must be a world continued and established, to be at once the theatre of its action, and the subject of its power ; that a prosperous, social state, with all the elements of happy civilization, just laws, established order, government gentle but strong, is not only a result wrought by religion, but the opportunity for religion to develop itself and work unmolested and unhindered ; that the chief evil attendant upon all systems of despotism or states of anarchy and revolution, is, that they accumulate obstacles in the path of Christianity, and that the grandest result of all true liberty is, that, under its auspices, the Word of the Lord has free course, and is glorified; that the Gospel is preached with greatest success, and the churches thrive, and multiply, when the civil power is so administered that we can "lead a quiet and peaceable life in all godliness and honesty,"—as I take into view all these facts and truths, then patriotism becomes impregnated with a new motive, redeemed from all association with that cheap and vulgar quality which is so much eulogized in vapid declamation, and wedded to religious ideas—learns to sing as in the sacred Psalm, "Because of the house of the Lord our God I will seek thy good."

The love of country, in times of trial and peril, needs to be invigorated and exalted by that class of motives which can be drawn only from our religion.

* At this very hour we are passing through scenes, which, for suffering and terror, we had supposed belonged only to the historic past. The sea has "wrought and is tempestuous." We are engaged in what has always been regarded as the saddest of all national calamities—a civil war. No Roman general, victorious in civil strife, ever received a public ovation such as was allotted to him who conquered a foreign foe; since, in his case, the success of duty was best honored by sad and reverent silence. Things which we have read of with pale lip, as occurring in other lands, have actually come upon ourselves, and men's hearts are failing them for looking for those things which are coming to pass. Thoughtful men

* Vide note, p. 219.

fear more than they utter. From causes which I need not attempt to describe, multitudes have fallen into despondency and gloom. Should this temper become prevalent, it would realize at once the worst mischiefs that ever have been imagined. What is needed now is a generous cordial of confidence and hope, stimulating the body politic into a state of tonic life, superior to all the depressions and dumb agues of temporary and local causes. And this can be administered only in one way. We need, at this moment, a large infusion of religious patriotism. We need to be lifted up to loftier conceptions of our nationality, as related to the providence of God in the progress of His eternal kingdom. I fear that too many frame their predictions and shape their conduct from the fluctuations of the Stock Exchange, and the reports of the daily bulletin. We must plant our feet on firmer ground than this, and lift up our eyes to higher objects. The events of a single day are but a brief parenthesis in the roll of historic ages. The stars above us are all in their places ; the ordinances of heaven are established in their faithfulness. God is on the throne, and heaven and earth shall pass away before one jot or tittle of His Word shall fail of its fulfilment. Far above all that is personal, or sectional, or partisan, oblivious to the petty differences of the hour, burying all subordinate questions of detail, emulating the high-souled deeds of our fathers, possessed of a magnanimous conception of our entire Christian nationality, as essential to the welfare of all races—Saxon, Kelt, African—black or white —to the interests of religion, to all the hopes of humanity in every portion of the globe—to the thousandth generation—far above and out of sight of all measures, mistakes, and successes of an hour—up and up must we rise, planting our feet on ultimate truths, standing steadfast and immovable in religious faith, " encouraging ourselves in the Lord," as did David amid the perils and disasters of Ziklag, and chanting our psalm above the voice of the storm. When Paul and his companions in their leaky ship were driven and tossed by the Euroclydon, his object was not to save the ship, but the lives of all she carried. Tossed and driven by this tempestuous wind, our purpose and endeavor is not to save ourselves —each for himself—but to save the ship freighted with such a priceless wealth. No one must be suffered to leave the ship, letting down a boat into the sea, and fleeing stealthily, as though they would do something about the bow : no one must be planning how to construct a raft out of the broken pieces of the ship when she has fallen apart : if the ship is among shoals and breakers, she must be saved : " better that we had not loosed from Crete and gained this harm and loss;" but let regrets and recriminations go by us now on the gale: every man must be at his post : let us unite our strength and wisdom : try every expedient, undergird the ship, shift her sails, take refreshment after a long abstinence, be of good cheer, and instead of running her aground, strike for the deep sea—bear off from dangerous shoals and soundings —make her strong, and tight, and staunch, from truck to keelson, instinct with life, obedient to her wheel ; so shall she save all who sail in her, and accomplish the voyage for which she was built, launched, and out-fitted.

There is a patriotism which is chiefly an unthinking

impulse, made up of memories and associations local to the soil where we began our existence—a natural affection, which has in it not one element of a religious quality. Were I asked to describe that love of country which is engrafted upon a religious stock, that compound affection which is illustrated in the inspired ode, used once and intended to be used always in public national worship, I should say, first of all, that it implies an intelligent comprehension of one's country as related to Supreme Providence, to the development of His historic plan, with reference to redemption and His one immortal kingdom. That which we have found to be wise in regard to our personal life and duty—fix the centre from which all acts should proceed and to which all acts should return—we are told is wisdom concerning the life of nations and the dramatic history of the world. This world does not swing in empty space, a dead, iron pendulum ; God is its Author, and Governor, and Life ; and all things, past, present, and future of our globe, are ordained in the interest and for the promotion of the kingdom of his Son. On a ten-inch globe or map representing our earth, you do not expect to find every lane of a city, or every creek of the country, but only a general outline of the world's configuration. We are not competent to decide upon every event, minute and episodical, how it is related to the grand unity of history, but we do know, because instructed by divine infallibility, that all things were made by Christ and for Christ ; that He who ruleth among the nations lifteth up one and casteth down another, with reference to that kingdom which is everlasting and to that dominion which endureth throughout all generations.

It is the root and foundation of our belief, that all the scenes of life's theatre are shifted with reference to the one drama which defines the object of the world's creation. It is on this root that our patriotism is grafted, and from this vital sap that it draws its sustenance. The love of our country grows intense, when we measure our nationality as related to that kingdom of Christ which is paramount, permanent, and universal. The Bible, in its historic parts, instructs us how the true life of all nations, from the beginning, was ordered in connection with the advent of Him who was the Desire and Hope of the world. This historic chain was not broken when revelation was closed, nor was Christ's rule over the nations terminated, when the pages of the Apocalypse were ended. He reigns now—and will reign forever. And this land of ours—its peculiar nationality—both are dear to us, more dear than words can express, because the product of historic forces in which we see and adore the hand of our Lord. To enhance the estimate of our nationality—we would repeat the brave chronicles of the past; we would lead you through the long galleries of recorded events, good and great ; recall reformations and revolutions which had a soul in them because born of love and duty and right : we would tell of up-heavings in the old world, of religious assertions and religious liberty; our own continent shut out and reserved till the right crisis ; the exodus of our ancestry inspired and guided by an educated religious conscience ; of the melting away and disappearance of savage tribes—the possession of a new hemisphere by a new order of men ; of a church ransomed and free from all political alliance—a church reformed and untrammelled in soul and limb ; of liberty regulated by law ; of institutions established by the people for self-government, self-protection, and self-improvement. We would repeat the old but never stale or wearisome story of the Constitution, the Union, our great and blessed nationality : as the fire kindles at the memories of the past and the hopes of the future—hopes identified with civilization, liberty, and religion throughout the earth—hopes which are the fruits of a long, long, and patient growth—the purchase of a vast and costly price,—standing on this high summit, we find no place nor possibility for despondency ; in possession of such a heritage, there cannot be a thought of throwing it away, or allowing it to be torn from us, or pausing to ask what it is worth, for it is above all price ; and so our patriotism, inspired and interpenetrated by our religion, takes up its cheerful Psalm : " Peace be within thy walls, and prosperity within thy palaces : because of the house of the Lord our God I will seek thy good."

And it is in this connection, in this chain of providential events, that we would religiously recall and honor the name and services of that great and good man who, by common consent, is recognized as the father of his country—the first President of our Republic, the founder and the representative of our free institutions. It is no common eulogium on such a man, that you cannot speak of his magnanimous patriotism, nor recall his words of warning and wisdom at the beginning and at the end of his public services, more especially the " pathos, grandeur, and parental love " of his Farewell Address, when, like Moses at Pisgah, with a bright vision of the future of his country, he gave his Deuteronomic counsels; you cannot do this without consciously or unconsciously framing a lesson, the very best for any times through which we are passing. We deprecate every thing which approximates to hero-worship, or exalting man as our trust and law; but we would shun, also, with earnest care, every thing like indifference to the gifts of God, especially the lives of men good and great, men of Providence, as they may be called, designed to be lights in the world, and safe interpreters of duty. Here is a name identified with our nationality; a name which never can be divided and subdivided into parcels to be distributed among dismembered States; the common property of the whole nation, and the symbol of that spirit by which our nationality must be preserved and perpetuated. We cannot recite the story now in detail; our children know it already, and their children and children's children will not forget it; for in his life and services, history had reached a new epoch, humanity a new development. I have said already, that a recital of what he was, and said, and did, was in itself a discourse for the times. The story of his peculiar training, the qualities of the stripling foreshadowing the virtues of the man; his preservation from dangers for a signal service for his country; exemplifying the true republican virtue of the olden time; offices seeking him, and he never seeking office for himself; honest, patient, and magnanimous, emulous of saving the country rather than winning the fame of a brilliant soldier; sure to win by Fabian wisdom, rather than risk every thing by hurling a column on needless danger; practising self-control greater than the taking of cities, when misunderstood and well-nigh sacrificed by military rivalry and political cabals ; showing Christian greatness in a willingness to serve rather than an ambition to rule ; instructing the country at the beginning and at the end, as one who believed and felt that our dependence was on Divine Providence, and that the foundations of our institutions were laid in morality and religion ; emphasizing, with the voice of a Hebrew Prophet or Christian Apostle, the philosophic truth, that the former could not exist without the sanctions of the latter ; warning, first and last, against party spirit, and sectional jealousy, and geographical preferences ; entreating, as a father doth his children, each and all, by mutual forbearance, to study the things which would edify the whole ;— as all this passes in review, we feel the glow of an assured confidence that the lesson of such a life was never intended for an hour, then to be swallowed up in chaos ; for it is a sign and pledge of a future deliverance and greatness, the model of a future conformity.   Nor can any man recount a tithe of such a record, without exclaiming, Oh, for one day of such a spirit now : oh, for one pulse, strong and brave, throughout this whole land, of that true, loyal, " sweet, cherished, hereditary " American sentiment which filled his honest heart : one more Farewell Address, inspired by wisdom and love, and listened to by all the people throughout all our borders, in reverent gratitude, ere he passed from the sight of man.

" Being dead, he still speaketh ; " and the gift of such a Moses is itself a pledge for the ultimate triumph of those principles which were represented and inculcated in his life. We delude no man with the false promise of a smooth, speedy, and easy vindication of our nationality. Every reason have we to suppose that it will be with us as with the people of Israel, in their education for their high destiny. They expected a quick and a short passage into the land of promise. So have we. They were impatient of obstacles and murmured aloud because of delays. So have we. They were to be forged and hammered into shape and strength. So are we. There are enemies, many and strong, hanging on our flank and rear; there is a sea, deep and wide, stretching itself across our path; Miriam and Aaron, the brother and sister of the nation's head, have proved disloyal, detaching themselves from their true leader; the High Priest himself has joined in with idolatries by which a host have been seduced; Korah, Dathan, and Abiram have incited a multitude of the people into bold rebellion; the waters which once were for refreshment have been turned into bitterness; Balaam has been summoned in God's name to curse Israel; spies have come back bearing an evil report to intimidate and deter, by false stories of giant foes and high fortresses:—but above us, around us, behind us, is a Power mightier than all, bearing us onwards, always onwards, in suffering and chastisement, onwards still, towards a promise which God has given. That household murmuring and disloyalty will be shamed and punished, even though it be not by the curse of leprosy; that idolatry will be repressed and reformed, and they who have practised it will be made to drink the ashes of the calf they have worshipped; that rebellion led on by the very kinsman of Moses will be subdued; some divine branch of sweetness will be cast into the bitter fountains of Meribah ; Balaam, in spite of himself, will be compelled to utter a blessing instead of a curse—" How goodly are thy tents, O Jacob, and thy tabernacles, O Israel ; " the disheartening report of the spies will be stilled by the strong voice of Caleb, saying, " Let us go up at once and possess it, for we are well able to overcome it ;" and though there is between us and the promised possession, a river, deeper, swifter, redder than the Jordan ; though the time be long and weary, even many years ; though Moses and Aaron may die, and many a soldier and priest may not see that for which he has fought and prayed ; though a whole generation, because of their unbelief, shall be buried in the wilderness ;—yet that river will be crossed, and the nation will go over dry-shod, bearing the ark of God with them ; and on the other side, the wilderness behind them, that vindicated nationality, that Christian Imperialism, will rear its monuments with the very stones taken out of the flood, and all the hills and valleys shall echo the songs of peace and universal thanks to God Almighty.*

A very defective notion of *religious patriotism* should I present, if I failed to say that the very tap-root of all Christian love for the country, is a principle of obedience to God.   In stating the truth on this part of my subject, we come in contact immediately with that question which defines the issue now before our country in this critical hour, involving not our welfare alone, but inevitably the peace and welfare of the whole world.   That question relates to the duty of citizens to the civil government of the country ; a subject so important as to be made the

* *Vide* Life of Rufus Choate, vol. ii. p. 423.

topic of frequent teachings by the Christian Apostles. The doctrine of the New Testament is briefly this: Government is an *ordinance of God*. It comes not by chance; it is not an invention of man; but an absolute necessity ordained by the Almighty, and as such is to be obeyed. "The powers that be are ordained by God," and whosoever resisteth this power resisteth the ordinance of God. So essential to the existence of society is government, in some form, that as religious men we are required by inspired authority to be subject to it, not only "from wrath" and compulsion, but for conscience-sake—through the power of a religious principle.

This doctrine of the Christian Scriptures is not for a moment to be confounded with those monstrous pretensions of tyrants, which allow no kind of protest against wrong, and forbid all attempts to reform and improve government itself by proper modes. Christian principles there are which, in certain cases, justify and necessitate the substituting of one form of government for another; and all admit that there have been revolutions, and may be again, which are sanctioned by religion. But no one of whom I ever heard, has ever pretended that the government established by the common consent of the country, benignant, just, and gentle, as we have thought it, was so despotic in its sway, so utterly subversive of all the ends for which government is instituted, or so stricken through and through with evils mortal to social order, that it became a necessity imposed by benevolence and religion, that it should be violently overturned.

There has sprung up in our country—and the mischief is not confined to any one parallel of latitude or longitude—

—a doctrine assuming the specious name of "ultimate convictions,"—which, reduced to simpler terms, means the opinions and preferences of individuals—which claims to be superior to all civil law, an authority higher than the constituted government of the country. There is a law of conscience—I speak of conscience well instructed, a dial set on a true meridian to the sun—which never should be treated with a slight. Whenever human governments require that of any man which an intelligent, honest, religious conscience pronounces to be wrong in the sight of God, the conduct of the Christian Apostles instructs him how to shape and decide his conduct. If his testimony for truth compels disobedience to the civil authority, he must bear the reproach of God patiently and firmly ; taking the consequences of his fidelity—suffering and death—upon himself in proof of his constancy to truth ; knowing that his martyrdom will be the means by which that truth will ultimately prevail. But no citizen is justified, on Christian principles, in being a seditionist ; striving to overthrow God's ordinance in government, simply for the gratification of his personal preference or passion. For consider, if the will, conviction, partiality of one individual is to be his supreme law, then the will and conviction of his neighbor, which are diametrically opposite to his own, are ultimate authority to him ; and who shall arbitrate between them ? What shall prevent violent shocks and collisions ? Your political thesis resolves itself into this : " every man does what is right in his own eyes." Society is at once dissolved into anarchy, and physical strength alone decides who and what shall be ascendant. We cannot magnify unduly this ordinance of God, a benignant government for our protection : and there is nothing at this hour between us and the surges of an angry ocean, but the Constitution which we have accepted as framed, adopted, and transmitted by our fathers. We have launched our earthly all upon the experiment of self-government, believing that governments are for the good of the people, and not the people for the pleasure and profit of the government. There is no need of inquiring into the original condition of the contracting parties ; we need not confuse ourselves with theories concerning the sovereignty of the several States ; since the people of all these separate communities, with wonderful unanimity, framed to themselves a certain form for the administration of government—" for a more perfect union, to establish justice, insure domestic tranquillity, provide for the common defence, promote the general welfare, and secure the blessings of liberty"—compacted themselves by a solemn agreement and covenant, established it in good faith, and confirmed it by provisions and oaths ; a form of government never claiming to be perfect, but self-adjusting, presenting the mode of its own safe and pacific correction, through the legal and orderly processes of legislation, judiciary, and convention, by which needful changes should be made, and wrongs redressed, and improvements accomplished ; and surely we shall search long before we find any ethical rule which can justify any party, however free and sovereign they may claim to be, breaking away from a compact into which they freely entered, simply on the ground of disgust with the result of a popular election, which they themselves had ordered to be held, and into which they had themselves entered as active participants.   The question thrust upon us, is, not whether we can consent to the loss of a certain portion of our national domain ; but whether we can, or ought to, consent to the destruction of our national existence.   If a chain composed of many links is broken in one place, it may be in another, and soon it will be detached into as many parts as there were links in its first composition ; and, this principle admitted, I see not what can save us from universal dissolution and chaos. I have revolved it much and long, in study by day and in watches of the night, and I cannot solve the problem, how, with such a doctrine of private preference, and ultimate convictions, protruded, allowed, and armed, we can ever be saved from the horrors which drenched the soil of France in blood, and rocked it to and fro with explosive revolutions.   So that, in the providence of God, we are thrown back inevitably upon the maintenance of our nationality, not in pride or ambition, but for self-preservation—the only barrier which keeps out the waves of the sea ; and thus our patriotism draws its vigor at last from the law of obedience to God.

All collateral issues aside, biding their own place and time, the question which we are called to settle, not for ourselves only, but for a waiting and troubled world, is the possibility of a self-governed nationality.   Our failure has been predicted ; by many desired ; some have laughed at our institutions, saying, if a fox should but scale the wall, it would tumble.   Meanwhile, with God's favor, our experiment has worked so well, and prospered so wonderfully, that it has reacted prodigiously on the Old World ; reforms have been begotten of our success ; and hoary despotisms have acknowledged and feared the effect of our institutions. There is not a crowned head in the world who has not heard the name of Washington, nor any people struggling for freedom who have not been cheered and encouraged by our example. Fond hopes would die all over the earth, if the experiment we have commenced should end so soon in disaster. Freedom would shriek in despair, if it should prove that our vast nationality had been dissolved, to gratify the will and ambition of an oligarchy. Every motive of self-preservation, of humanity, of liberty, of religion, compels us to a most earnest expression of loyalty. We must honor Government ; we must stand firm on our Constitution, as the only security of property, freedom, and life. It is no time, when a ship is in mid-ocean, and struck by a hurricane, to attempt to take her to pieces and rebuild her on another model. Now is the time to prove the strength of her timbers, and, by our brave deportment, to show our confidence in our institutions and our God. " Let us gird up the loins of our minds, be sober, and hope unto the end." These inspired words well describe the temper by which, in such a time, we should be governed ; *firmness, sobriety*, and *hope.* It is sad to see the sufferings, anguish, bereavements, and deaths of the hour ; but it makes us sadder still to think of the future, if our failure should entail on coming generations transmitted hostilities, strifes, and woes. If the principle for which we are called to testify is good and right and religious, then its vindication is worth all which it may cost. The suffering we endure, because of it, is the price we pay in its honor. Our duty is stern and solemn, but how can we avoid it?   It is Brutus delivering his own sons unto death, for the honor of law and magistracy.   It is Abraham offering up Isaac at the summons of God.   It is Jephtha sacrificing his own daughter, kissing her fondly as he consigns her to doom, exclaiming:

> " I could not love thee, child, so much,
>   Loved I not Honor more."

It is the Christian law of vicarious suffering, according to which, all which is good and valuable is made sure only by the endurance of mediatory pains.   If great truths are to be wrought out of our history, for the good of the world, the world must see how high an estimate is placed on them, by God and man, in the degree of suffering which is borne, in cheerful trust, for the sake of their vindication.   Every thing small, selfish, corrupt, must be consumed out of us so as by fire.   " As many as I love I chasten," says He who is Lord of the Church and King over the Nations.   We may not prove ourselves worthy of immediate success ; the tide which seems to be rolling in and onwards may surge backwards for a season ; but truth will only gather force for a later swing ; the difference between right and wrong is essential, and God is pledged to the final triumph of the one, and the defeat of the other ; and we cannot have a firmer basis of confidence than this.   Our wisdom, our duty, it is, to draw motives of conduct, not from the fluctuating events of the day, but from eternal verities, the stability of that Kingdom which never can be moved.   It were easier to think of swinging the Alleghanies on their base, dividing the continent in another direction ; of turning the great rivers of our land about, so as to run to another point of the compass, than to imagine the overthrow of those great laws which involve the ultimate welfare of our race, in the eternal kingdom of the Redeemer.   That kingdom is not the mere decoration and support of governments and nations ; but governments, nationalities, law, liberty, all things sublunary, are for the never-ending and illimitable Kingdom of our Lord.   Here, then, have we a standing-place, high and strong.   The floods may lift up their waves, but the Lord God Omnipotent reigneth.   Parts of His ways He has disclosed, to guide our feet and confirm our faith.   Patriotism is inspired by religion.   Because of the house of the Lord our God, we seek the good of our native land.   We will honor God, and all His ordinances.   We will pray for His protection, and seek for His blessing ; grateful for what He has done for our fathers, we will seek His favor on us and our children.   Guided by His word, cheered by His promises, we will continue our march, hoping unto the end; knowing, beyond a doubt, that the world, under the power of its Maker, is rolling on towards universal love, peace, liberty, harmony, and joy.   Nor is this a blind confidence, for God is with us only as we are with Him.   And they who live in later ages of time, will take up the very Psalm which we chant to-day, and sing it with a thousand-fold better conception of its real meaning ;—DELIGHT IN GOD, AND IN THE LAND WHICH THE LORD OUR GOD GIVETH US.

OUR FEET SHALL STAND WITHIN THY GATES, O JERU-SALEM.

JERUSALEM IS BUILDED AS A CITY THAT IS COMPACT TOGETHER :

WHITHER THE TRIBES GO UP, THE TRIBES OF THE LORD, UNTO THE TESTIMONY OF ISRAEL, TO GIVE THANKS UNTO THE NAME OF THE LORD.

PRAY FOR THE PEACE OF JERUSALEM: THEY SHALL PROSPER THAT LOVE THEE.

PEACE BE WITHIN THY WALLS, AND PROSPERITY WITHIN THY PALACES.

FOR MY BRETHREN AND COMPANIONS' SAKES, I WILL NOW SAY, PEACE BE WITHIN THEE. BECAUSE OF THE HOUSE OF THE LORD OUR GOD, I WILL SEEK THY GOOD.

LULL IN THE STORM.

And while the day was coming on, Paul besought them all to take meat, saying: This day is the fourteenth day that ye have tarried and continued fasting, having taken nothing. Wherefore I pray you to take some meat; for this is for your health: for there shall not a hair fall from the head of any of you. And when he had thus spoken, he took bread, and gave thanks to God in presence of them all; and when he had broken it, he began to eat. Then were they all of good cheer, and they also took some meat.

ACTS 27 : 33–36.

XII.

LULL IN THE STORM.

In the first Book of the Eneid we have a description, in Virgil's liveliest manner, of a furious storm on the sea, by which the hero of his epic, with all his fleet, was brought nigh to destruction. Eolus and all his crew of winds had broken loose from their cave of rocks, and lashed the sea into foam ; nothing could stand before their boisterous rage ; the seams of the ship yawned, the oars snapped ; some of the vessels fell over into the trough of the sea, and arms, furniture, and men, washed overboard, were drifting about in the yeasty surf; when, suddenly, Neptune lifts his placid head out of the deep, surveys the scene, sends back the winds to their prison, puts to rest the stormy billows, disperses the congregated clouds, brings back the sun, and creates a bright and blessed calm ; even as when sedition rages in a great city—this is the poet's own illustration—and a mob is raging through the streets, and stones and clubs are flying through the air, if by chance they should see some man, remarkable for his benevolence and wisdom, instantly they are still, giving him their attention, while he soothes their passions and counsels them to peace. This poetic scene not inaptly illustrates the effect produced on all our minds by the return of this halcyon day of our American calendar.* It finds us in mid-ocean, contending with angry gales and surges. We are conversant with the perils, the passions, the burdens, and the sorrows of a protracted war. Yet such are the memories and associations connected with the day, that we are not surprised to find the wondrous effect it has in hushing us into tranquillity and making us happy. Frequent are the occasions when fasting and lamentation are most becoming. Happy for us that such days have been observed by our ancestors, with a degree of earnestness and patience that surprises us, their degenerate offspring. The learned Lightfoot has left us a record of the manner in which a Fast-Day was observed by the parliamentary Assembly of divines to which he was attached during the civil wars of England. "This day," writes he, "we kept solemn fast in the place where our sitting is, and no one with us but ourselves, the Scotch Commissions, and some parliament men. First, Mr. Wilson gave a picked psalm, or selected verses of several psalms, agreeing to the time and occasion. Then Dr. Burgess prayed about an hour; after he had done, Mr. Whittacre preached upon Isa. 37 : 3, 'This day is a day of trouble.' Then, having had another chosen psalm, Mr. Goodwin prayed ; and after he had done, Mr. Palmer preached upon Ps. 25 : 12.

* Written in the year 1864—the gloomiest period of the war. In accordance with a felicitous suggestion, arrangements were made for a special observance of the annual Thanksgiving, that autumn, by the whole army, supplies most generous and abundant being sent to all the camps, by citizens at home.

After whose sermon we had another psalm, and Dr. Stanton prayed about an hour, and with another psalm, and a prayer of the prolocutor, and a collection for the maimed soldiers, which arose to about £3 15*s*, we adjourned till the morrow morning."* This, indeed, might be called "*laboring* in word and doctrine." "Other men labored, and we have entered into their labors." If there are times which call for depletion and humiliation, there are other times which demand cordials to stimulate, refreshments to strengthen. What a beautiful incident was that, when the apostle Paul, himself a prisoner for Christ's sake, stood on the deck of a drifting ship, in the stormy Adriatic, when "neither sun nor stars in many days had appeared, and no small tempest lay on them, and all hope that they should be saved was taken away, and there had been long abstinence from food, even fasting for fourteen days "—and addressed the crew in these words : " Sirs, ye should have hearkened unto me, and not have loosed from Crete, and to have gained this harm and loss. And now I exhort you to be of good cheer, and take some meat, for this is for your health ; for there shall not a hair fall from the head of any of you." And when he had thus spoken, he took bread, and gave thanks to God, in presence of them all. He whose counsel had been despised, he, in that black and tempestuous night, the ship pitching and rolling, *giving thanks* to God, in the presence of those despairing men, and persuading them to take food and be of good cheer !

Precisely this is what we are invited to do by the ap-

* Lardner's Works, vol. 13, p. 19.

pointment of this day. It is a festival of gratitude, in the lull of a storm ; and we intend to take meat, give thanks, and be of good cheer. A smile comes to-day over the grim visage of war. The camp is converted into a domestic festival. The homestead sends of its plenty to the soldier in tent and trench. Let the hand loosen its grip, for a few hours, on sword and musket, and the snow-white flag float from every dwelling and every church, while for one day a whole nation devotes itself to the delightful occupation of fostering and expressing sincere gratitude to Almighty God.

To be thankful and happy when all is propitious and peaceful, implies nothing to our credit. The great art is to be cheerful and hopeful when affairs appear to be in perplexity and gloom. Among the many fantastic conceptions of our most prolific modern writer, Mr. Dickens, is a character whose passion it was to meet with troubles and disasters sufficiently serious to give something really creditable to the habit, on his part, of an irrepressible merriment. Once, according to the author, he was on the eve of finding what had been his ambition for a long time. That was when he emigrated to America, and sought a new home, in a new settlement, on one of our Western rivers, among sharpers and dirty politicians and bilious fevers and mud and bowie-knives and tobacco and fogs and swamps and braggings, and American eagles flying sky-high, and men sitting about as if their organs of observation were in their feet, tavern-brawls, commendations of slavery, bad whisky, and a lank, cadaverous, yellow, corpsy population who would insist on calling their town by the name of Eden—there at last it was that he began to indulge in some measure of self-complacency, because in such extremes of misery he was able to maintain his usual overflow of animal spirits. To be contented in the midst of peace, prosperity, and abundance, is a small virtue. The absence of contentment in such circumstances, would, indeed, be a crime ; but something good and great is there, when a weak mortal wrestles, through the live-long night, with the angel who strives to give him a fall, continuing his bravery, even when the sinews of his strength have been withered, and compelling the mysterious form to leave him a blessing, ere he relaxes his hold.

In Boswell's *Life of Johnson*, Mr. Wilkes is introduced as entertaining a company with the description of a sermon which he had heard in the Highlands of Scotland, in which the preacher inveighed with the utmost vehemence, for the space of two hours, against the evils of luxury, when there were not more than three pairs of shoes in the whole congregation. Appropriateness is the foremost rule of successful speech. Instead of picturing to myself a state of affairs remote and unreal, I intend to keep in mind a vivid impression of the actual condition of our beloved country. Were we inclined to a desponding and discontented temper, we might find material enough for complaint. A civil war, which for magnitude—the extent of territory which it covers, the number of combatants it involves—throws into shade every rival ; a national debt rolling up, within the space of four years, to a sum already equal to twice the number of all the inhabitants of our planet ; the graves which have been crowded with hundreds of thousands of the most vigorous youth of the continent, taken from the arts of peace, and from happy homes to a red and hasty burial ; the uncertainties and apprehensions which still attend our unadjusted strifes ; all these might be our chosen themes till our hearts were wrung with agony, but not one of them would be an appropriate topic for a day of gratitude, save as we can discern good evolved out of evil, the blackest clouds unfolding an edge of gold and crimson. Vain is the attempt to force mirthfulness upon those who cannot forget the causes of grief and apprehension : a nobler art is that which, confessing the presence of great sorrows, can infuse into them the radiance and warmth of great consolations, and by a divine alchemy can extract material for gratitude out of the very dregs of bitterness. Let us look at things, not as they might be, not as we wish them to be, but just as they are, in their complexity of good and evil, sweet and bitter ; and let us invite the blessing of Heaven upon a people, who, in the very throes and anguish of their trials, have more to excite their gratitude than any other nation beneath the smile of the Autumn's sun. Though our common mother, our honored country, mourns the loss of many children, she is not to us like Niobe, petrified in torpid despair, but, like many a mother whom we have seen exalted and ennobled by losses and trials, more tender, more generous, more fertile in all goodly intentions towards the living, by reason of her memories of those whom she has buried. We need not for a moment to be puzzled by the riddle of Samson : "Out of the eater came forth meat, and out of the strong came forth sweetness," for, if we are wise to know and prove it, bees will be seen to swarm from out of the ribs of the dead lion, making honey for us and our children, sweeter than any from the " thymy heaths " of Hymettus. Small claims has he to Christian bravery, who rejoices only when skies are bright and tranquil. " I will sing of mercy and of judgment," said the Psalmist ; and a mind properly attuned to their harmony, will discern material for religious joy amid the severities of Providence.

There is one incident in Hebrew history which serves as a warrant for a special observance of an annual festival in " troublous times." Nehemiah, the governor of Jerusalem, was as little inclined, by natural disposition and circumstances, to hilarity as any man that could be named. The leader of an expedition designed to rebuild the prostrate city, he was perplexed with care and trouble. Sanballat and Tobiah, the leaders of a rival and unfriendly colony, after they had tried taunts and insults, formed a confederacy with the Arabians and Ammonites, and took up arms against the patriotic band who were fortifying Jerusalem. As if these foreign stratagems and assaults were not trouble enough, the governor was pestered by dishonorable and traitorous persons in the city, who took advantage of the public distress to exact usury, and make exorbitant contracts. In these depressing circumstances, the wise ruler, fearing that the people would be disheartened, determined to try the effect of a little recreation and festivity. It seemed to him that they would all be the better for unstrapping the load of care, and invigorating themselves with the sweet cordial of religious joy. So this care-worn official issued a proclamation for a festival. He bade the people to drop trowel and spear, provide themselves with branches of the pine, the palm, and the myrtle, and enjoy a little season of cheerfulness and charity, hospitality and thanksgiving. "Go your way, eat the fat, and drink the sweet, and send portions unto them for whom nothing is prepared : for this day is holy unto our Lord : neither be ye sorry : for THE JOY OF THE LORD IS YOUR STRENGTH." This proclamation was issued on the eve of the "Feast of Tabernacles," and was intended to reëstablish that ancient festival. This was originally of divine institution ; it had been long and happily observed by the Hebrew nation, through all the vicissitudes of their history, and it was intended to subserve very important ends in that illustrious community. It was a festive occasion altogether. The time for its observance, corresponding to our October, was the most beautiful of the whole year—after the heats of the Summer solstice, and before the "former rains," the most favorable time for general travelling. The feast was held in and about the metropolis, whither all adult males resorted from the various tribes. The mode of its observance was singularly picturesque. The people left their usual dwellings, and constructed tabernacles—hence the name—or booths and arbors, out of the "boughs of goodly trees," especially of the evergreen, so many varieties of which were found in Palestine. The whole court of the Temple, the roofs of the houses, the area of the streets, and the adjacent fields, were covered with these graceful structures. On the evening of the first day, there was an illumination, which threw a golden light over this most animated and joyous scene. The city wore the appearance of a camp, and yet not with the usual accompaniments of a camp—weariness and watching and armed preparation; all was hilarity and delight. Thither the tribes had come up, from the valleys of corn, of milk, and honey, appearing before God in Zion. No more should it be said that heathenism alone had provided days of festive worship, for the "modest and reverent solemnities" of Israel had appointed a season of joy, alike simple and pure, in utmost contrast with the bacchanalian orgies which resounded in the courts of Chemosh and Dagon, the insane laughter of Sidonian worship, and the monstrous pomps of Babylon and Egypt. Now was the hill of Zion fairly ablaze with pleasure and joy. The harp and the viol were heard in the land, the tabret and the cymbal, stringed instruments and organs, and high above them all were the voices of a whole nation, chanting together those high-sounding psalms which had been prepared by their Poet-King. The waving of palms, the flush of joy overspreading every countenance, the choral music, conspired to make the Jewish Feast of Tabernacles the most remarkable among all the observances of men, for pure, well-regulated, and religious joy.

What now was the intention of this national festivity? Merely for the overflow of animal spirits? Was it a provision for general holiday, with nothing ulterior to the act of recreation? Far from this. It had a definite object and meaning—chiefly to commemorate the earlier events of their own annals, even the time when their fathers dwelt in nothing but movable tents, the nomadic period of their history, when God brought them out of Egypt into their own goodly land. Conjoined with this act of commemoration, the feast was to testify gratitude for the ingathering of the harvest; to furnish an occasion for the reunion of friends, the interchange of hospitality, the bestowment of kindness on the poor, the widow, the orphan, and the stranger; and, above all, to foster a spirit of nationality, by bringing together the different tribes, and so fusing down the rough edges of sectional prejudice. This great Hebrew nation was divided into several groups, quite distinct in several particulars, as to rights and inheritances, taking names from their several progenitors. As these, with their distinct geographical lines, bearing banners inscribed with various names and emblems, were brought together once in the year, to form acquaintance and interchange civilities, how certain was the effect of their natural festival to obliterate local interests, and to blend the many tribes into one strong sentiment and heart of nationality, in the use of the same songs, the expression of the same religious faith, and the joyful worship of one and the same God.

Every civilized people has some festive custom by which to celebrate the ingathering of the harvest. What object is better fitted to produce gladness and praise? The fruits and grains which are hustled about in markets and on the docks as if they were the most vulgar things, are not the product of human art, but the gift of a bountiful Father. How stupendous this miracle of abundance of food, provided by His hand, every year, every day, and several times in every day for every living thing! Talk of miracles as belonging to remote ages in the past! Behold this marvel of the revolving year. The work of the husbandman complete, Winter comes, and seals the earth in silence and cold. The streams are stiffened and still, the ground is hard as stone, and buried out of sight in masses of snow. The sleet and the hail are abroad, the birds have fled, and verily it seems as if nature were dead, and wrapped up, stiff and stark, in its white and glistening winding-sheet. Weeks revolve, Orion and the Pleiades keeping watch, like angels at the sepulchre of Christ, when the icicles begin to trickle from the roofs of the houses, and the snow-bunting appears with its soft chirp, and the ice melts in the rivers, and the streams are free and frolicsome, and, as the sun ascends higher in his circuits, the green grass makes its appearance, and the winter-grain shoots up all over the fields, and the birch-leaves show themselves, and the " home-loving and divorceless swallow " has come back to its haunts, the sweet violets are by the wayside, and the bright marigold in the green meadows, and the fresh earth yields itself gladly to the march of the plough, and the trench in the garden and the furrow in the field take to their bosom the sacred deposit of the seeds, and all the air is perfumed with the blossoms of the orchard, and the green blade of the corn is up, and men sleep and wake, knowing that it will grow without thought of theirs, by the mysterious life which God imparts to its every cell and tissue ; and Summer comes with his fervent heat, and the dews distil, and the showers fall, and lo ! a continent is crowned with all kinds of grains and fruits ; the ground is teeming with its treasures, the soft wind of the west plays through the tresses of the corn, and skims over ten thousand acres of bending wheat ; and soon Autumn has come, with its glorious pomp, its harvesting and its plenty, and its imperial coronation of the year, and there is no stint to the munificence of our heavenly Father— bread enough and to spare in his great house.   The eyes of all wait upon Him, and He giveth them their meat in due season—the ox and the sheep, the ant and the bee, the wild beast in the forest and the nimble squirrel, the sparrow and the pigeon darkening the sky with their swift and vast caravans, and men, women, and children, in great cities, in great armies, in great fleets, in the house, by the way, all over the earth, fed daily, hourly, by this vast miracle of an universal Providence. Well may the holy Psalm utter the words, Praise the Lord all the earth, ye dragons and all deeps, fire and hail, snow and vapor, stormy wind fulfilling his word, mountains and all hills, fruitful trees and all cedars, beasts and all cattle, creeping things and flying fowl, kings of the earth and all people, both young men and maidens, old men and children.   Let them praise the name of the Lord, for His name alone is excellent—His glory is above the earth and the heavens.   When Handel's Messiah was first performed, in 1780, in London, the audience, exceedingly affected by the music in general, when the chorus began, " For the Lord God omnipotent reigneth," were so transported that all, the king not excepted, started to their feet, and remained standing till it was ended ;* and the world ought to be transported with delight as in harvest-songs they speak of the wondrous works of God, and *abundantly utter* the memory of His great goodness !

* Forbes' *Life of Beattie.*

Next to the ingathering of the harvest, the event of the year which should elicit our liveliest gratitude is the preservation of our institutions amid all the commotions of the times, by the good providence of Him who bears up the firmament by no visible support. The issue of our recent presidential election was watched with profound concern by multitudes at home and abroad. It was, in the intelligent judgment of many, as if the fate of republican institutions trembled in the scale, for all time and for all people. The decent and orderly manner in which the election was conducted, the promptness with which the minority, two millions of men, acquiesced in the decision of the majority, exceeding their own number only by some two or three hundred thousand voters, the tranquillity which instantly succeeded a most stormy agitation—has not only strengthened our own faith in our own institutions, but has presented before the world a spectacle of sublime self-control which is entitled to more than a passing allusion, even a most considerate and philosophic analysis.

An election is, by the very signification of the term, the putting forth of one's own will and preference. It is only in certain stages of civilization that such an expres sion of the individual will is tolerated or allowed. Let us not forget what toils and fermentations of history were necessary before that new phase of government was reached in which a whole people are permitted to make expression of their personal preferences in the administration of their own public affairs.

According to the familiar proverb which we wrote, when children, in our copy-books, "Many men have many minds." So long as men have distinct individuality, their wills must often work in opposite directions. Shakespeare makes one of the citizens, in *Coriolanus*, to say, " We have been called of many, the *many-headed* multitude ; not that our heads are some brown, some black, some auburn, and some bald; but that our wits are so diversely colored ; and truly, I think, if all our wits were to issue out of one skull, they would fly east, west, north, south; and their consent of one direct way, would be at once to all points of the compass."* Hence this great interpreter of nature reasoned that popular consenting— in other words, a government based on free voting—was a solecism and an impossibility. Beginning with his premises, we reach a different result. We accept the first fact, as to the " many-headed multitude." The next fact, the logical inference from its freedom, we admit also ; and a very important fact it is, if any one would analyze and interpret rightly the working of our free republic, that there will always be some occasion for the expression of different opinions and determinations. To express this idea in a more homely phrase, there will always be something about which to quarrel. You meet it first in a country-town, in a parish-meeting. The thing in dispute is the building of a new school-house, the laying out of a new road, the location of the post-office. There being no imperial authority to direct, every man in the town, of course, has an eye on his own accommodation and his own property ; no one is willing to be wronged or incommoded ; and so parties are formed, and there is any

* *Coriolanus*, Act 2, Scene 3.

amount of hard talking, and faction, and threatening; but the town-meeting comes about, the "selectmen" are on hand, a moderator is chosen, the votes are dropped, the decision is announced, and, with the exception of the few grumblers who are always threatening to move out of town, every body acquiesces in the result; the village relapses into its wonted tranquillity, till somebody's will starts a new project, and the whole hive is roused again in the excited play of rival interests and preferences. This is precisely what we mean as essential to the idea of liberty,—the free working of divers wills. The same thing occurs, on a larger scale, in national affairs. So long as the nation is not dead, but alive, and in progress and growth, it is a matter of necessity that there should be the putting forth of individual wishes and intentions, which, for noise and force of collision, is proportioned to the magnitude of the questions at stake and the interests supposed to be involved. Now it is a question of democracy as opposed to federal centralization; now it is the tariff; the rival claims of agriculture, commerce, and manufactures; now a national bank, and the removal of deposits to a national treasury; now it is antimasonry, now the colonization of the blacks, and now the abolition of slavery; now it is the legalized suppression of intemperance, and now the forth-putting of native Americanism in opposition to all foreign influence, political or religious. So it ever has been, and so it always will be; it is involved in the very conception of liberty, as represented in general suffrage, that there should be the free and unobstructed working of many wills, in every conceivable direction. From this freedom results parti-

12

sanship, in the working together of those who are of the same mind, and from the opposition of parties comes clashing, debate, noise, and all the varied measures which can be devised by which one party may carry the day against the other. So loud is the sound, so passionate the manner, so vehement in language and behavior, that those living in other countries, unused to such exhibitions, predict only one result—the overthrow of the government, a revolution terminating in bloodshed and universal anarchy. To all which there is but one answer, for such as disbelieve in free institutions : Danger is not in noise, but silence ; not so much from what comes out of men's mouths, as from that which is crowded down into their smothered hearts. The steam rushing and roaring from an open valve terrifies the timid by its frightful noise, but the escape is the sign of safety ; the peril is when the valves are shut, and the steam is pent up within the strained and banded boilers, and the boat shoots swiftly through the still waters ; then is the time to expect fatal explosions. We are not blind to the perils of liberty, for they are many and portentous ; but, in providing an antidote, you must not strangle liberty itself, nor forget that this is its essential quality—that there should be, throughout the whole mass, a free expression of the elective will of all. Did you never watch, on a Summer's day, the gathering of two great clouds, in the west and the north ? Blacker and blacker do they roll up, with muttering thunders in their bosom, covering the face of the sky, when, suddenly, as they meet in mid-heaven, there drops one bright flash, so smooth in its descent as to excite the sense of the beautiful amid the terror of the scene, followed instantly by one sharp, rattling volley, and then comes down the rain ; and when the clouds are emptied, the sun breaks out, and the meadows give forth a goodly smell, and those masses of cloud hasten towards the western horizon, exchanging their inky black for every brilliant hue, reflecting the glory of the setting luminary which they could not obstruct. Even so great states and territories are agitated by great public questions, affecting, as they believe, the welfare of the country, the condition of posterity, and the prospects of the world ; every breath blows the fire of faction to an intensity of heat, like that of a furnace ; the press, the public meeting, are inflamed with passion, and such are the rumblings of the gathering hosts, and such the up-turnings of the " discolored depths " of the sea, that every foreign spectator anticipates the last spasms of the republic ; but the day of election has come, and these four millions and a half of men, all over the land, put themselves in motion, yet as decently as if going up in orderly procession to Sunday worship, armed with nothing but those small pieces of white paper, which, one after another, are dropped into the ballot-box,

> " Soft and still
> As snow-flakes fall upon the sod,
> Yet swift to do a freeman's will,
> As lightning does the will of God."

The sun goes down—the telegraph announces the result—the earth has neither exploded itself, nor dashed any other orb into fragments, but it wheels in quiet obedience to the centripetal force ; and a defeated minority, with no change of opinion or will, practises conformity to the great law of constitutional morality—peaceful acquiescence to the majority—that sacred sentiment for which we are now battling in the eye of the world. The habit is so familiar to ourselves, that we do not pause to reflect how sublime it is, what majestic developments both of conscience and intelligence it implies—this alliance of self-assertion with self-control—this utmost freedom of will with loyalty to the supremacy of law, order, and authority.

Having said so much in the way of analyzing our own methods and vindicating our own habits, chiefly with reference to others, who do not understand us as we understand ourselves, it is well, in review of these recent and pregnant scenes, to say something with reference to ourselves. In the advice we give, perhaps we shall be thought to resemble the impudent mountebank in the *Tatler*, who, when Britain was shaken by an earthquake, advertised to the country-people certain pills for sale, which "were very good against an earthquake." Quite an absurdity, it may be thought, to prescribe for popular commotions and national ferments. But, beautiful and hopeful as is the play of free forces, seriously a national election, as now conducted, is a terrific trial of the national character. It is most devoutly to be wished, that we may never adopt it as our rule, "that all is fair in politics;" that there was less of that hyperbolical mode of speaking and writing previous to an election, which must be construed as a figure of speech to redeem it from the name of falsehood; and that there was more of the calm candor which relies on sound argument rather than hard and tough expletives. The names which political parties have attached to each other, in this country, during the last thirty years, the like of which are used in no other country in the civilized world, are shocking to public decency; and we need not be surprised, so long as we apply them as familiar terms of description to our own "kith and kin," that we are regarded by foreigners, who have never visited our shores, as only removed a degree or two from the savages, whose grotesque nomen-clature we have imitated in our political designations.

The very definition we have given of *liberty*, implies the necessity of weights and balances to check and counteract the full swing of the will, lest it fly off into excess. Its natural tendency is to ambition, to pride, to self-glorification, to obstinacy of purpose : to make it safe, it must have a large infusion of that virtue for which neither the Greek nor Roman languages had a name, till the New Testament writers coined the new word, *humility;* that quality which, with no meanness, defers to the will of others, especially in graceful subordination to all rightful authority on earth and in heaven. Let us be grateful that there is in our land so much of intelligence, so much of educated conscience : our only peril for the future is involved in the inquiry whether we have enough of both to protect us from the assertion of self-will, in its manifold forms of dishonesty and corruption, ambition for place and power and emolument. We are told that in Turkey it was a custom, when any man was the author of notorious falsehoods, to blacken the whole front of his house, so that an ambassador, whose business it is, in the words of Sir Henry Wotten, to "lie for the good of his

country," has had this mark set upon his house, when he
has been detected in any piece of feigned intelligence
that has prejudiced the government or misled the minds
of the people.* Following this singular conceit, I have
sometimes imagined what a curious effect would be produced if all the habitations of our countrymen were
painted in colors representative of the men who live in
them. If all those who deal in falsehood and forgery
pernicious to the public welfare had their houses black
as falsehood itself, and those infected with jealousy and
prejudice and envy had houses of sickly yellow; and all
ever suspected of enriching themselves at the public expense were ensconced in houses green as the backs of
our paper-currency; and all addicted to fanaticism, ma-
lignity, and revenge, had their houses crimson as blood;
while those only who practised a true candor dwelt in
houses corresponding thereto—the very word signifying a
pure whiteness—it is quite certain that we should have
a good deal of polychromatic ornamentation, and a sort of
architecture, if not too funereal, that would not be without its good effect on the morals of the country.

To have a republic, you must have a community of
good men; since a republic, by its very terms, is the ag-
gregate of individual wills. One of the sages of antiquity, as the result of his political observation, has left
on record this prescription, "*Abstine a fabis*" ("*Abstain
from beans*"). The reference is not to any article of
dietetics; but beans, white and black, being used by
voters as we use printed ballots, Pythagoras meant that,

---

* Addison, iv. 461.

if one would maintain his peace of mind, he must not meddle with elections. This is no rule for an American citizen. Abstain from elections, and the republic falls to pieces, since its distinctive organization depends altogether on the expression, in some sort, of the elective will of those who are themselves the commonwealth. Grateful for past blessings and escapes, there is no lesson more pertinent, more important for future duty, than that good men, foregoing their apathy and reluctance, must charge themselves with care and responsibility towards the State, exercising their own choice intelligently, independently, decidedly, or there is but one alternative—the surrender of the country, through ever-recurring elections, to the greed, the venality, the selfishness of the multitude ; and that is an entombment of the republic from which there is no resurrection.

But we will not dwell long enough even on this one word of caution to cause a shade of sadness on a day of gratitude. We have not been given up to destruction. We are not called to deplore reverses to our arms, but to celebrate past successes. Whatever opinions may exist as to policy and management, there was never a time when the purpose of the nation, God helping us, to defend its own life and maintain its own honor, was more general and more decided than at this very hour. Allegiance is a legal conformity, and may be compelled by outward force. Loyalty is an uncoerced and unbought grace, with true love in its heart, and so is patient and strong, ready to do or endure whatever will fortify and bless the country to which it clings with undying devotion. And surely, if ever there was a cause which might naturally be supposed to draw towards itself the sympathies of all generous spirits in the world, and the blessing of God Almighty, it is the purpose of a free and benignant government to preserve itself, and uphold the supremacy of law, and this with no vindictiveness or wrath, but with that calm repose which indicates the consciousness of a good cause, and power adequate to its accomplishment. For the first time in our existence as a nation, we have of late a coin bearing upon its face a religious sentiment— *In God we trust.* Brave old Latimer, more than three centuries ago, preached before King Edward the Sixth, on the happy issue of a new shilling, having for its inscription the fine motto—*Timor Domini fons vitæ vel sapientiæ*—a sentence which, the preacher hoped, would be printed on the heart of the young king in choosing his wife and all his officers. If the sentiment now in common circulation on our coin is but deeply impressed on the hearts of the nation, that God is our trust, we may be released from all vaticinations or apprehensions as to that future which still is veiled, assured that the final issue will be right. So let us take our meat in the lull of the storm, and be of good cheer, thanking God and taking courage.

LIBERTY AND LAW.

As free, and not using your liberty for a cloak of maliciousness;
but as the servants of God.

1 PET. 2 : 16.

12*

XIII.

LIBERTY AND LAW.

THE period of Hebrew history which followed the death of Joshua is described as one in which "every man did that which was right in his own eyes." Though the incidents which illustrate this state of anarchy are recorded in the appendix of the Book of Judges, and not at its beginning, with which they synchronize, yet it is agreed by the best chronologists, Jewish and Christian, that the incidents themselves took place in the year 1406 B. C. The exodus of the Hebrew people from Egypt, under Moses, was in the year 1491 B. C. Then was it that Moses and all Israel chanted that song upon the shores of the Red Sea, which will stand to the end of time, like a monumental shaft, in honor of a great deliverance. Subtracting the one date from the other, we are surprised to find how nearly the result corresponds to the space which separates the Declaration of American Independence in 1776 from the present time.

It seems to us incredible that a people so distinguished by the favor of Divine Providence ; so recently delivered out of Egyptian bondage, with signs and wonders so extraordinary, and guided into the occupancy of the fair land which for so long a time had been promised to them and their fathers, should so soon, if at all, relapse into lawlessness, irreligion, and heathenism. We should have supposed that, with such memories as those which characterized their national history, and these so fresh and recent, they would have been sure to adhere to all those political and religious laws which were their security and honor and blessing. With what nation had God dealt as with them? Yet twenty years only had passed since the death of Joshua—the leader of the nation, the viceroy of God, who had been a personal witness of all the marvels which had signalized their history from the date of the exodus; scarcely a decade of years had been finished since the last of those venerable men had died, who had participated in the scenes of the wilderness, and the occupation of the national domain; when the whole people, as if smitten with frenzy, cast away their eminent prerogatives, secured to them at such a cost, and, like swine trampling on priceless pearls, abandoned themselves to anarchy and idolatry. Then occurred those scenes of rapine, violence, carnage, and barbaric cruelty, terminating in most fierce and bloody wars between tribes once linked in firmest concord, which cannot now be read without a blush for human shame and sighs for human folly.

The method, as it would seem from this episode of history, as well as from the whole drama of history itself, by which the Almighty educates nations for a high civilization, is to allow them to experiment for themselves, according to their own ways and devices. There is a shorter, easier, and more economical method, within the reach of all, if they would but adopt it; even to regard the requirements of God with implicit faith and obedience. But when men will bolt out of the right way, and will do that which is right in their own eyes, though it be antagonistic to the will of the Supreme, there is but one way, even that they should make trial of their evil courses, and be made to feel, in their own experience, how evil they are, and how tremendous the consequences of every infraction of the Divine code. Such was the result of this portion of Hebrew history. It was well, both for themselves and for the world, that a nation, bent on the experiment, should make one trial of what it was to be without any lawful magistracy. It was not necessary that the experiment should be repeated. The lesson was burnt deep and ineffaceable into the national convictions. Sensualism, brutality, internecine wars, barbaric invasions, so far prevailed, that at length necessity, the instinct of self-preservation, suggested various remedies. Persons remarkable, at first, for physical strength and courage, presented themselves as rallying-points for the assertion of right, the vindication of justice, and the protection of the innocent. Such were the "judges" of Israel—Othniel, Ehud, Deborah and Barak, Gideon, Jephthah, and Samson—rude compounds, as we should say, of the warrior and the magistrate, yet the offspring of necessity, and the strong helpers of the people, out of the morass of anarchy, into somewhat of order and law, gradually shaped into permanent magistracy, and culminating at last in the splendor of the Hebrew monarchy.

Why should not every man be allowed to do that which is right in his own eyes? Why should not mere *will* and *feeling* be a sufficient authority for the actions of individuals and communities? All have an intuitive apprehension that such a state of things cannot be allowed ; that it would be sure, if tried, to bring about a general wreck and ruin of the race. Yet all may not be able to give such an answer to this question as would satisfy one who forms his opinions and regulates his conduct on ethical and religious grounds.

The question is invested with special importance, in our own times, and in our own land, because of the tendency here to deify the ideas of *personal rights, personal freedom,* and *personal independence.* Every thing in our institutions, in our literature, in our manners, has long tended to stimulate these ideas to the utmost. We have had any number of discussions and treatises designed to prove that individual opinion was the highest arbiter of truth and duty, and that every man's own intuition was the ultimate standard of what is right. The whole tendency of our national life and thought is to foster this spirit of personal liberty and independence. Nor are these qualities to be spoken of with disrespect. They are most essential elements in the grand compound of human civilization. Combined with certain other elements of law and order, they form the very highest development of humanity. What are the other elements so essential? What are the limitations which must be fixed to the exercise of personal freedom? This is the very gist of the question. This is only proposing, in another form, our original problem : Why may not every man do that which is right in his own eyes?

Man is not an independent existence, but a part of a

living organism, which we call society, by which he is connected with other individuals in indissoluble relations. This is a necessary condition of things, dependent not on our choice, but without our choice, on the will of the All-Wise. We hear much of the *social compact*—an expression used by those who have reasoned concerning the origin and laws of human society and civil polity; and since we must have terms to represent ideas, there is no objection to this phrase, if we use it with a discreet perception of its import. The point to be guarded in the use of the word *compact*, or any of its equivalents, in the definition of society, is this : organized society is not the *voluntary* concourse of individuals, but a providential necessity into which we are born, without our knowledge or consent. It is not of his own will that every child enters the world subject to an authority higher than his own. He is introduced, at his birth, into a social state which necessitates his subordination to a preëxisting order, in the shape of parental government. In like manner, without his consent at all, he is born into the civil polity, a condition of things which depends, not on the voluntary associating of men, but on absolute necessities imposed by the Being who has given us an existence. Without this beneficent organization, which we call *society*, the human race could not exist at all ; certainly it could not exist with any possibility of civilization and culture and development and progress and happiness. The State represents the great ideas of order, security, right, justice, and humanity, as the necessary condition of all morality. There must be order as the basis of all right relations ; and order consists in obedience to positive laws, as a necessary condition, ordained by the Almighty. It is in this sense, that the Bible defines the *powers that be*—that is, civil government—as ordained of God ; asserting that resistance to this (without just cause) is resistance to God himself. In asserting this, the inspired Word does not represent that government is a cast-iron, immovable, unchangeable power, to exist in all ages and all countries, in one and the same form. It has itself applied spiritual and reformatory power which tends to make governments better, more just, and more humane. It instructs those who govern, that they too are under divine obligations to act without wrong, or cruelty, or oppression ; and the great problem of society, through solemn centuries, has been so to adjust these two forces, the freedom of the individual, and the order of society, as to secure the greatest amount of all that is right, and just, and peaceful, and happy. In the progress of events, it has sometimes happened that the one force or the other has been in excess ; that there has been an uprising and outbursting of popular liberty, which has overturned superincumbent authority, creating, for a season, confusion, disorder, and revolutionary violence, till government could readjust itself on a better and wiser basis ; while, on the other hand, the Ruling Power has often asserted itself with such vigor and severity as to bear down all personal liberty, forbidding all motion, or peeping, or protesting, till stimulus, hope, and life, have died out of the individual man.

Amidst all these alternations there has been an actual progress through these compound forces of *freedom* and *order*. The pendulum has swung to and fro, and the index-finger on the clock of time has been moving on and round. It has been our boast—or, if the word suggests too readily the national fault of self-complacency—it has been our sober belief, that, as the result of all preceding experiments, and the general improvement of the race, under the auspices of education and religion, in our own land, at length, there had been attained a form of government which secures, in happiest combination the world has ever seen, the largest amount of personal liberty, with the most reliable expression of order, protecting person and property. If either of these forces has been in danger of running to excess, it surely has not been severity on the part of the Ruling Power. The theory of our form of civil government is the right of free men to govern themselves, by laws which they have, from their own intelligent choice, themselves enacted and recognized. This peculiar form of social polity exists under what is called a *constitution*—a written constitution; that is, a system of rules, and principles, and ordinances, by which the government shall be administered, and these adopted by the people themselves, and not a gift conferred by a monarch; and, to guard against all sudden caprices, the whims and passions of an hour, these rules and ordinances are engrossed in an instrument, which prescribes the orderly method by which, at any time, the document itself may be altered and improved.

The principle which underlies a government so constituted is, that the people themselves are so intelligent and virtuous that they can be trusted with the power of self-government. Whether this be true, in fact, of our

own population, is the very experiment which we are trying before the gaze of the world. The theory itself,
whatever the issue of its first great trial,—what does it
leave to be desired? What could man ask more than
this : the right to prescribe for himself the rules and ordinances by which government shall be administered, and
the order of society shall be secured? Could the imagination of man go farther than this? The Constitution of
the British Realm is not a written instrument, in the
hands of the people, to be read in schools ; it consists in
an accumulation of historic precedents, of established
usages, recognized as fundamental law; but not *written*
at all. For what has France been struggling through all
her dynasties and revolutions, but that there should be
granted to her some *octroyée* through imperial favor, which
would secure to her citizens more of personal right and
freedom? What more would Italy desire, sighing for
unity, than the permission to govern herself according to
a written constitution? I will not speak of Spain and
Austria, where the genius of order has reigned so long
and so tyrannically, that individual freedom and courage
are almost smothered out ; but how would Hungary and
Poland, in which the seed-thoughts of our Protestant
faith have been planted so deep, prolific already in noble
purposes and struggles, how would they clap their hands
for joy, if, at last, they could only attain their long-lost,
long-sought right, of prescribing and administering their
own constituted government?

This privilege, enjoyed by us, is no sudden attain-
ment, but the fruitage of a long, slow, deep-rooted growth.
It is the issue of historic causes. It has been purchased

at a great price. We who enjoy it might think that it had always been in existence the same as now. In fact, it is of recent origin. At what a cost of time, and heroism, and martyrdom, and suffering, and blood, has it passed into our hands. Consider what has already been accomplished under its auspices. It has secured all which is implied in order, with the least possible restraint consistent therewith, on the freedom of the individual. It has wronged no man. It has oppressed no man. It has never brought one man to the scaffold or the prison unjustly. It has secured to a vast population all their rights. Through this large domain any man—nay, any woman—could travel, unmolested, without espionage, without passports, and without a suspicion of harm. All forms of lawful business were protected, and a vast nation had started forth in a career of unprecedented prosperity, with no kind of restraint save what they had imposed on themselves for their own peace and comfort, as if to show to the world, at last, what a people could be and do, under the auspices of freedom, industry, education, and religion. Surely, if ever there was a people under every conceivable obligation to love their country, to obey its laws, to be loyal to its constitution, it is the people of these United States. If the Word of God, fresh from its inspired origin, abounds with commands to " honor the king," to " obey magistrates," to revere authority, to pray for all who represent the ruling power, when that ruling power existed in the shape of heathen emperors, irresponsible and despotic, what emphasis belongs to the same precepts in this stage of society, when government, constituted by the people themselves, represents the heaven-born law of order, with the very minimum of restraint upon personal liberty?

Our question is answered; not on grounds of mere policy and expediency, but by the eternal laws of Providence, and the principles of revealed religion. To do that which is right in our own eyes, without regard to lawful order, is to strike ruthlessly at the vitals of society, and demolish the necessary safeguards of all human interests and possessions.

That there is a right reserved to nations to change and revolutionize civil government, we concede. But that right, like every other, must be justified by morality. It exists only when government has been perverted from its proper ends, to such a degree that redress can be obtained in no other way. It is when the wrongs perpetrated by government are mortal and incurable; so that the very principle of order which the State represents, the very ideas of justice and right and humanity and happiness which are symbolized by the Ruling Power, demand a change to be made, even at the expense of a temporary inconvenience, peril, and suffering; a parenthetical evil for the sake of an ulterior good; amputation and cautery for the sake of the life. Till such a case is presented, every act of resistance to civil government is denounced as immoral and unchristian.

What is the cause assigned for *this* revolutionary movement? Was it incurable through constitutional processes? Was it of such a grievous nature that there was no remedy to be hoped for through the ballot-box, legislature, and the judiciary? Was it of such a deep-seated and malignant character that it became necessary, for the sake of the common good, to incur all the risks and expenditures, perils, sufferings, and woes of Revolution and War, that it might be extirpated?

As these questions have been asked, so must they be answered before all the civilization of the world. Contemporary nations await the plea, and posterity will pronounce its judgment. Manifestoes, declarations setting forth the reasons for the act, have already been issued by some who have taken part in it. Others have contented themselves with falling back upon certain alleged rights, without assigning any reason at all, failing to plead at the bar of public judgment. That these reasons are inadequate, and some of them contradictory; that, compared with the issues involved, all of them are frivolous, will, I think, be conceded by all who pronounce a calm and dispassionate verdict, and who have little heart to deal in mere invective and denunciation. To say the least, such an attempt to overthrow the government of the country was *gratuitous;* altogether unnecessary, in view of any real or imaginary wrong; and if gratuitous and unnecessary, how criminal and wicked.*

The question forced upon an incredulous and reluctant country, was nothing but the existence of its own nation-

---

* The best testimony on this subject, because removed from the possibility of prejudice or misjudgment, has been presented in two addresses, on two occasions, by the same person, the Vice-President of the Southern Confederacy. In the first, delivered in the State of Georgia, when discussing before his fellow-citizens the right and expediency of secession, he denounced the act as unnecessary, and ruinous; declaring the whole project to be the scheme of ambitious and disappointed politicians. The second, delivered more recently,

ality. That there had been a highly exasperated feeling, which was to be deplored, was true. But if this was to be allowed as adequate cause for disruption, why might not some other excitement and displeasure in some other direction prompt other States to fly off at a tangent and array themselves as foreign and hostile bodies? The difficulty lies in this—that we are to be forced to recognize a right of voluntary withdrawal ; which implied of necessity national suicide. If one part could withdraw, why not another? Nay, facts already show that the question was not to be confined to States, but that one portion of a State could claim a right to separate from the rest. If States from States, why not counties from States, and towns and cities from counties, and individuals from towns —tell us where this process of dissolution and disintegration shall end? It has no end short of the destruction of the whole social system—the dissolving away into chaos of that constituted order, which is the definition and purpose of the State, leaving the dismembered parts to a condition of anarchy ; every man doing that which

after he had himself been swept into the vortex of which he had warned others so earnestly before, in which he has given us an elaborate declaration of reasons, aiming even at a philosophical analysis and defence of the new Republic, asserting that slavery, as a normal condition, was its corner-stone ; that this indeed was contrary to the opinions of Washington and the fathers of the country, and that it had been reserved for this day to discover this truth, as the basis, religious and philosophical, of a new social organization. And here he rests his plea. It is not strange that when this address was republished in the city of Paris, by an American citizen, it was pronounced by the Press a forgery, not to be credited till authenticated by the affidavit of a French consul !

is right in his own eyes. The curtailing of our national domain is not the question; the circumscribing of our vast domains is not the issue—that might humiliate, but it could be borne; the life of our nationality might still be intact. But the tremendous question is—and we cannot evade it—how the right of voluntary separation, at mere will, upon mere feeling, can be conceded to the several parts, larger and smaller, without consenting to a principle which would be sure to recur again in other issues, and at some other caprice, till the whole civil polity, the entire social fabric, had crumbled to pieces. The question on trial, therefore, is the very existence of lawful government,—and that government, the very one which has made us the envy of so large a part of the world—self-government, under the auspices of liberty and virtue.

This is the issue which is now joined. It is not a warfare of one section against another. It is not a warfare against slavery, however, directly or indirectly, that may be involved in it. We hold ourselves still bound by constitutional obligations on this as on all other subjects. It is not a warfare for political ascendancy, for partisan preferences. It is not a warfare for territorial conquest, for the lust of subjugation. The very idea is as absurd as for the eye to attempt to conquer the ear, or the foot to subjugate the hand. It is simply, solely, honestly, for the defence of constitutional government, as the only breakwater against inevitable faction and feud; the only surety for order and justice and humanity. It is for the maintenance of the common weal; the health and vigor and life of the whole nationality. It is to uphold what we believe is of essential service and benefit to all alike. It is to decide whether we can abide in peace and unity, under lawful magistracy, or whether, at every gust of passion, or every whim of feeling, we are to be dismembered into contemptible factions, and dissolve away into absolute lawlessness. Nothing is demanded of one member of the body which is not demanded of all. Nothing is demanded of any, more humiliating or more unreasonable than subjection to those self-imposed laws which have conferred on the whole country such boundless prosperity, and which have never inflicted a wrong on any.

This is, as I believe, the one issue, in view of which we are now making history for ourselves and the world. We must meet it in the spirit nurtured by our religion. We must meet it with the temper of men who have been taught in the school of Christ, to bear all personal affronts with meekness—smitten on the one cheek, to turn the other also ; but who, when great interests are at stake for posterity and for the race, are inspired by an unselfish and manly energy, counselled by our religious faith, to withstand in the evil day, and, having done all, to *stand*. War is, indeed, a tremendous necessity. Gladly would we have cut off our right hands, and plucked out our right eyes, if we could have spared our native land the direful visitation. Since these events have come upon us, since we are not spared the trials which we had fondly believed belonged only to the past and the remote, let us seek to extract the lessons which will secure for us a better and wiser prosperity. There has been a too general laxity of habit in regard to law. As a people, we have erred before God in this respect. It has not been in one latitude alone that men have trifled with legal authority, and evinced a disposition to spurn control. That Liberty which we have almost defied, has been conceived, with a flushed cheek, and loose ungirded dress, conferring license on her worshippers to do as they willed. The Liberty which we honor, is a reverend form, the first-born of Virtue, wedded to order, girded with truth, with a chaste smile, and a strong right arm. If it must be that our faith in the capacity of self-government, under the auspices of the Christian religion, is to be tried by fire, then let it be tried, but not consumed. Sir Archibald Alison has pronounced the American Constitution a failure, and recommends a national Church and a national monarchy as the remedy. History does not roll backward after this manner, but onward always, purifying itself as it flows, by the effervescence of contrary qualities. Our faith does not lead us to abandon our nationality as a failure ; it only instructs us, if it need be by fire, then, so as by fire, to purify its properties, and amend its defects. Grateful for the memories of the past, with no bend of shame in our coat-armorial, hopeful for the future, with an ever-increasing trust in Divine Providence as our distinctive quality, we look forward and upward, above and beyond the dun smoke of the battle-cloud, to a more serene and tranquil sky, which sooner or later is sure to come. We will pray and hope and look for nothing worse than this—that the whole population of these United States may gladly subjugate themselves to constituted law ; that nothing may be defeated but that which imperils the good of all ; that nothing may rise to the ascendancy but that which is right and just and humane ; that all causes, come whence they may, which tend to exasperate and irritate and vex, may be removed, and that the people in every portion of the continent, identified in history, in interest, and in hope, may study the things whereby they may edify one another; that peace, on such a basis, and with such purposes, may speedily return, so that, as the tender grass springeth up after the rain, all that blesses and beautifies life may reappear with a fresher and surer growth; that confidence and credit, scared away by the noise of arms, may return; that suspicion and fear may fly away forever; that commerce and all the arts of peaceful life may resume their wonted channels; that education and religion may bestow on all their divine blessings and strength; that liberty may grant and secure the privilege to do all that is right and good, and that only; so that the sun may reappear holding its steady sway along the western sky, neither going backwards, nor hiding itself in clouds: but as the vapors which strive in vain to conceal the heavenly luminary along its daily path, become afterwards the instrument of reflecting its light, in most glorious effulgence, so will we hope, believe, and pray, that all the trials through which we are now passing, or are destined yet to pass, will only contribute to enhance the glory, which, according to the word of the Almighty, is sure to come in the Latter Day.

INDEPENDENCE NOT SECESSION.

In righteousness doth he judge and make war.

REV. 19 : 11.

Manus hæc inimica tyrannis
Ense petit placidam sub libertate quietam.

ALGERNON SYDNEY.

XIV.

INDEPENDENCE NOT SECESSION.

IT is common to celebrate the birth of our national independence with every demonstration of popular joy. So it was predicted by one of the authors of the immortal Declaration—it would always be celebrated with bonfires, and illuminations, ringing of bells, and salvos of artillery.

Special reasons gave to this anniversary, the present year,* an extraordinary zest and importance. We have reached a new epoch in our national existence. We have passed through a second birth. Delivered from great perils and pains, we are just entering a new period of our history. Not less important is the termination of our great civil war, than was the beginning of our independent nationality. Separated by an interval of nearly a century, the two events are immediately related. They have their resemblances and their contrasts. Both are part of one great historic development. " Deep answers unto deep at the noise of God's water-spouts." Our nation's birth and our nation's vindication are connected

* 1865.

directly with human rights, liberty, and welfare ; and are important acts in the progress of the kingdom of our Lord on the earth.

As such, they deserve to be celebrated, most devoutly, by an intelligent and religious people. They demand something more of us than holiday amusements, and noise, and pageantry, and exuberance of animal spirits. There should be a thoughtful consideration of causes, and principles, and divine laws. There should be a wise looking at the past and the future. Above all, there should be a most devout study of divine providence—its unfoldings and intentions in connection with our history. We cannot adjust ourselves wisely and vigorously to our duties as citizens in this Christian Republic, if we are not well informed as to the principles of divine jurisprudence which are to be acknowledged in our peculiar nationality.

While Washington commanded that the manifesto of national independence should be read at the head of every division of the army, the clergy, of their own impulse, performed the same office, with a very general unanimity, from their pulpits.

Those who aided and abetted the recent rebellion, at home and abroad, claimed that it had, for its origin and defence, the same rights and principles as those which were involved in that Revolution which secured to us independence from the Old World, and which is now universally celebrated as an act of wisdom, and righteousness, and honor. Was the one event right because it was successful? Is the other to be branded as crime merely because it was defeated? Or, did the one suc-

ceed because it was right, and did the other fail because it was wrong? What are the laws of right and
wrong as applicable to such subjects? What are the
principles, in the code of Christian ethics, which make
one revolution rightful and obligatory, and another
criminal and unjustifiable? Surely, we are in a most forlorn condition if we are not able to render a good and
sufficient answer to questions like these. Such matters
should not be left to caprice, to prejudice, to passion.
They come within the range of divine laws. These laws
are capable of exact statement. We cheerfully undertake
to define them. We hold that what is generally known
in history as the American Revolution—the act of separation from the British Government—was right, not because
it succeeded, but that it succeeded because it was right
—right in itself, right in accordance with divine laws ;
and therefore it deserves to be commemorated with
gratitude, and all who accomplished it with immortal
honor. We hold that the recent attempt to revolutionize
the government of this country was wrong, criminal, unjustifiable, notwithstanding the numbers even of good
men who were involved in it ; that in its inception, and
in its progress, it was at variance with the revealed law
of God ; and that it has been overtaken by defeat, and
will be remembered as an offence, because it was gratuitous, and against the statutes of the Almighty. Such language might pass for mere breath, if unsupported by
proof. Proof we propose to furnish. It will be my object, in this chapter, to verify the statements now made ;
presenting, in form, the contrasts between the two great
events in our history—the first and the latest—with the

reasons which crowned the one with success and glory, and doomed the other to defeat and ignominy. Sad for us and for the world will it be, if we do not rightly interpret the lesson which has been uttered in the terrific voices of war, and written, large and distinct, in human blood.

We begin what we have to propose on this subject with the inspired affirmation that government is a divine ordinance. "The powers that be are ordained of God." We are all aware of the manner in which this doctrine of revelation has been perverted and abused. Despots have cited it as the basis of their authority. Nothing is here said or implied as to the *form of government.* The expression is very general. The reference is simply to government. Civil government is a power for human protection. The authority for such a power proceeds from the Almighty, who has ordained that society could not exist without it. It does not spring, therefore, in an ultimate sense, from the consent of the governed. Surely, the right of parental government does not proceed from the consent of the child, who is born under domestic authority. It results from the will and ordinance of God. The object of government is, not the aggrandizement of those who administer it, but the welfare of those over whom it is extended. It is an agent for human protection, security, and well-being. Divine benevolence being its authorship, human happiness is its object and end.

From these premises we infer, *first*, the duty of obeying and conserving and honoring civil government, so long as it is administered with reference to its prescribed object; and, *secondly*, the right and the duty of modifying and changing government when it is perverted from its ordained uses into an instrument of wrong and oppression, and organizing a new and better form of administration which will conform to the legitimate intentions of civil government. These premises and inferences cover the whole ground pertaining to our subject. They prove the right of revolution in certain circumstances. They define the circumstances in which alone revolution is right. They inform us when attempts at revolution are wrong, a crime against society and against God.

The right to revolutionize government inheres in the very purpose of government. Mark the word : to *revolutionize* government, not to abolish government, not to destroy all government, since the necessity of some government is a divine ordinance for human welfare ; but to change its form, its method of jurisdiction—removing one and substituting in its place another which is better.

When is it right to revolutionize government? We answer : *when the existing government has so far failed of its legitimate object as to be an instrument of wrong, unrighteousness, and suffering.* Then, and then only, is it right and proper, in accordance with the divine law of benevolence, that it should be altered and set aside, and another form of government organized, which will the better promote the protection, safety, and happiness of the people. The process of change may require suffering. It may involve an appeal to arms, and the shedding of blood ; but the result contemplated,—redress of wrong, the removal of evils, the increase of happiness, the greater good of the whole,—justifies the stern and violent proceeding. Christian Benevolence smiles on an act which, proceeding from such a motive, tends to such an issue, and honors it with her blessing and sanction.

Such, we hold, were the circumstances which justified the American Revolution, and shed immortal renown upon those who conducted and accomplished it. It did not spring from mere passion. It had a better basis than a simple preference. Our fathers did not rebel against the mother-country because they did not like a monarchy, and because they thought they should like another form of government. Many of them were strongly attached to the ancient traditions of the ancestral land. They had no desire to inaugurate a new and independent government, provided the evils from which they suffered could be redressed. They began with protesting against those evils. They desired that they should be reformed and abolished. They remonstrated against abuses. They expostulated with the British Parliament and King. They were not wild and malignant insurgents. They were reformers, in the best sense. They knew not when they began how far their protestations would lead. They petitioned, they entreated. They sought for relief. They were subject to wrongs which amounted to oppression. There were those in the British Parliament who themselves protested against the wrongs inflicted upon the American Colonies. The eloquence with which Chatham plead the cause of our fathers, insisting on their rights, still echoes in the annals of the British Senate. But all these remonstrances and expostulations were in vain. Redress was denied. At length, the evils complained of reached such an enormity, that the duty and wisdom of resistance were revolved by our fathers. They did not precipitate revolution. They weighed well the cost. In their immortal manifesto they acknowledged that "existing governments should not be changed for light and transient causes." They regarded it as better to suffer wrong, while the wrong was tolerable, than to expose the country to all the sufferings and woes of revolution. But when abuses and usurpations were so multiplied as to prove that the government which originated them was perverted into an instrument of oppression, they could not evade the conviction, that it was their duty to set it aside, and provide other methods and agencies for their security. Then was it that they made their appeal to God, and to the "judgment of mankind." They made an expression of the reasons which justified their resistance to the long-established government, and their purpose to provide another. This was the design of the Declaration of Independence—to assign the reasons which impelled them to make this painful and violent separation. Those reasons, as they are recorded in the immortal document, are *twenty-seven in number*. We hold that they are good and sufficient. They are of such a character as indicate a radical perversion of civil government. They prove that the government by which those wrongs were perpetrated, instead of being an agency to protect and to bless, was itself an instrument of tremendous mischief. Its perversion was so complete and incurable, that nothing remained for good men and true but to set it aside, and adopt what was better. Their action was prompted by no antipathy of races, by no prejudice of classes, by no impulse of passion, by no ambition of power. It was a calm, intelligent, rational conviction on their part that the government under which they had lived had so far failed of the object for which government was instituted, that the common welfare, benevolence itself, demanded that a change should be made, by a revolution which might cost sacrifice, suffering, and blood. We do not propose to repeat, compare, and weigh, the several reasons assigned by our fathers, for the assertion of their independence. They are all on record. The wrongs of which they complained were not superficial. They imply a total subversion of the divine ends of government. Instead of being an organized power to protect, to bless, it was an armed power to irritate, annoy, oppress, and curse. And for those radical mischiefs there was only one radical and efficient cure. The government itself must be thrown aside, and another, just and benignant, be organized in its stead. This was what our fathers undertook and accomplished in the American Revolution. Their acts stand approved by the divine law of love. It is justified by the legislation of Him who is the ordainer of governments for man's welfare. That which is the end and design of government was the warrant for the change of government. The men who inaugurated the Revolution were called by the parent government — rebels. We regard them as reformers, righteous and heroic; and applaud their doing, not for its success, but for the great principles and laws of benevolence which prompted and conducted the achievement in the interests of human rights and human happiness.

We pass now over an interval of fourscore years, to the recent attempt to revolutionize the government of this nation, from which we have so recently emerged. That the government founded by the people of this country, nearly a century ago, was absolutely perfect, it would be false to affirm. That it was good, perhaps the best which in the circumstances could have been constructed ; that it was just, and liberal, and benignant ; that its aim was to promote the general welfare ; that it was, in fact, administered through a series of years, in the spirit with which it was organized ; that, through all changes of party and organs, it looked to the rights and security and good of the country, in the general tone of its action : these are facts which we affirm to be true, beyond all question or contradiction. These are the things which have made our government the theme of general panegyric. We will not now compare it with other governments. We will not expose ourselves to the imputation of lauding it with indiscriminate eulogy. It is enough that we take these facts for our premises : that the American Government was to be regarded as the divine ordinance for the good of the American people ; that it actually accomplished the end for which it was instituted ; and that, therefore, it was the religious duty of all to conserve and honor it, until it could be demonstrated that it was so perverted in spirit and acts, that the law of benevolence demanded that it should be revolutionized and overthrown.

It is from these premises that we start in our religious reasoning. Was the American Government an instrument of wrong and oppression ? Did it fail of the object for which civil government is ordained of God ? Who ever pretended that it did ? Dissatisfaction has frequently arisen in view of particular measures. Parties and sections have been disaffected by the failure of favorite projects. When majorities rule, minorities will always grumble and complain. But who has ever alleged that the Federal Government of this great nation was an instrument of mischief, of oppression, and of wrong! To prove to the satisfaction of all that no such necessity existed, as did exist in that original Revolution we commemorate, we confine ourselves to a few witnesses, whose testimony cannot be ascribed to prejudice.

The first of these is Mr. Jefferson Davis, who, in the Senate of the United States, in the year 1860, used these words : " This is the best Government ever instituted by man, unexceptionally administered, and under which the people have been prosperous beyond comparison with any other people whose career has been recorded in history."

The second is Mr. Alexander H. Stephens, of Georgia, who, in the year 1861, expressed himself, in the convention of his own State, as follows : " I must declare here, as I have often before, what has been repeated by the greatest and wisest of statesmen and patriots in this and other lands, that the American Government is the best and purest, the most equal in its rights, the most just in its decisions, the most lenient in its measures, and most aspiring in its principles to elevate the race of men, that the sun of heaven has ever shone upon. Now, for you to attempt to overthrow such a Government as this, under which we have lived for more than three quarters of a century, in which we have gained our wealth, our standing as a nation, our domestic safety while the elements of peril are around us, with peace and tranquillity,

accompanied with unbounded prosperity and rights un-
assailed, is the height of madness, folly, and wickedness."

The third is Henry A. Wise, then Governor of Vir-
ginia, who, in the year 1859, sending this sentiment to a
public gathering in Richmond : " The Union and the
Constitution of the United States as they are—the country, the whole country "— descants, even to rhapsody, on
the magnificence of the idea thus embodied, which made
" him, an unit, the possessor of the whole Union with its
pride, and its greatness, and its immortal annals," con-
cluding with these words : " If any would not love such a
country, let him have no country to love ; and if any
would array this country's parts against each other in sectional division and strife, let them have no inheritance in
the whole—the grand, great whole—but let them selfishly
have a single small space for their safe keeping, a house
made for treason, felony, or mania, a prison or a mad-
house."

This is testimony from the right quarter and of the
right quality. It might be reinforced in the same line
to any degree. But it would be superfluous. Whatever
was the reason alleged for the recent attempt at revolution, it was not this—that the American Government was
so perverted from the proper use and end of government,
that duty required that it should be changed and set
aside. If this reason did not exist, then the endeavor
at revolution, we will not say on political, but on Christian
grounds, was unjustifiable and criminal. No one, to our
knowledge, has pretended to prove that such a reason
existed. There was any amount of exasperation because
of other things ; recriminations based on other grounds

were hurled to and fro through the air ; but who, in any part of this country, or of the world, ever undertook to show that the Government of the United States was so despotic, so wicked, so cruel, that a regard for the general welfare—which is another expression for benevolence—required that it should be overthrown? We plant ourselves firmly on this ground. For the present, we hold in abeyance every other consideration. We confine ourselves strictly, for the moment, to this one. It is a ground on which all believers in the Bible, and all sincere friends of order, of law, of good government, and well-regulated liberty throughout the world, should stand together. It is the ground on which we justify, on our part, the war in which we have been engaged, in defence of the national life. Just now, we hold ourselves to this single issue. We endeavored to preserve that government which we knew deserved to be upheld, both for ourselves and for all mankind, against the assaults of men who sought to destroy it. Reasonably did we anticipate the sympathy and support of all friends of good government throughout the world in this righteous struggle. We did not expect the sympathy, either of despots or anarchists. It would not have disappointed us if the Emperor of the French had withheld his sympathy from our purpose to maintain, at any cost, our constitutional government. The world at large may have forgotten, in the brilliant success of the man, his art, his policy, the tremendous crimes by which he vaulted to his present position at the head of the Empire. But there are those, on both sides of the sea, who will never forget the scenes which occurred in Paris between the 2d and the 4th days of December,

1851, when he who was the President of the Republic, by a deliberate plot, called a *coup d'état*, drenched the Boulevards with innocent blood, and stained his own name with the infamy of perjury, that he might wear, for a season, the title of Emperor. No reason was there, why we should have expected the sympathy of such a man, who had revolutionized the government of his own country with criminal ambition to exalt himself, in our upright purpose to maintain our own good and lawful government ; but reason enough there was why we should expect no qualified sympathy from our ancestral land, whose traditions and history are so intimately related to good government, to true liberty and pure religion. Religious assemblies and Parliamentary debates have assigned as a reason why England stood aloof from our defensive struggle, that it was not designed nor prosecuted on our part with the intention of overthrowing slavery. That is true. This war, so far as the loyal States are concerned, was not begun nor prosecuted with that motive ; however true it was, that slavery ere long became involved in the sweep of the whirlwind. It is true that the inhabitants of the Northern States did not rush to arms for the purpose of destroying slavery. They could not have been united on that issue. They were united in the solemn purpose to defend and perpetuate the National Government. On that issue, they had a right to expect the good wishes and the blessing of all right-minded men throughout the world. For the moment, we keep to this issue and no other. What would the friends of human society, the friends of good government—men who believe neither in anarchy nor despotism—friends of order, of law, of liberty, of religion—what would they have had us to do, in the interest of the human race, but resolutely to resist all attempts to overthrow a government so good and genial as our own? The end has not come as yet to this great strife, so far as its issues are sure to affect and involve the future of other nations; but woeful would it have been for all the prospects of the world, had this gratuitous and unjustifiable attempt at revolution been successful. We had reason to expect that all candid minds—freed from jealousy and from fear—purified from the sympathy with the two extremes of tyranny and agrarianism—would have cheered, with one voice of approval and of prayer, this noble intent to uphold, at any expense of treasure and blood, this great ordinance of God for human welfare—a government which, by universal consent, was true to its benevolent intent. Where was the spirit of Hampden and Russel and Milton at that critical hour? Why was it not given out as in the sound of many waters in aid of a cause which, sure as any truth, involves the welfare of the world? By what spell was it that in public life, even in that Britain whose history and literature are so affluent in apostrophes to constitutional law, those who advocated our cause with full-voiced sympathy were so few, and those who looked at it askant, with suspicion, with ill-concealed disapprobation, were so many and so strong? These are questions which one day will demand an answer. We intend to have it known that we are true to our ancestral traditions; that we have not forgotten the lessons of British history; that we have not parted with all faith in the teachings of Providence and Revelation; that we threw off one government and undertook one revolution because that government was perverted into an instrument of wrong and oppression ; and that we have defended another government and defeated another revolution because the government was just and good and lenient, and that revolution aimed to destroy what God has ordained that we should honor and conserve.

No one familiar with the history of this country can question that, in one way or another, slavery was the cause of this recent commotion. To write out this history ; to define the position assumed by extreme men on either side ; to describe the measures and acts by which feeling became exasperated and inflamed, would be superfluous. We content ourselves with repeating the remark, that the destruction of slavery was not the motive which united the loyal States of the country to commence and prosecute the expensive war which God has crowned with success ; but, inasmuch as they who inaugurated armed rebellion against the National Government risked this institution of slavery on the issue of the war, by a series of events which were foreseen by none at the beginning, but which now appear to all as the special interposition of Providence, that system which was the root of all our public calamities, has been, by universal belief and consent, utterly abolished, and the whole land—North, South, East, West—admitting it now, will rejoice in it with universal gladness. God has wrought more than man had devised.

The completeness, the thoroughness of this victory in behalf of good government, is amazing. Nothing like it is to be found in history, when we consider the extent of our territory and the numbers arrayed on either side. Of one thing now, we are assured—the respect, the honor, the gratitude of all liberal minds, and all friends of free government throughout the world. Our cause is their cause. None have occasion to regret the issue of this war, but those who were apprehensive of the growth of liberal ideas and just principles in reference to civil government. The common people throughout the whole of the Eastern hemisphere, earnest for governments which will protect and bless them, heard of it gladly. The great leaders of religious and civil liberty throughout the world have made it the occasion of eulogy and of thanks. None are more certain to rejoice in it, as a measure looking to the permanent peace and prosperity of the country, after the exasperations of the hour have passed away, than those who were deluded into the vain attempt to revolutionize the government and destroy our nationality in the interest of human slavery.

The result we have reached has been at a vast expense. We cannot say, even when we compute the number of graves or the hosts of crippled and mutilated men who demand our respect and honor in the streets, that the price has been too great. All great achievements in the interest of the human race are accomplished through suffering. Our fathers suffered, but not in vain. We have suffered, but not in vain.

The sentiments appropriate to the times are not pride, insolence, and ambition, but gratitude, faith in God, faith in our institutions, and a resolute purpose to keep that faith with ourselves, and with the world, in the interest of law, liberty, and all goodness. We are entering upon a new historic epoch. It is with us as with the world emerging from the flood. That flood had enriched the earth with its vast deposits—to be improved by a better culture. We are not the same nation, in many respects, now that we have come out of this war, as when we went into it. We have no fear that such a war will ever be repeated, so long as the sun and moon endure. We rejoice that this has been decided in our own day. We have proved and settled it that liberty does not mean the absence of law; that the best and largest freedom does not imply the destruction of government. If we have had great deliverances, we must now meet great responsibilities. With victories in the field there must be the greater and sublimer victories of peace. We must conquer the resentments of the defeated, by conquering our own. We must be careful that constitutional law is not weakened nor dishonored by the hands of those who have achieved its vindication. Grave questions are on our hands, demanding wisdom, humanity, moderation, religious patriotism. If many of us are prone to think that mistakes have been made in our country, by the allowance of *universal suffrage*, the most they can be expected to concede is, that its exercise should henceforth be impartial. We like the expression *impartial* suffrage better than *universal* suffrage. Whatever qualifications may be thought proper for the high and solemn duties of a voter, let those qualifications be allowed to work impartially, without regard to color. Those qualifications existing, let none be denied the right of voting, because of the complexion of the skin; and, on the other hand, we may well hesitate to confer that right on any, because they are black, when wanting the qualifications which are expected of others.

Some questions which are destined to convulse the nations of Europe we have already settled. The time is certain to come when our sympathies will be looked for and valued. They will never be withheld from what is good through any spirit of retaliation. The sympathies of the American people will always be with free institutions, with liberal governments, with the rights of the people in Church and State ; and never will they be given to any class of men, who, under whatever name, agree in thinking that the many are to be held subservient to the few, and that the object of government is to aggrandize the oligarchy by whom it is administered. Government is for the good of all the people ; and a religious people will always conserve it as God's ordinance for the happiness, and not the harm, of society. Thoroughly imbued with this conviction, mindful of our history, knowing well the sublime events out of which it sprung, and those yet sublimer events which it foreshadows ; grateful to the Almighty for our earlier and our latter deliverances, we pledge ourselves to the great work of educating and Christianizing this ever-increasing population ; before the world we pledge our sympathy and aid to the great cause of liberty, of good laws, of humanity, of good morals, of true religion, of universal brotherhood and peace.

AMERICAN NATIONALITY.

He maketh wars to cease.   Be still, and know that I am God.
The Lord of Hosts is with us : the God of Jacob is our refuge.

Ps. 46.

XV.

AMERICAN NATIONALITY.

MANY instances of national thanksgivings are recorded in history. There is that most memorable deliverance of Israel from the bondage in Egypt, the miraculous passage of the Red Sea, upon whose shores the tribes, with Moses and Aaron and Miriam for leaders, with timbrels and dances, joined in a song of gladness and triumph, which elsewhere in Scripture is associated with that chorus which will be shouted at the last, by all the followers of the Lamb on the sea of glass. Our ancestral history is marked at every stage by these occasions of thanksgiving by a whole people. Edward the Third, the night after the famous battle of Cressy, issued orders, not only for abstaining from all insulting of the conquered and all boasting of their own valor, but for returning thanks to the Divine Giver of the victory. After the decisive battle of Poictiers, and the victory of the Black Prince, eight days successively were appointed by his father to be observed throughout England, for solemn and public thanksgiving. Few scenes in history are to be compared with that after the battle at Agincourt, where the gallant Henry the Fifth, with a small army,

14

routed the immense forces of France, when the king ordered the 115th Psalm to be repeated in the midst of his
victorious army, and at the words " not unto us, not unto
us, but unto thy name, be the praise," he himself, his
dismounted cavalry, his entire army, with all its chivalry,
fell to the earth upon their faces, ascribing to the Almighty
all the glory of their victory.

When the Spanish Armada, bearing such menaces
against Protestantism and liberty, was so terribly destroyed by a tempest upon the sea, not only was there a season
of national thanksgiving throughout England, but Queen
Elizabeth directed a medal to be struck, with the inscription, " Afflavit Deus, et dissipantur."

Later still, when England was distracted and convulsed
by a rebellion, in the interest of the Pretender, representing the House of Stuart, that synonym for bigotry and
despotism, against the House of Hanover, on the final
termination of the eventful strife which "secured every
thing to be esteemed, and delivered from every thing
that could be apprehended by a Protestant and free
people," a day was set apart for public thanksgiving, the
extraordinary observance of which has been preserved in
the charming description of Addison.   Not now to speak
of those many occasions for thanksgiving which were
observed by the feeble colonies of America, in view of
special deliverances which must have persuaded even
Atheism to believe in a Superintending Providence, there
was one which deserves a particular mention as appointed by the first President of the country.   It will be remembered that, shortly after the American Revolution,
and the formation of the Federal Constitution, chiefly

owing to burdensome taxation consequent upon the war, and to misconstructions of the name and the spirit of liberty, there were several attempts at unlawful insurrection against the government by armed forces in Massachusetts and Pennsylvania—attempts which to us, at this distance, seem to have been contemptible, but which at the time occasioned no little anxiety to the friends of order. On the complete suppression of the spirit of rebellion, which occurred during the lifetime and the office of George Washington, he issued a proclamation for National Thanksgiving, affixing to it, with his own signature, the seal of the United States—a document which cannot be too frequently recommended, for the excellence of its sentiments and the beauty of its expression.

NATIONAL THANKSGIVING.

A Proclamation.

By the President of the United States of America.

When we review the calamities which afflict so many other nations, the present condition of the United States affords much matter of consolation and satisfaction. Our exemption hitherto from foreign war ; an increasing prospect of the continuance of that exemption ; the great degree of internal tranquillity we have enjoyed ; the recent confirmation of that tranquillity by the suppression of an insurrection which so wantonly threatened it ; the happy course of our public affairs in general; the unexampled prosperity of all classes of our citizens—are circumstances which peculiarly mark our situation with indications of the Divine beneficence towards us. In such a state of things, it is, in an especial manner, our duty as a people, with devout reverence and affectionate gratitude, to acknowledge our many and great obligations to Almighty God, and to implore Him to continue and confirm the blessings we experience.

Deeply penetrated with this sentiment, I, George Washington, President of the United States, do recommend to all religious societies and denominations, and to all persons whomsoever within the United States, to set apart and observe Thursday, the nineteenth day of February next, as a day of public thanksgiving and prayer, and on that day to meet together and render their sincere and hearty thanks to the Great Ruler of Nations for the manifold and signal mercies which distinguish our lot as a nation—particularly for the possession of constitutions of government which unite, and by their union establish liberty with order; for the preservation of our peace, foreign and domestic; for the seasonable control which has been given to a spirit of disorder in the suppression of the late insurrection; and generally for the prosperous course of our affairs, public and private; and, at the same time, humbly and fervently to beseech the kind Author of these blessings graciously to prolong them to us; to imprint on our hearts a deep and solemn sense of our obligations to Him for them; to teach us rightly to estimate their immense value; to preserve us from the arrogance of prosperity, and from hazarding the advantages we enjoy by delusive pursuits; to dispose us to merit the continuance of His favors by not abusing them, by our gratitude for them, and by a correspondent conduct as citizens and as men; to render this country more and more a safe and propitious asylum for the unfortunate of other countries; to extend among us true and useful knowledge; to diffuse and establish habits of sobriety, order, morality, and piety; and, finally, to impart all the blessings we possess, or ask for ourselves, to the whole family of mankind.

> In testimony whereof, I have caused the seal of the United States of America to be affixed to these presents, and signed the same with my hand.

[L. S.]   Done at the city of Philadelphia, the first day of January, one thousand seven hundred and ninety-five, and of the Independence of the United States of America the nineteenth.

GEORGE WASHINGTON.

By the President:
  EDM. RANDOLPH.

Happy would it have been for the American people, if the counsels of this Proclamation had at all times inspired and governed our entire population. Never was there a people having such occasions and obligations for gratitude to God Almighty, as the inhabitants, and all the inhabitants, of this country, invited again by their President to sit down together at a national love-feast, and speak together of things which pertain to our country's life and unity and strength and glory. I say this with a full knowledge of many things to be regretted and deplored in the past; with the memory of many things, in every direction, which never can be approved and justified; without abating or modifying, in one jot or tittle, our previous judgment in regard to many measures, and many utterances of individuals, and sections, and parties ; with a full and fresh conviction of all the woes and burdens connected with that war out of which we have just emerged ; remembering the untold numbers, and those among the flower and vigor of the land, who have been swept into gory graves by the tornado of battle ; all whose names will never be known, till the earth and the sea give up their dead, at the trump and muster-roll of the Last Day ; with a most vivid impression of the many families who observe this day with weeds on their persons, and vacancies at their hearths and tables ; keeping before me, too, the fact, that large portions of our country cannot speak of victory and triumph, but are conversant with defeat and disappointment, chagrin and impoverishment, with little disposition to festivity, and we know not what antipathies and hostilities still rankling at the heart ; with the fullest persuasion as to the gravity of questions yet on our hands, undecided, pregnant with momentous issues for the future of America ; not forgetting how many things have been said and done which we could have wished had not been, how many things there are now, and may be and will be, probably, contrary to our own preferences and judgments,—yet with all these abatements, and shadows, and apprehensions, we say it again, and that with the profoundest convictions of its truth, never was there a country having so much to stir the gratitude of a whole people, as our own dear, torn, bleeding, reunited, regenerated America. If, after the manner of the ancients, who chronicled celebrated events with appropriate medals, we were to symbolize our country at the present time, we would represent her with a tear in her eye, for her dead children—a tear, not like those of Niobe in cold despair, but glistening with the pride of self-sacrifice for a cause great and good ; and notwithstanding that tear, radiant, calm, strong, cheerful, attended by the two forms of Security and Hope, the one, as the old Roman coins present her, leaning against a pillar, conscious that its strength cannot be moved ; and the other, "jocund, tip-toe," with her robes drawn back, in the posture of walking, as not to be encumbered or delayed, when pressing forward in a brighter and more magnificent career.

Wishing to avoid every thing like cheap and vulgar declamation, and to present something like a true analysis of *American Nationality*, with the reasons for rejoicing over its preservation, and the method and spirit by which it is to be perpetuated, let us briefly allude, by way of preface, to the wonderful changes through which we have recently passed—changes so astounding as to task our own senses and credulity. Had it been told us one year ago, when we met, as it were on the deck of the ship, tossing and thumping among the breakers, just where and what that ship would be to-day, tight and taut in hull and rigging, the battle and the storm both passed, and halcyon days returned, with smooth seas and bright skies, and the nation's flag high at the mast-head, undimmed, untorn, unblemished, not one of us would have believed the half of what is now fact and truth. According to the curious calculation of Sir Isaac Newton, the comet of 1680 imbibed so much heat by its approaches to the sun, that it would have been two thousand times hotter than red-hot iron had it been a globe of that metal ; and that, supposing it as big as the earth and at the same distance from the sun, it would be fifty thousand years in cooling down to its natural temper! Considering the ferments and excitements into which we have been wrought during the last four years of war, and the intense heat of the passions in all parts of the country, many entered into very curious computations of how many years, some despairing of any thing short of several centuries, before we should cool into comfort and moderation. Was there ever a transition so sudden, so general, so complete as that which, within a few months, has taken place in our affairs? There is a deep meaning in the fact, of important use, as testimony, when we come to speak of the history and elements of our nationality, that those who had taken arms against the government at last so promptly and universally abandoned a struggle which they saw to be useless ; for, notwithstanding words of passionate hostility, there was a latent love and pride for the old flag, which could not be exterminated, making that submission at last easy and complete, which never would have been reached at all, if there had been no misgiving at heart as to the rightfulness and necessity and honor of their cause. The war has ceased. I do not say that all which Tacitus meant by his expression, *recentibus odiis*, the yet fresh resentments, passions and prejudices of contemporary antagonists, have entirely disappeared ; but war, with its flames and desolation, its musterings and its shoutings, its shocks and din, and garments rolled in blood, has ended, and ended so that, as we believe, it will never be renewed, on that issue, so long as the sun and the moon shall endure. According to that inimitable description given us by Virgil in the first book of the Æneid, Military Fury is shut up in the temple of Janus, and laden with chains, sitting

High on a trophy raised of useless arms.

The immense armies which were mustered for the service of the country have been disbanded. Contrary to many predictions, domestic and foreign, they have returned to their pacific pursuits, quietly and softly as the snows massed on the mountains melt away in the spring and trickle down in streams which fertilize a continent. And to-day, notwithstanding all forebodings, and threats, and reasonable expectations, and precedents, there is not a single man throughout our vast domain who is in armed rebellion against the lawful government of the country. Not only is there no army, no ship, no fort, no regiment, no corporal's guard, but not one roving squad, not one guerrilla band, in all the fastnesses of the mountains, not one soldier, not one citizen, of any description, in arms and array against the government of the United States; and such is the change of affairs, and such the dearth of news consequent upon the change, that we, who a few months ago held our breath as we read of hundreds of thousands engaged in deadly conflict, and had our minds in the highest pitch of expectation day and night, now languidly open our morning papers to find a whole page headed with startling capitals to catch the eye, covered with the harmless advertisement of a sewing machine, a quack medicine, or the important intelligence announced by the telegraph—amused at its own feat—that a fishing sloop from Massachusetts Bay has arrived at

14*

Fortress Monroe; that the travelling agent of the old Peace Society has begun a new course of lectures; and that some dozen or two of adventurers and refugees, some of whom were dressed in Federal uniforms, have been shaking fists at each other from the opposite banks of the Rio Grande.

We should not say that the highest state of national prosperity was indicated by the entire absence of all exciting causes, according to the old Dutch conception, in which life moves on like the canals of Holland, " no breakers, no waves, not a froth-bubble on the surface," men and animals together never in a hurry, slow and sleek and heavy; or, in accordance with the Chinese idea, stamped on the very faces of the people, representing the flat, monotonous life of we know not how many centuries; nevertheless, when a people who are excitable to the last degree, like a swarming hive, buzzing and humming, when roused by alarms, have subsided into that condition in which they have nothing to report out of the ordinary course of events, it betokens that the flood of waters has abated, that the swollen streams have returned to their quiet channels, that the bow is out in the sky, and the meadows give forth a goodly smell.

It is of our *nationality* — our *American nationality*, as preserved and vindicated, that I treat, as the great event of the hour. Other things there are of which we may be proud, for which we should be thankful, but this is the one fact which sheds importance on all others, and which so defines and describes the true issue of our civil war, if not to all just now, yet to all ere long, to the

entire North, South, East, and West of our common coun·
try, that it will be the occasion of devout and fervent gratitude. It is this spirit of nationality which has prevailed and
triumphed. By this, I do not mean that there has been,
or is now, or will be, complete unity of sentiment in regard
to public measures, or the administration of public affairs,
but it is of comparatively small account what differences
of opinion may exist in regard to all subordinate matters,
so long as there is above all, beneath all, an honest at-
tachment to the national life, and an undivided purpose
that it shall be preserved. A serpent with one head and
many tails, will glide through a thicket much easier than
another serpent with many heads and one tail. Differences of opinion, likings and dislikings, attractions and
repulsions of party—differences running to all widths
between slavery and anti-slavery, and I care not what beside—these are only the caudal extremities of our growth
and motion ; and it is because at the other end, leading
the whole movement, there was but one head representing
the purpose and spirit of our nationality, that we have
worked our way safely through the tangled thickets without wounding or tearing off any portions of the body,
and dragging after us into the common triumph the many
tails of discord, which, had they been foremost, would
have torn us apart into many bleeding fragments.

Cicero recommends Pompey to his countrymen, on
the ground that he was always fortunate, and so great
was the importance attached to *success* by the Roman
people, that some of the emperors adopted the title of
Fortunatus among their highest designations. It is not
merely because the interest *we* have espoused has been

crowned with success, that we are called to unite in thanks before God ; but on the higher ground, that the nationality which has been re-asserted and reëstablished involves interests of the highest magnitude to every part of our country, to generations yet unborn, and to all the prospects of Christian civilization throughout the whole world. It is upon this high table-land that we would take our stand. Something of an effort may be required to reach it. Inasmuch as many are always prone to confound petty details with ultimate inductions, private grievances with vast public interests, I must ask each one of my readers, under the inspirations of the hour, to put out of his mind every thing which pertains to party and section, every thing of local partiality and personal preference, and to rise to those summits whence we can calmly and dispassionately survey the goodliness and greatness of our American nationality. As I shall speak of what is implied in that term, I beg him to take off his eyes from the eddies and back-water of the stream, from the drift-wood and weeds—every thing that is unsightly which is borne along on the surface—and survey awhile the depth and breadth and length and magnificence of the Great River itself, which maketh glad the city of our God. Differences of opinion exist among intelligent citizens as to the origin, the causes, the conduct, the men, and the measures of the war ; and nothing is so long-lived as ancestral prejudices and educated partialities. We are told of the old Tory of former times, who could not be accosted by a neighbor in the street with the usual remark about the weather, without replying that there had been no good weather since the Revolution. Judging from the style adopted by certain men and newspapers, we should infer that there was a faction existing in this country, consisting of the President, the Senate, the House of Representatives, and the Supreme Court; and that whenever there happens to be a majority of one opinion, Congress has no power to make laws. Here is a man who has nothing to say or do but grumble about matters which are only incidental and parenthetical to the great movement. One can see nothing but the temporary suspension of the writ of Habeas Corpus; another groans under the burdens of taxation, and revolts at the injustice of the income tax. One thinks it a very hard matter that his rebel cousin, when taken prisoner, was not treated like a gentleman, with fine linen and sumptuous fare; and actually complains because an army, marching through a country in hostility, did not leave every thing just as nice and genteel as after a pacific parade. It is no secret that some men entertain opinions of the widest extremes in regard to slavery. One goes the length of regarding it as a divine institution, to be conserved and perpetuated and, of course, seeing little else than misery and wrong and poverty and woe in the sudden liberation of the slaves; while at the opposite side are those who regard the extinction of slavery as the sole issue and object of the war; who, oblivious of the sentiment recorded on a certain occasion by President Lincoln, "with slavery or without it, *the Union* must be preserved," hold every other occasion for gratitude subordinate to this, that African slavery is forever abolished. Outside of all these conflicting opinions, beyond and above private complaints, personal disappointments or congratulations, prejudices, passions, traditions of place and education, we sweep a wider induction and climb that higher ground, where law and duty, loyalty and love, memory and mercy, justice and hope, patriotism and religion, invoke all the people to praise for the continued and invigorated life of the nation.

Am I required to explain what is meant by our nationality, and how much it includes? It would not be possible within the compass of a chapter to combine and retain all the thoughts and memories which come rushing upon us, at the proposal of such a question. We should feel obliged, in framing a full and correct answer, to unfold the true theory as to the object and import of civil government as a divine ordinance, with a careful statement of the reasons, which, on ethical grounds, justify one revolution, because government is perverted and oppressive, and condemn another as wanton and criminal because government is benignant and liberal; with some delineation of the enormous consequences which would ensue upon the admission that governments pronounced to be good may be assaulted and resisted at the whim and passion of any. We should be constrained to go back, through ancient protests and memorable struggles, to historic roots and forces, to lay bare the vital origin of our nationality, leading you through the galleries of the past, and bidding you to look at the faces of great men, and the pictures of great events. We should take you to Geneva, and Frankfort, and Leyden; and repeat what was accomplished in Britain in successive protests against despotism, the history of the long Parliament, the achievements of Hampden, and Cromwell, and Harrington, and

Pym, and Sidney, and Milton, and Russell—America in embryo, Jacob struggling with Esau in the womb of British history, America on British soil,—and the birth of liberty after long and perilous throes—liberty not flushed and licentious, but chaste and severe, wedded to law, the pledge of order and peace. We should be sure to tell you of what stuff the American colonies were severally composed, what extraordinary conjunctions of events, what reservations of this American continent, till the right moment in the dramatic movement ; how the colonies distinct in origin and character, were from the first attracted, by a common instinct of self-preservation, together ; how separation from the Old World was accomplished throughout by a *Federal* sympathy and power—in the words of Hamilton : "The Union and Independence of the States, blended and incorporated in one and the same act ;" of the independence of the country, declared by the American Continental Congress, and fought to a successful issue, in and by the union of all the States ; one in heart, one in toil ; how notwithstanding the cabals, of small men, North and South were interfused and intermixed, now a Northern general commanding in Southern battles, and now a Southern general in the Middle and Northern States, while out of the centre of the continent, as representing the heart of the whole movement, and presiding over it, arose that august form of Washington, who knew nothing, thought of nothing but the whole country, and so the independence of America was achieved by the union of America. Then we would rehearse the history of our national Constitution, the reasonings of that extraordinary man, Alexander Hamilton,

the right hand of Washington, who was so quick to foresee that a league could not serve as a government; that
confederacies, having subserved their time and purpose,
were to give place to an organized nationality; how that
nationality arose, not by a timid mending and patching
of the old articles, but by the higher action of a direct
representation of the People of all the States, assembled
in conventions, a new Government and a new Constitution, which, leaving undisturbed many rights and powers
of the several States, assumed the grander and more imperial, the sole right of making war and peace, of diplomacy,
the issuing of coin, the only coin of the country supersed-
ing all State mottoes and devices, with *E pluribus unum*
upon its face, the adoption of a national flag, and so the
birth of a full-grown and blessed nationality.   We should
be sure to repeat to you, as the exponent of that time and
history, the counsels of Washington, our American Moses,
in his farewell address, that sweet and noble Deuteronomy of our annals, with its warnings against sectional
jealousies and geographical distinctions; his noble heart
beating to its last throb in pride and love and hope for
the American Nation.   With wonder should we tell
how the country grew and prospered, how the flag was
borne upon every sea, and was a protection to every
citizen; how territory was enlarged and populated,
a vast tract of country, known as Louisiana, large
enough afterwards to be partitioned off into several
states, was ceded by France, to what?—to whom? To
Arkansas? To Missouri? They were not yet in exist-
istence; but to the United States. We would dwell
on the marvellous ease with which the Federal

Constitution adapted itself to new territories, and new exigencies, and so commerce flourished and agriculture smiled, and the arts prospered, and peace reigned, and the fourth of July was celebrated North and South, and East and West, and the foot of every child marked time to the simple, soul-stirring old music of our nationality. Nor should we leave out of account how, as exciting questions arose, and sectional collisions were imminent, men were prepared for the emergency, whose names belong no more to States but to the Nation; HENRY CLAY, whose sweet, persuasive, and limpid speech, in defence of all that was national, was like his of old, on whose lips the bees of Hymettus were said to settle; and that other form, grand, imposing, never to be forgotten, as one who, by his special study and eloquence, made ready the country for that struggle out of which it has just emerged, DANIEL WEBSTER, known as the Defender of the Constitution, and whose matchless words, on more than one occasion, so moved the heart of this whole people, that, long after his argument was finished, they turned towards him, in breathless delight, as Adam to the discourse of the angel;

> " The Angel ended, and in Adam's ear
> So charming left his voice, that he awhile
> Thought him still speaking, still stood fixed to hear."

If any thing more were necessary to complete the conception of our nationality, I would bid you glance at the geography of America, and mark in what direction run the ranges of its mountains and its great rivers, the outlets of commerce—physical characters, in which God Almighty has written out the unity of our nation; and

when, by all these lessons of history, these memories
of the past, remote and recent, we are possessed of
some idea of what is meant by America—America
as a whole, as an organized and distinctive nationality—let us remember that the progress of events is
not to be arrested or reversed, that history is not to be
turned backwards, according to the sagacious sentiment
which John Hampden adopted on his coat of arms,
" *Vestigia nulla retrorsum* " ("No steps backwards ");
and when all this is full in your mind, I ask you what
shall we think of the conduct of men, in any quarter,
speaking disparagingly of our nationality; what of the
audacious crime of striking at the heart of such a government, wantonly and without cause ; and what is your in-
stinctive sentiment in regard to men who would peep the
name of a State in contempt of the grander name, the
United States of America; who had wrought themselves into such a frenzy of the imagination that they
were willing to lower the national flag to a foreign protec-
torate ; that men could be found who had so far forgotten the pride and honor and independence of their
country, that, to accomplish their unnatural purposes, they
actually crept round, through Nassau and Canada, British
provinces, to ask for sympathy and aid from British
authority—hanging all their hopes on British recognition,
fawning about the British ministry, and crawling for protection under the paws and the tail of the British lion.
Thank God, the nation lives ! If we never understood it
before, we know, we feel that we are a nation now. Our
independence, at last, is completed. Henceforth we shall
make our own laws and our own language. If we choose

to adopt a new word expressive of a new thing, we shall
certainly do it at our pleasure. We shall be Americans
throughout ; we shall manufacture our own goods, cast our
own cannon, enact our own notions, honor our own flag,
do things in our own way, dispose of our own criminals,
hang our own rebels, and dispense justice or mercy according to our own convictions, as lawfully expressed by
the chosen authorities of the country, without regard to
malcontents at home, and without asking permission of
any body abroad.

Does any one hesitate to give praises, loud and hearty,
for the preservation of our nationality? They may not
admit it just now, in the suddenness of their reverses, and
the uncooled ardor of their passion ; but no portion of
the country has more real occasion for gratitude over the
issue of the war, than the very States by which the war
was inaugurated. We shudder to think what consequences
must inevitably have ensued, sooner or later, if they had
succeeded in the purpose of breaking away from the
Federal Union. Does any man in his senses, who knows
any thing of human nature, of history, of America, believe
that a confederacy, based on the very principle of secession, could for any time be held together by that principle? Would not the very centrifugal passions, which
whirled them out of the sphere of nationality, have
entailed the certainty of subsequent explosions, throwing
them into contemptible fragments with petty rivalries,
intestine wars, imposts at every border, custom-houses
and guards at every boundary ; without dignity, without
security, without strength, without a common flag? Well
for them, and for us all, that the ever-recurring revolutions

of Mexico and of South America have not been brought nearer to us, to be repeated on our own soil. Grateful should we be, that this question has been settled, in our own times, and is not to be bequeathed to our children. Nor is there less occasion for gratitude, that the maintenance of our nationality is for the interest of well-regulated liberty throughout the world. It has proved that liberty is not weakness but strength ; that our nationality is the strongest of all governments, because its roots are in the hearts of a free people. It was because they doubted this fact of the strength of a democratic government to protect itself against internal foes, that our success was doubted by foreign powers. But the result has demonstrated, to the delight of all friends of free institutions throughout the world, that our nationality was never so strong as when enemies out of its own household rose up against it ; when the very head of the country fell instantly by cruel assassination ; and that, to-day, it stands self-poised, calm, and triumphant.

Had the issue of this war been otherwise, leaving us fractured and despicable, the shadow on the dial of Time would have gone back we know not how many degrees, and wails and dirges would have been tolled off in all the turrets of the air. God has been merciful unto us, and blessed us ; that his way may be known upon earth, his saving health among all nations.

Thus far I have confined myself purposely to one topic, the preservation of our nationality, from the clear conviction that, in every event, the best thing for the white man and the black man, the Northern man and the Southern man, and every man in America,

Europe, Africa, and Asia, was that this free republic, this constitutional government, which unites liberty and order, should be maintained inviolate. It was from this conviction, that, with all our innate abhorrence of human slavery, as entailed upon this country by the mother land, against American protests and expostulations, many were disposed to counsel moderation and patience, and time for the working out of remedial, rational, and legal methods. But how marvellous are the ways of God, transcending all our wisdom and forethought! Who of us ever dreamed that in our day, as the result of unanticipated events, slavery would be exterminated, and that the Southern States themselves would take part with the majority of all the States, by a legal amendment of the National Constitution, to secure its complete extinction! It was here, as it has always been, in the wisdom of Divine Providence ; crime was made the instrument of its own defeat ; reviving the lesson of the old fable, that they who fight against the gods, blow fire and ashes into their own faces ; and they who sought to dethrone the lawful government of the country, were buried under their own Ossa and Pelion. Slavery has killed itself in America. Let all the people say, Amen. Henceforth it cannot be an element of national politics ; henceforth its removal will be for the national peace and purity and morals and honor. So let us thank the Almighty for an issue which has been of his own working, far above all the wisdom and power of man. The cancer is cured, but the man lives ; the defect in the façade is removed, but the Temple stands stronger and firmer than ever.

That the loyal people of this country are, on every ground, disposed to be magnanimous and lenient to those who called themselves our enemies, needs not be argued. Whether enough has been done in the way of solemn justice, to mark public abhorrence of the crime of wanton rebellion, to stamp it with infamy forever; whether the hanging of a few miscreants, convicted of arson, and cruelty to prisoners, is a sufficient assertion and vindication of justice, in view of the tremendous calamities which have been brought upon the American people by this rebellion, may safely be left to the decision of those who are invested with constitutional authority and power in the premises. But in regard to the Southern people, many of them misled and wronged, patience, kindness, magnanimity without stint—on one condition—and but one: *good faith* and honor and loyalty now to the government of the United States.   Every thing can be forgiven ; every thing can be healed ; every thing can be restored, if there be complete confidence as to the sincerity of the oath of allegiance to the National Flag and Constitution. To ask that every man should say that at no time had he any sympathy with the movement which overspread his whole State, to demand that men should accomplish the feat, surpassing all achievements of jugglery, of swallowing themselves bodily, that in an instant there should be a complete reversal of all habits of thought, and liking of institutions to which they were attached from birth, is too much to expect of mortal imperfection. But what is demanded, and that most reasonably, is that, accepting the issue of the appeal to arms which they invoked, they should now abide by the issue in duty to the national government. Time and patience and social intercourse and commerce will accomplish the rest. If I am not mistaken, words have fallen in some quarters, sometimes from fair lips, reasoning under prejudice, that the oath of allegiance was merely a form, a matter of policy, to be taken with mental reservations, and private evasions and intentions, by which it may afterwards be broken. The taking of this oath is no *coup d'état*. Let there be so much as a suspicion that it is not taken in good faith, and the foundations of civil society are dropped out. Euripides, the great tragic poet of Athens, once introduced a person into a play, who, being reminded of an oath he had taken, replied, " I swore with my mouth, but not with my heart." The impiety of the sentiment set the audience in an uproar. Socrates, the friend of the author, swept out of the theatre in indignation. And Euripides himself, so great was the offence, was publicly accused and arraigned and brought to trial, as having suggested an evasion of what was thought the most holy and indissoluble bond of society.*

Social changes impose new social obligations. Those who have been suddenly, by the convulsions of the war, thrown up out of slavery, are to be the wards of the national justice and humanity. We cannot yield assent to all the theories which have been put forth in regard to their immediate and unconditional rights of suffrage. It has been argued, for example, ingeniously, but sophistically, that suffrage is a natural right. If it is so, when

* Freeholder, p. 420.

does it begin? at birth? when a child can hold a piece of paper? Does it belong exclusively to one sex? Plainly, suffrage is not a natural but a political right, and the time when it shall be exercised, and the persons by whom it shall be exercised, are and must ever be fixed by the civil power—the State itself. What more can be asked, or conceded, in regard to this right of suffrage—the most sacred and high and solemn that a freeman can hold,—but that whatever qualifications an intelligent community shall prescribe, the same shall be allowed *impartially*, without distinction of color. More than this would be to overturn the old foundations of intelligence and virtue on which our free institutions are built.

God grant that the kindly sentiments which gratitude inspires may foster the purpose, hereafter to do every thing that an intelligent, self-governed Christian people can do for the honor and interest of our whole country. Well may we adopt the sentiment worn as a frontlet by a great man in former times : " Serve God and be cheerful." * Not content with what is generally understood by being good citizens—honest, just, and true—we should cultivate more the specific and grander affection of patriotism. Exercising the rights of freemen to criticise public men and public measures, as we would not mislead foreign observation, or harm and mislead ourselves, let us, in a higher region, and with a mightier sentiment, be sensitive to all which affects the honor of our nationality. There is something to be admired in that which has occurred in the civil wars of history, that before bat-

---

* Inservi Deo, et lætam.

tle commenced, the pavilion or the position of the king should be designated, so that no harm should come to his person who represented the life of the nation. Something to be honored, is the custom of the Persian ambassador to the countries of Western Europe, bringing with him a sod of his native soil, to be looked at every day, so to be reminded of the country with whose honor he was entrusted. Without counselling any thing which is romantic and vainglorious, let us be grateful for the land which God has given us, the Constitution bequeathed to us, the Government given to us anew, as preserved amid unprecedented trials, grateful for the names and services of great men, the principles, ideas, and successes, which America has furnished already as a succor and hope for other nations, and confident as to what Christian liberty will yet do for the world; the cross symbolizing what Christ has done for individual man; the flag what Christian men may do and organize for themselves; that flag to-day the same which rustled over us in our childhood, to be the same for ever, we trust—changed only as new stars shall come out upon its azure firmament, but losing none; let us rise above all the asperities, the griefs, the perplexities of the hour, and rehearse, we and our children, now and always, those grand old words of the Hebrew poet, which inspiration has left us for the very purpose of expressing, as no other words ever can, our love for our whole country and our religious convictions as to the relations of our unbroken, united, harmonized America to the world:

GREAT IS THE LORD, AND GREATLY TO BE PRAISED IN THE CITY OF OUR GOD, IN THE MOUNTAIN OF HIS HOLI-

NESS. WE HAVE THOUGHT OF THY LOVING KINDNESS, O GOD, IN THE MIDST OF THY TEMPLE. ACCORDING TO THY NAME, O GOD, SO IS THY PRAISE UNTO THE ENDS OF THE EARTH ; THY RIGHT HAND IS FULL OF RIGHTEOUSNESS. WALK ABOUT ZION, AND GO ROUND ABOUT HER : TELL THE TOWERS THEREOF. MARK YE WELL HER BULWARKS, CONSIDER HER PALACES : THAT YE MAY TELL IT TO THE GENERATION FOLLOWING. FOR THIS GOD IS OUR GOD FOR EVER AND EVER.

THE PAST AND THE PRESENT.

Say not thou, What is the cause that the former days were better than these ? for thou dost not inquire wisely concerning this.

ECCLES. iv. 10.

XVI.

THE PAST AND THE PRESENT.

IT would seem that even in the days of Solomon, some were disposed to disparage their own times, and to sigh for those which were gone. They appear to have assumed that the "former times were better" than their own; an assumption which the Preacher affirms not to be true. It amuses us, when the old gouty count in Gil Blas persists in saying that the peaches were not so good as they were in his boyhood. But when the disposition assumes the grave form of discontent with what is present and actual; complaining of one's own day and generation as the worst that ever was known; we are taught both by reason and Scripture to pronounce the habit as most pernicious, for it is grafted upon a falsehood. Bad as the times may be, they are better and not worse than those behind us, and the poorest use to which we can put our time and faculties, is to be querulous over those affairs to which we are personally related, and to stand, in what is called the "barrenness of these degenerate days," Janus-faced—one countenance, that which is turned to the future, elongated, scowling, and sombre; while that which looks to the past, has an expression of wishfulness, smiles, and satisfaction.

There is an illusion in regard to the memories of the past, which ought to be corrected by a sober judgment. It is easy to make the correction so far as it relates to our personal life. We recall the period of childhood, as one of peculiar happiness. We find delight in recurring to the time when, as children, we were welcomed and blessed under the roof of our first and earliest home. There is good reason why the bright picture should be hung up in the gallery of the memory : the house, the cheerful fire, the generous table, the cordial greeting, love sincere, confidence unsuspected, contentment complete, the crystal ice, the new-fallen and resplendent snow; or, that other pleasure, of which a popular writer has said, nothing is to be compared with it—" A Child's Midsummer Holiday—the time, I mean, when two or three of us used to go away up the brook, and take our dinners with us, and came home at night tired, dirty, happy, scratched beyond recognition, with a greasy nosegay, three little fish, and one shoe, the other having been used as a boat, till it had gone down with all hands out of soundings." * So it has been gravely asserted by the same author that this was the very happiest period of life ; and that no man ever " experiences such pleasure after fourteen, as he does before, unless it be in the novel sensation of his first love-making." The illusion, so common, is easily explained. Conversant with care, pressed with burdens peculiar to itself, manhood looks back to the time when care was unknown, and burdens and toils were not so much as thought to exist. Life mature is put in contrast

* Charles Kingsley.

with life immature, in the strong points of their dissimilar-
ity, and so the balance is carried to the wrong side. The
griefs of childhood, real, far more real, than our ripened
and stronger life remembers, are forgotten. The shades
in that bright Mosaic are left out. Nothing is accounted
for or remembered, but the bright hues of careless pleasure. We drop out of the drag-net of time the sand,
the sea-weed, the drift-wood, and all which we retain is
the tinted shell, with its smooth and polished lips, its
lining of pearl, and its soft murmurs of a receding and
unwritten music.

Then, again, the personages change their places, and
pleasures vary. You cannot crowd a full-grown man
into the dimensions of the boy. The child has himself
become a man ; and his enjoyments are of a new name
and form. He who was once welcomed home as a child,
now has the pleasure and honor of extending a welcome
to his own children, who are thus the instruments of
giving him a double joy, his own and theirs reflected upon
his larger heart. Spring, summer, autumn, and winter
are not the same ; each has its uses and its enjoyments,
and the latest are the richest in fruit-bearing, harvesting,
and reward. Some pleasures there are which, like some
diseases, we can have but once. Talk of the first love-
making as a memorable epoch of life, from which one is
receding ; it is a fit utterance for a poetaster, for it is a
fiction. The man, ripe in years and experience, if his
heart be pure and true and honorable, will tell you how
his heart has grown deep and broad and large, as another life has grown into unity with his, in the passing
of many summers and winters of diversified events.

and that to him the gray curl which now rests on the forehead sanctified by time, is more dear and more beautiful than the brown and raven tresses which crowned that brow of rose and ivory, on which boyhood printed its first kiss of pride and passion.

The illusion which cheats so many in the estimate of their present life, affects their judgment in regard to the past and present of nations. Their knowledge of history is limited to some fiction of life and manners which they have received from ballads and romances. They will insist on placing the "golden age" in times when, in fact, kings lived less sumptuously than a prosperous farmer to-day; and men and women with titles of nobility were destitute of comforts which are now within the reach of the common laborer. In spite of all evidence, thousands imagine to themselves the social state of past centuries as more agreeable and happy than that in which we are now living. They are charmed with the "merry England" of Queen Bess, because their only notion of that England is derived from the splendid panorama of Kenilworth. They have read the description of an English inn, as given by Izaak Walton, the walls covered with ballads, the brick floor swept to tidiness, and the sheets scented with lavender, such as the honest and quiet fisherman frequented when coming in from the brooks and meadows, and immediately he imagines the England of Walton's day as a Paradise of cleanliness, comfort, and contentment; when, in fact, the majority of tenements had not even a chimney, and floors were generally colored brown with a wash made of soot and small-beer, to hide the dirt; and the filth and discomfort of houses, as described by Erasmus and Hollingshed was so great as, in their opinion, to be the cause of fatal epidemics ; and in London, taverns were designated by flaming signs of Blue Boars and Golden Lions and Saracens' Heads, because such a vast proportion of the people could not read names and numbers, and so were dependent for direction on some form palpable to their senses, the more grotesque the better.

It is difficult for us even to imagine what period of time, or what stage of history, men disaffected in the days of Solomon had in their eye, when they pronounced them better than their own, which was the very culmination of their national polity. Could it be that any were so deluded as to wish that they could exchange their condition for a state of anarchy, when every man did what was right in his own eyes ; when there were no roads, nor arts ; when an ox-goad, or the jaw-bone of an ass, were the most efficient implements of war, and the dissevered limbs and joints of a mutilated woman were sent through the tribes as the best summons to battle ? or, earlier still, had a nomadic life of tents, and flocks, and pastures, its peculiar charms ? It is hard to say what age they would imitate, or what state of things they would propose for an example. A glory was it, surpassing all which ordinarily falls to the lot of mortals, to stand on the shores of the Red Sea, when it had been crossed, as it was by Israel, and chant their songs of praise and deliverance to God Almighty. But these were the very men, with God for a protector, and his promise for a cordial, who looked backward and sighed for the green meadows of Egypt, with nothing better than onions and vassalage.

15*

In 1679, a period of wonderful heroism, labor, and austerity, in our country, a convention was held in New England to inquire what was the crying sin which had incurred what was called the judgment of God on the colonies, and the unanimous conviction was that it was to be ascribed to the luxurious and intemperate habits of what they pronounced a backsliding and downward age ; and this at a time when modes of living were so rigid and austere as now to excite the sense of the mirthful ; when Lady Moody lived in a house nine feet high, and Governor Winthrop expended on official dignity about as much in a year as an ordinary gentleman of our time in a month. Mr. Addison has given us, in one of the numbers of the Spectator, a humorous description of a valetudinarian who was bent on being sick, and reducing himself by spare diet and profuse sweating, but who all the time, in spite of himself, was growing decidedly corpulent. " At first it might seem strange," says Macaulay, " that society, while constantly moving forward with eager speed, should be constantly looking backward with tender regret. But these two propositions, inconsistent as they may appear, can easily be resolved into the same principle. Both spring from our impatience of the state in which we actually are. That impatience, while it stimulates us to surpass preceding generations, disposes us to overrate their happiness. It is, in some sense, unreasonable and ungrateful in us to be constantly discontented with a condition which is constantly improving. But in truth, there is constant improvement precisely because there is constant discontent. If we were perfectly satisfied with the present we should cease to contrive, to labor, to endeavor, to fight with a view to the future. And it is natural that, being dissatisfied with the present, we should form a too favorable estimate of the past. In truth, we are under a deception similar to that which misleads the traveller in the Arabian desert. Beneath the caravan all is dry and bare, but far in advance and far in the rear is the semblance of refreshing waters. The pilgrims hasten forward, and find nothing but sand, where, an hour before, they had seen a lake; they turn their eyes and see a lake where an hour before they were toiling through sand. A similar illusion seems to haunt nations through every stage of the long progress from poverty and barbarism to the highest degree of opulence and civilization. But if we resolutely chase the mirage backward, we shall find it recedes before us into the regions of fabulous antiquity."* Pertinent is the apostrophe of Charles Lamb : " Antiquity ! thou wondrous charm, what art thou ? that being nothing, art everything ! When thou *wert*, thou wert not antiquity —then thou wert nothing, but hadst a remoter *antiquity*, as thou calledst it, to look back to with blind veneration ; thou thyself being to thyself flat, jejune, *modern !* What mystery lurks in this retroversion! The mighty future is as nothing, being everything ! The past is everything, being nothing." †

In drawing a comparison between times present and past there is an important advantage in taking a survey of a considerable period of time, as the whole or the half of a century. The movement of society is by actions and

* *History of England,* vol. I., p. 396.   † *Elia,* p. 23.

re-actions. It is not like the current of a rapid river, always running on in the same direction. Rather is it like the swing of the ocean when the tide is rising. A wave comes in, breaks, and rolls back. No one would imagine, from a single glance, that there was progress at all. Fix your eye steadily for half an hour on one point, and you will perceive, with all that flux and reflux of the waves, the progress of the tide is onwards and upwards. Just so is it with history. Examine it in small and detached portions, a year, five years, and it is like a single wave, which disappoints you by its recoil. Take fifty years, the flats and the sea-grass are out of sight, and you are struck with the difference between low ebb and a full tide. Important events require time for their own elucidation. You cannot judge of them by their first appearance; you must wait and see their ultimate effects. Events have roots, branches, and fruit. They do not ripen in a day. Sir James Mackintosh was not a weak and fickle man because of a difference of judgment in his earlier and later writings upon the French Revolution. This change of opinion was the necessary result of advancing time, and so was the proof of serene wisdom. Who can doubt that Edmund Burke, if now alive, would write very differently, on the effects of the French Revolution, from what he did in the year 1790? The progress of half a century gives an entirely new aspect to events which appear disastrous or hopeful in their first occurrence.

"The present enlightened age," is an expression which has already attained to a cant currency; and many, so deftly rebuked by Douglas of Cavers, regard it with as much satisfaction, and the past with as much contempt, as if, like Love in Aristophanes, it had been hatched from the egg of Night, and all of a sudden had spread its radiant wings over the primeval darkness.* Other centuries have been marked by great events. We call events great only from the results to which they lead. Other men have labored, and we have entered into their labors. We and our children gather fruit from the trees which they planted with fear and trembling. The roots of those institutions which distinguish our own times lie back in other centuries. But there is one circumstance which gives to recent years, and the position from which we survey them, a decided pre-eminence. The older the world is, the more apparent becomes the design of its Maker. The comprehensive study of history is like the ascent up a mountain,—the higher you climb the more you see. It is like the progress of a drama,—the farther you advance the more you comprehend of the plot ; as events thicken the better do you discern their bearing on the catastrophe.

The close of the last century was marked by the most astounding changes. It was a time of general war and convulsion. It seemed as if God had arisen to shake mightily the earth. Men's hearts were failing them for fear, and for looking for those things which were to come to pass. A great part of the eighteenth century is remarkable for the European wars of succession. Ere the century closes, wars of a very different description,—wars of principle,—compared with which the contests of the

* Douglas on the Advancement of Society.

house of Hapsburgh were children's squabbles, convulse the world.   At the first movement of the popular mind in France, the friends of humanity rejoiced.   Great abuses were reformed, and good men were hopeful.   But the huge mass set in motion could not be stayed.   The detent was wanting, and everything whirled and whizzed to a premature and disastrous stoppage.   Commotion, pro- scription, confiscation, bankruptcy, civil war, foreign war, revolutionary tribunals, guillotinades, blood, chaos, fol- lowed each other in rapid succession.   A military despo- tism rises from the confusion and threatens the independ- ence of every State of Europe.   As the century opens, Napoleon was certainly the most remarkable personage in the world.   We have now reached a point of time when we can pronounce with some deliberation upon the general effects of his extraordinary career, and of that great revolution in the midst of which he emerged. There was too much of terror and of mystery in those events, at the time of their occurrence, to allow men to judge with calmness.   There was then scarcely one honest friend of liberty whose ardor was not damped and whose faith in the high destinies of mankind was not shaken.   It is now our deliberate opinion that the French Revolution, in spite of all its follies and crimes, its atroci- ties and sacrifices of human life, was a great blessing to the world.   Deliverances were wrought, though amid plagues, and signs, and wonders.   Demons were exorcised, even though they raged and foamed, rending and tearing their miserable victims.   The Colossus of war who be- strode Europe, was a rod of iron, by which the Almighty dashed in pieces the old despotisms of the world, like potters' vessels. Nations were lifted up from under the heavy oppressions by which they had long been stifled. A revolutionary spirit was abroad all over the world. Mountains did not stay it, nor did seas stop it. A new idea was thrown into the heart of society, which, of necessity, produced explosions and the greatest of changes. That idea was the rights of subjects,—the inalienable freedom of man. The world had heard enough before, in all forms, of *the divine right of kings.* The " Rights of Man " was the title of the book published by Thomas Paine, then in England, in reply to Mr. Burke, who, in his Reflections on the French Revolution, was for defending old establishments, notwithstanding their abuses. But those establishments, political and ecclesiastical, went down as at the breath of God's nostrils. Daylight was admitted into the most dark and hopeless regions. Bodies which had been regarded dead as the mummies were magnetized with a new life. Wars were not confined to the English Channel or the Rhine ; they were carried into the remote East, and were a day of resurrection to the slumbering nations. The French army invades Egypt. " Soldiers," says Napoleon to his troops, " from the summit of the pyramids forty centuries look down upon you ! " The advancing column rolls over the plain of Esdraelon, and their flushed and excited commander looks out upon the strife from the top of Tabor, where our Lord was transfigured. The concussion is felt throughout the Ottoman Empire. The Spanish colonies in Central and South America begin a series of struggles for their independence. A large force is sent against them, and after a long and bloody contest the Spaniards are expelled, and their former possessions are created into many republics, of divers fortunes and prospects. The civilized world was thoroughly overturned and overturned, and society began to be organized on new principles, and pervaded by a new life.

It is true, there was a reaction. The spirit of popular liberty met with checks and rebuffs. The House of Bourbon is re-established. The battle of Waterloo re-stores exiled kings, prelates, and aristocracies. "The battle and its result," said Robert Hall, "seemed to me to put back the clock of the world six degrees." But it was only as the recession of a wave or two. The ocean was not dammed up. It was inevitable that other revolutions should come. In 1830 they came again, with less of cruelty, less of mistake. In this year the Belgians secure their independence, and a new Constitution is formed by the representatives of the people according to which a new King is elected. In Switzerland an aristo-cratical government is exchanged for a democracy. At the same time political commotions arise in Germany, and constitutional charters are secured for Saxony, Han-over, and the electorate of Hesse. A general desire for liberty pervades Italy; and there are insurrections in Bologna, Modena, and Parma. By the Revolution of the Three Days the Papal priesthood of France is again over-thrown. In the very same year a revolution occurs at Warsaw; troubles and dissensions break out in Greece; a new organization takes place of the relations between the nobility and burghers of Russia; a general desire of representative government prevails in Prussia; and the opposition in the British Parliament, backed by the people, are strenuous for those national reforms which were carried under the Grey Ministry, two years after. Nor was this the end. Recent events are but reverberations of the first explosion. At each repetition of the struggle much has been gained, and former errors and excesses avoided. Louis the Sixteenth was beheaded, and his wife, the pride of courts, inhumanly murdered. Louis Philippe leaves the Tuilleries, the Queen on his arm, unmolested, a crowd of revolutionists opening to let them pass. In a few instances, Hungary and Italy, we have been disappointed as to results. But the end has not come yet. There has been a succession of changes in the right direction; and the face of the world to-day no more resembles what it was at the close of the last century, than the post-diluvian earth was like its appearance before the flood. There are more written constitutions defining and securing the rights of subjects, than ever existed in the whole history of the world before. The increasing intelligence of society has operated most beneficially upon the ruling powers. The greatest despotisms are forced to recede when they encounter national sentiments. The veil of separation which the Orientals wisely spread before their monarchs, and behind which they have remained like idols of dark origin and uncertain attributes, has, in continental Europe, been rent to the bottom, and kings are held answerable to law, justice, and humanity. The late King of Naples was compelled to plead at the bar of public opinion, in reply to the letter of Mr. Gladstone concerning the atrocities of the Neapolitan prisons; and the Emperor of Austria did not disdain, in his recent speech at the imperial dinner in the Hotel de Ville of Paris, to explain and defend his pacific policy.

Perhaps the most striking change which has occurred, and this in connection with that revolution and that personage in France of whom we have spoken, is in the condition and prospects of the Papal Power. Think of it as it was when kings stood barefoot at the gate of the Pontifical palace, or meekly held the stirrup of the Pope's palfrey; and nations forsook their own anointed and hereditary monarchs when censured and excommunicated by the *soi-disant* successor of St. Peter. France became imbued with infidelity. That country which from the time of Charlemagne to the present hour has been most intimately allied to the risings and fallings of the Papal power,—whose *vocation*, according to Lacordaire,* is the defence and propagation of the Papal Church,—it was in France that the spirit of infidelity appeared which was destined to eat like a canker into the heart of the Papal domination. That infidelity began with opposition to Papal pretension and Papal cruelty. It was allied with the nascent spirit of liberty. Had it not been for this it would have passed away like the Deism of England,

---

* C'était la nation franque, et la nation franque était la première nation catholique donnée par Dieu à son Eglise. Ce n'est pas moi qui décerne cette louange magnifique à ma patrie ; c'est la papauté à qui il a plu, par justice, d'appeler nos rois *les fils aînés de l'Eglise.* De même que Dieu a dit à son Fils de toute éternité : Tu es mon premier né ; la papauté a dit à la France : Tu es ma fille aînée. Elle a fait plus, s'il est possible ; afin d'exprimer plus energiquement ce qu'elle pensait de nous, elle a créé un barbarisme sublime ; elle a nommé la France le *Royaume christianissime*—" christianissimum regnum."—*Conférences de Nôtre-Dame de Paris,* p. 440.

without leaving any deep furrows in the soil of the coun try. But so it was that French infidelity was provoked into being by political abuses, cruelties, and pretensions, in the name of religion. The true secret of its power was in the zeal with which it espoused the cause of jus·tice, freedom and humanity ; till in French literature, and French politics, humanity, justice, and freedom became identified with infidelity. The French language, at this time, was the medium of European intercourse. It was spoken at all the courts of the Continent, from the English Channel to the Bosphorus. The infidelity of Paris thus met with a rapid and universal dissemination. It spread like the air over the whole of Europe. It was an assailant which no police could stop. Freedom from superstition was counted an honorable distinction, a frontlet of divine inspiration. By means of some inexplicable power, the altars of religion were deserted, the mysteries of religion were performed in vacant cathedrals, and the priests themselves smiled at their own credulity. At this juncture there arose out of the tumultuous elements of European society that great aspirant, whose military and political tactics were destined to complete what infidelity had begun. To the eye of Napoleon the Pope of Rome was little more than any other sovereign and man. He summons the Pontiff to Paris. The Pope threatens him with excommunication. Napoleon heeds it no more than a whiff of snow when crossing the St. Bernard. The bull of excommunication was issued. It was only the advertisement of Pontifical imbecility. When Gregory VII. excommunicated Henry IV. of Germany, his subjects felt themselves absolved from all alle-

giance to their sovereign, and fled from him as if he had
been smitten with the pestilence. When Pius VII. excommunicated Napoleon, not a corporal left the French
army. Undiverted from his purpose, the "man of destiny" strips the Pontiff of political power. The Papal
dominions were annexed to France. The French flag
waves from the castle of St. Angelo. The title *King of
Rome* is conferred by the French Emperor upon his infant son ; and he builds for him a sumptuous palace on
the Quirinal hill. The Papacy was brought so low as to
be an object of pity rather than hatred or dread. The
time came for reaction, as might have been predicted.
The Pope was reinstated by the allied sovereigns. Exiled prelates came back to Paris, and the form of the
prostrate Church was lifted up. To the eye it has been
recovering from its shame and depression. With all
which the Papal See has regained, it bears no resemblance to its ancient power.   Had it not been for foreign
protection, the present Pontiff would have been thrown
into the Tiber by the inhabitants of his own metropolis. If a Pope is to continue to reign as a temporal
Prince, it must be with some show of justice and freedom. He must be the patron and defender of human
rights. Christian faith, which at the close of the last
century was driven out from continental Europe, has returned with a better discrimination. Men may be skep-
tical as to the Papacy without renouncing belief in Chris-
tainity. Multitudes now deride and scorn the pretensions
of the Roman Pontiff and his Church, without vaulting
over into the deism of Robespierre or the frightful atheism of Clootz. In the latest revolution of Paris, the

crucifix was borne in advance of the crowd, and Jesus Christ was hailed as the great apostle of Fraternity, Equality, and Humanity. The next action is already in progress, and millions will learn to discriminate between Christianity and Ecclesiasticism, convinced that there is a religion which does not oppose reason and justice and progress, but is the grand ally and defender of all which concerns the true welfare of man.

The sun of the last century went down amid murky clouds. Terrible signs flashed their lurid light across the darkened skies; hecatombs of human lives were sacrificed; but who can doubt that, as a consequence of these unusual commotions, the century now passing is distinguished above all its predecessors for the increase of liberty, the security of chartered rights, and, as a necessary result, a greater amount, present and prospective, of intelligence, industry, peace, order, and prosperity. These convulsive events were as the tornado tearing up the old forests by the roots, or the ploughshare overturning the soil. It was the day of preparation; and now we turn to the seed-time and the harvest, the golden fruits which are waving on a thousand fields.

A new power has been brought into operation in the principle of *voluntary association.* Men have clasped each other's hands, and by means of united strength have accomplished what before had been left to solitary hopes, and individual force. The world had not been wanting in good men in former centuries; but their agency, to a great extent, has been individual and independent. There are traces in their writings of irrepressible longings after better opportunities for aggressive action. No sooner had the great changes to which we have adverted taken place, than sagacious men felt the impulse to unite their services in the propagation of all truth, and the reform of all abuses. No recesses were suffered to remain unexplored ; pretensions are questioned, claims investigated, and inquiry, by its ceaseless and corrosive action, is wearing away those fetters of the mind which keep its faculties dormant, and limit the range of its powers. Bishop Burnet greatly applauds the plan projected by Oliver Cromwell, for instituting a council in opposition to the Propaganda Fide at Rome. But it has been well demonstrated that the power of voluntary association, which combines the efforts of all who are favorable to a good cause, is mightier in its results than any influence which a single monarch could exert ; and individuals every year accomplish far more splendid deeds than entered into the imagination of Cromwell, in his truly noble conception. Thirty years ago, Dr. Channing took occasion to write against this increasing power of association, lest it should impair individual freedom and responsibility. Wherever there is power, caution should attend its use. It is a poetic fancy to suppose that all the beauty of private beneficence belongs to the days of Sir Roger de Coverley, English squires, and patriarchal estates. We believe there is more of private charity now, than there was before associated power began to change the face of the world. This is an influence which supplies deficiencies of individuals and of governments, in attaining ends which they cannot reach. It is a greater discovery than the mariner's compass. There is no object to which this power cannot adapt itself, no resources which it may not ultimately command ; and a few individuals, instead of being isolated as were good men before, can lay the foun· dations of undertakings which would have baffled the might of those who reared the pyramids.*

The isolation of nations in former ages, was obviously intended by God. He defeated the purpose of those who sought to centralize power on the plains of Shinar. Diversities of languages, a range of mountains, a river or a sea, separated and secluded tribes and nations. Quick and easy communication is a feature of these times of fraternity and humanity. Little did the first observer, who watched the rattle of the lid on a tea-kettle, from the power of confined steam, dream what changes would be wrought in the world by that new agent, which then forced itself on his attention. Little did James Watt, the Duke of Bridgewater, Earl Stanhope, his eccentric sister, Lady Hester, and Robert Fulton, when experimenting upon several scientific properties and practical uses of vapor, conceive that they were God's agents for bringing about some of the greatest moral revolutions of the world. When at last, in the year 1807, Fulton succeeded in getting under weigh the little steamboat Clermont, with her head up the Hudson—a few are yet living who remember well the jeers and jests of the day,—highly gratified as he was with the success of his experiment, little did he imagine that he was giving to the world a providential agent, which, by the stroke of a piston, was to diffuse knowledge, liberty, and religion over all the earth.

* Douglas on the Advancement of Society in Knowledge and Religion.

Read the almost plaintive words of Richard Baxter, —the scarcely uttered hope cherished by him that the time might come when access could be had to the Orient, —and say if God's hand is not in this unlooked-for propinquity of the nations. Along the Bosphorus, this new agent is breaking down the rigidity and breaking up the apathy of the Turk. Doubling the Cape of Good Hope, it has startled the sleep of the Bengalese and Chinaman. By its unconscious working in the Mediterranean, the Black Sea, and the Eastern Oceans, it has done more to diffuse intelligence, liberty, and life than any other providential power whatever. It is a power which does not belong exclusively to commerce. Commerce! Why, it is itself God's agent. The great sea was not intended to be a mere manufactory of whale oil, or a road for the transportation of cotton and tobacco. It is a highway of emerald and sapphire for the footsteps of Christianity. Henceforth, nothing is done in a corner. Nothing is too remote to escape attention. The steamers which crowd their way through stormy seas, the roads of iron which bind whole continents together, the clicking wires which run their electric net-work through the air and beneath the ocean, are the great nerves of human sympathy, and are destined to the high office of uniting the whole race of man in a loving brotherhood.

Nothing which is familiar to us strikes us as wonderful. Surprise wears away in time from the greatest discoveries and inventions; and we send thought through the air, and ride in carriages without horses, and in ships against the wind, just as carelessly and composedly as though such things had always been. Fletcher, the old dramatist, was counted as half crazy when he put into the mouth of Arbaces this ranting promise:

> "He shall have chariots easier than air,
>   Which I will have invented : and thyself,
>   That art the messenger, shall ride before him
>   On a horse cut out of an entire diamond,
>   That shall be made to go with golden wheels,
>   I know not how yet."

The wonder of the promise has long ago been realized ; and if the poetry of the dream should yet come to pass, and locomotives cut from solid diamonds, and car-wheels wrought from gold, should become common, we should ride after them with as little surprise as now we walk beneath the azure and the gold of God's glorious firmament. Who can forget the feeling of *awe* which came over him, when for the first time he received a telegraphic dispatch from a distant city, transmitted from New York to New Orleans actually in advance of time itself ! This approaches spiritual power more nearly than any thing we have seen and handled.

The authors of the *Spectator*, the *Tatler*, the *Rambler*, had no conception of the modern newspaper. This is one of the most wonderful and powerful agents of our times. It is dumb, yet it tells us of all which is done upon the earth. It bears in its own name the initials of the four points of the compass, N. E. W. S.—news. It is the great dial-plate on the clock of time. Go to the archives of an Historical Society, and consult an old newspaper ; let it be a file of the *Boston News Letter*, commenced in April, 1704, the first ever published on this Western continent. Read of African slaves in the

16

town of Boston,—perhaps a fresh cargo of stout-limbed Guineamen have arrived in a Newport ship : turn rapidly over the leaves of the volume ; your eye catches a succession of great names and events,—Benjamin Franklin resisting the censorship of the press, and making the lightning of the skies a pastime for himself and his son,—tribute money, unjust taxation, mutterings and rebellion, Lexington, Bunker Hill, Revolution, Independence, Confederacies and Constitutions, Fulton's humbug, commerce, arts, peace, prosperity, enterprise, expansion. May we not rightly call the smutty chronicle the index finger of Providence pointing to the hours on the chronometer of history ? An artist expends great time and labor in painting a panorama, and crowds find delight in gazing upon the canvas ; yet is it of a limited space,— a ruin, a river, a city,—Thebes or Jerusalem, the Nile, the Hudson, or the Mississippi. But a newspaper is a daguerreotyye of the whole world,—its warrings, parturitions and diplomacies, its buyings and sellings, its governments and revolutions. The huge telescope of Sir John Herschel is so swung that it reflects all the distant wonders of the sky, which sweep across its lenses, upon a small horizontal table under the eye of the observer ; and analogous to this, a newspaper brings all the occurrences of remote continents under your astonished and delighted eye.

Up by the North Pole, among seals, whales, and icebergs, we can just discern a scientific party endeavoring to force from Eternal Winter its ancient secret, and to ascertain if there be not a new way of getting round this small globe we inhabit. In Africa are as many more, quite as vigorous and persevering in seeking to discover whereabouts certain rivers take their rise. Away on the Tigris are others digging up old Nineveh, perhaps the bones of Tiglath Pileser himself; while that spot on the shores of the Pacific, resembling the life and activity of an ant-heap, is a vast company of what Bunyan would call muck-rakes, scrambling for gold. Yonder is Professor Teufelsdröckh demonstrating to a gaping auditory, that "society is founded on clothes," that man is God, that it is better to walk on your head than feet, or any other conceit that bewildered logic may happen to play with. Are you fond of seeing harlequins, the daily journal will please your fancy. Do you like spring-vaulting and tumbling, politicians will surprise you with feats of agility. If you prefer ledgerdemain, the wire-pullers will show you enough of sleight of hand ; and if tragedy is to your turn, the incendiarisms, the murders, the woes and the wars of this sad world call for no crocodile tears. And if you have learned to look at all things with the calm eye and sober judgment of a Christian, the thing which most interests and delights you is the conviction that God presides over this great stage of life, and that events transpire under his direction. Though the actors are not automata, yet their several parts are all worked into one great design : scenes the most startling, disappointments the most depressing, follies the most extravagant, are all overruled by an All-wise Master, and are hastening on a catastrophe which will be so joyous and wonderful as to fill heaven and earth with grateful applause.

The newspaper is the peculiarity of an age of inter-communication, an agent of human sympathy. What else lies at the bottom of this conception but a just idea of man's fraternal relations? It is the cheap correspondence carried on between all members of the human family. What a man puts into a newspaper on the other side of the globe, is on the supposition that it will interest the rest of the family on this continent. As we learn more of our fellow-men, we feel a kindlier interest in them. We rejoice in their prosperity, sympathize in their calamities, and cheer on their struggles for the right and the good. There are now too many newspapers abroad to allow a man to live like a snail. They enlarge the world to our knowledge and our love. Why is any thing made public but on the belief that it will be of interest to many others? Why is it announced in your paper that Isaac and Rebecca were married on a certain day last week, but on the supposition that it will give you pleasure to know it? And when, lower down on the sheet, under that startling word *Deaths*, your eye runs along, always with apprehension lest it fall on some well-known name, and reads that the aged father, the young child, the beloved wife, the rich, the poor, the admired, the honored, and the beautiful are gone, is it not taken for granted that even strangers will heave a sigh for the afflicted, and the world respond in sympathy to the incursions of a common foe? Read in this light, the commonest advertisements which crowd our papers have a kindly odor about them. Say not, with a cynic sneer, as though you were doubtful whether there was any thing honest in the world, when a store-keeper advertises his wares, that it is all sheer selfishness; for if it is pleasant to one to announce a fresh supply of tallow or wool, hardware or muslins, is it not just as pleasant to some other one who wishes to know it? When a brace of young partners in trade insert their virgin advertisement, informing the world how happy they shall be to wait on customers, can you read it without entering into their fresh hopes and giving them your blessing in their new career? Business advertisements! Waste paper! You know not what you say. Those ships which are to sail to every harbor in the world, those fabrics which have arrived from every commercial mart on earth, this iron from Russia, tea from China, wool from Smyrna, fruit from Malaga, coffee from Cuba, cotton from Georgia, sugar from Louisiana,—do they not preach to us at the corners of the streets, at the entering in of the gates, on our docks, and in our custom-houses and exchanges, sermons on the mutual dependence of mankind?

Charles Lamb has a very humorous conception, in a letter to an acquaintance at New South Wales, on the difficulty of corresponding in a free and friendly manner with one at so great a distance, comparing it to the effort of talking through a tube to the man in the moon. It was a playful conceit; for, in sober judgment, the facilities for communication between distant parts of the earth have destroyed the old confusion of ideas about longitudes, latitudes, and differences of time; the tubes are connected between the different apartments of our Father's house, as they are in our modern architecture, so that the freshness of sympathy and ardor of love are not lost in the great and dividing sea. How much time elapsed before the exploit of Leonidas at Thermopylæ was known west of the Tiber we cannot divine. Scarcely was the first blow struck by Garibaldi, before every eye was turned, every ear alert, every heart alive; for the daily visitant at

our dwellings made all personal spectators and participa-
tors in the scene.   The school-boy in Vermont and Ohio,
in his weekly declamation, has rehearsed with emotion
the noble sentiment of Blum on the morning of his exe-
cution :

> " Whether it be the scaffold high,
>   Or in the battle's van ;
>   The proper place for man to die
>   Is where he dies for man."

Patriots struggle not alone.   What occurs on the
Arno or the Tiber rouses the sympathies of all mankind.
Nor do these expend themselves in useless emotion.
They create a sentiment, and establish a law to which all
actions must be referred and by which they must be
judged.   The more of ubiquity is given to what men do,
the more certain is it that they will be held accountable
for what they do.   " They that be drunken are drunken
in the night."   The frantic cruelties of the world's Cali-
gulas and Borgias were perpetrated in darkness ; but as
light spreads, and the conviction gains ground that what
is done to-day in a closet will, ere the sun rises, be pro-
claimed upon the house-tops, that conviction must work
for the suppression of cruelty, for the shame of tyranny,
and the triumph of truth and goodness.

That freedom of opinion, of which the newspaper is
the symbol, is looked upon by many with apprehension.
There is no subject concerning which men are so slow of
heart to believe as *liberty*.   At first even good men are
afraid of it.   They handle it as they would an animal in
a cage.   They open the door by little and little.   They

are afraid to let the bolt fly clear back, and let go of the chain and the collar for ever. Had the band of Pilgrims who founded the Massachusetts colonies, who, for the sake of freedom of conscience, sacrificed homes, churches, and universities, foreseen the time when papers advocating infidelity, agrarianism, Fourierism, prelacy, the Papacy, the wildest and the most arrogant follies of Church and State, would everywhere be tolerated, they would have started back aghast ; and we know not but such an unexpected glimpse of the concealed purposes of Providence would have led them to hail the Mayflower as she weighed her anchor, to take them back for shelter under the surplice of Archbishop Laud. In the year 1723 the newspaper called " *The New-England Courant*," established by James Franklin, as an organ of independent opinion, was censured, interdicted and stopped, " except it *first be supervised.*" " I can well remember," writes Increase Mather, then more than fourscore years of age, " when the civil government would have taken an effectual course to suppress such a cursed libel." You cannot stop the sun at the horizon. If men are dazzled by liberty, the proper cure is liberty. There can be no true freedom for what is good, except there be freedom for what is bad. The best mode of refuting sophistry and mischievous opinions is to let them come forth to the light. We have no wish that enemies should sap our foundations in secret, and spring a mine on us stealthily. Let them think aloud. It is better to give vent to mephitic gases into the air than confine the explosive elements in subterranean galleries. If a man really intends to overturn and re-organize society, advocating community of property, the dissolution of the family, reducing the human race to a herd of animals in broadcloth, let him avow his purpose in a public newspaper, and if the result be not the complete frustration of his scheme, the demonstrated futility of his project, it will only be as there is no power in truth, and no right in equity. Truth never has suffered in a fair and open discussion. Weapons which seem to pierce her ethereal form through and through, leave her spiritual body unharmed. There is many a man with a conceit in his brain, for whom the best prescription would be that he should publish it. For the mischief done to the unwary we greatly deplore that so many vipers should be brought out from the kindling fires of freedom; but, because of this, we cannot consent that the fires should be put out and we be left to freeze on desert islands. When the warm sun of summer is up, it brings all unclean and creeping things to life. The grass is full of all manner of vermin; so is the bark of great trees. The adder crawls out of his hole to bask in the glowing heat, but whole harvests of grain overtop and conceal the mischief; the forests are growing taller and taller, and fruits are ripening on every tree. Just so is it beneath the genial warmth of freedom. If incidental evils are developed, if the loathsome agencies of infidelity are warmed into life, do not forget that beneath the same vital heat the rich verdure of a continent is springing up higher and higher, and the trees of righteousness, the planting of the Lord, are striking their roots the deeper and spreading out their fruitful boughs to the ends of the earth.

Now we see the bearing of providential agencies in

increased facilities for international intercourse on the prospects of the world. America is no longer the unknown and remote land it was when discovered by Columbus. It is near to all the world and all the world is accessible to it. Regarded as the home of hope and freedom, furnishing ample room in which stifled millions may breathe and live, immigration has set in like the tides of the sea. The immigrant, finding his most sanguine hopes surpassed, has reported to those behind what he has seen and accomplished. Millions on the Rhine have heard of it. France and Switzerland, Norway, Belgium, Holland, Ireland, Wales, England and Scotland, . Italy and Hungary, Poland and Sweden, have all experienced that electric sympathy which has reacted from the log-cabins which their emigrant population have reared in the new settlements of the New World. These last are not beyond talking distance with their old homes. St. Louis is within ear-shot of Hamburg. The wires touch between New York and Berlin. Indeed, we cannot judge of events by their first appearance. Look at the Puritans of England, when suffering under the Five-mile Act, and you might esteem them the objects of Divine displeasure. But the world was not to come to an end until God had most gloriously vindicated his justice in the ultimate honor and prosperity of those who, for a time, were called to the endurance of suffering and hardship. These institutions which are now stretching away to the setting sun ; these blessings which brighten and enlarge around us, are but a part of those results which Providence has connected with the fortitude and fidelity of the noble men who, ages ago, willingly suffered in testimony

of truth.   The extent of our territory, and the growth of
our institutions, can surprise none more than ourselves.

One cannot but be amused in reading a book on
America, by an English, French, or German traveller, even
though he aims at great accuracy; for before he can reach
home and pass his volume through the press, his statistics are all obsolete.   A single jar changes the whole
kaleidoscope.   On the shores of the Pacific a nation has
been born in a day; a populous State, inhabited by the
young, the enterprising, the bold and energetic, looks out
from the "Golden Gate" upon the astonished East; and
this from a territory which a few years ago was not
known by name to the Republic, itself the abode of semi-
civilized vagrants.

But the greatest of changes have been moral.   The
effect of the Revolutionary war was most disastrous on
the morals of the country.   Voltaire has said, "Put together all the vices of ages, and they will not come up
to the mischiefs and enormities of a single campaign."
Added to these common effects of war, French infidelity
had been imported, and the virus had spread, infecting
many of the leading men of the country.   The deistical
writings of Ethan Allen and Thomas Paine had acquired
an immense popularity, all the greater from the memory
of Ticonderoga, with which the former, and the political
treatise of "Common Sense," with which the latter was
associated.   The scale is now turned.   The sentiment of
the nation is decidedly in favor of Christianity.   The
secular press, to a great extent, recognizes and honors it.
The old falsehood that infidelity is necessarily associated
with freedom and progress, is here abjured.   Christianity

has her ablest advocates in all departments of intellectual and physical science; her firmest believers among the intelligent friends of popular progress. Statesmen and merchants, men of thought and men of action, have gradually been working their way to the conviction that the Christian religion is the best aid and promoter of secular improvement, and whatever is done to give to its institutions a broader basis, is a sure pledge of all national prosperity.

All the agencies for good which have been mentioned are yet in their infancy. Their power will be reduplicated in time to come. Progress for the future, under these organized and providential instrumentalities, must be vastly accelerated. It is the certainty of yet greater advancement which gives to our times the brightest aspect. What recoils and reactions may be thrown into intermediate history, we cannot predict. That such things should occur in our career accords with the general course of Divine procedure. But episodes stop not the drama, nor eddies the current of the stream. The course of the world and the country is onward and onward still. Remote deserts unknown to us in the solitudes of the West will soon smile under the culture of happy freemen. Flocks of sheep and herds of cattle will supplant the elk and the buffalo. Natural obstacles to intercourse will be removed; the Rocky Mountains will be tunnelled, and the two oceans will be joined together. The banks of our rivers and the shores of our lakes will shine with opulent cities; commerce will whiten our waters; agriculture cover a continent with wheat and corn, and places now unknown to civilized man will resound with all the hum and stir of busy life. The school-house and the church, those engines and hopes of freemen, will be reared fast as the forest drops before the march of enterprise.

The day of universal jubilee will surely come. Every year bears the world nearer to its promised Sabbath. Generations pass from the earth, but time does not stop. Man and the world he inhabits are subject to change, but the Word of the Lord endureth for ever. The rocks may be worn away by the encroachments of the sea, the mountains levelled by the attrition of ages, the stars may lose their light and the sun his glory, but the promise of God standeth sure and changeless on its immovable foundations. "HE SHALL COME DOWN LIKE RAIN UPON THE MOWN GRASS : IN HIS DAYS SHALL THE RIGHTEOUS FLOURISH, AND ABUNDANCE OF PEACE SO LONG AS THE MOON ENDURETH. HE SHALL HAVE DO-MINION FROM SEA TO SEA, AND FROM THE RIVER UNTO THE ENDS OF THE EARTH. HIS NAME SHALL ENDURE FOR EVER; HIS NAME SHALL BE CONTINUED SO LONG AS THE SUN : AND ALL NATIONS SHALL BE BLESSED IN HIM. BLESSED BE THE LORD GOD, THE GOD OF ISRAEL, WHO ONLY DOETH WONDROUS THINGS, AND BLESSED BE HIS GLORIOUS NAME FOR EVER, AND LET THE WHOLE EARTH BE FILLED WITH HIS GLORY. AMEN AND AMEN."

DR. HODGE'S THEOLOGY.

Systematic Theology.

BY CHARLES HODGE, D.D., LL.D.,
OF PRINCETON THEOLOGICAL SEMINARY.

Three vols. 8vo, tinted paper.   Price, vols. I. and II., $4.50.   Vol. III., $5.

IN these volumes are comprised the results of the life-long labors and investigations of one of the most eminent theologians of the age.   The work covers the ground usually occupied by treatises on Systematic Theology, and adopts the commonly received divisions of the subject,—THEOLOGY, Vol. I.; ANTHROPOLOGY, Vol. II.; SOTERIOLOGY AND ESCHATOLOGY, Vol. III.

The plan of the author is to state and vindicate the teachings of the Bible on these various subjects, and to examine the antagonistic doctrines of different classes of Theologians.   His book, therefore, is intended to be both didactic and elenchtic.

The various topics are discussed with that close and keen analytical and logical power, combined with that simplicity, lucidity, and strength of style which have already given DR. HODGE a world-wide reputation as a controversialist and writer, and as an investigator of the great theological problems of the day.

SPECIAL NOTICE.

Volumes I. and II. of DR. HODGE'S *SYSTEMATIC THEOLOGY are now published.   Vol. III. will be ready early in November.*

*** *A supplementary volume, containing an analysis of the whole work, prepared by* Prof. A. A. HODGE, *of Alleghany Seminary, an index of topics and also one of Scriptural texts, is in course of preparation, and will be issued early in* 1873.

SCRIBNER, ARMSTRONG & CO.,
654 BROADWAY, NEW YORK.

PROSPECTUS

OF A

Theological & Philosophical Library

EDITED BY

HENRY B. SMITH, D.D., AND PHILIP SCHAFF, D.D.,

Professors in the Union Theological Seminary, New York.

————o————

The undersigned propose to publish a select and compact Library of Text-Books upon all the main departments of Theology and Philosophy, adapted to the wants especially of ministers and students in all denominations.

Some of the works will be translated from the German and other languages; others will be based upon treatises by various authors; some will be written for the Library by English or American scholars. The aim will be to furnish at least one condensed standard work on each of the scientific divisions of Theology and Philosophy, giving the result of the best critical investigations, excluding, however, such histories and commentaries as extend through many volumes.

This scheme is not presented as final, but as indicating the aim of the editors. If sufficient encouragement be given, no pains will be spared to make the project complete, and thus to meet a great and acknowledged desideratum in the apparatus for study. On all these topics every student needs, at least, one good work. To supply this will be the aim of our Library.

The various volumes will be published in the best style, on reasonable terms, and as rapidly as the nature of the work and the encouragement of the public will allow.

The editors will be assisted by eminent scholars of various denominations, who will respectively assume the literary responsibility for the volumes prepared by themselves within the general plan and aim of the library.

————

NOW READY,—THE INITIAL VOLUME

IN

The Theological and Philosophical Library.

UEBERWEG'S HISTORY OF PHILOSOPHY.

Vol. I.—*History of the Ancient and Mediæval Philosophy.* By Dr. Friedrich Ueberweg. Translated from the fourth German edition by George S. Morris, A.M., with additions by Noah Porter, D.D., LL.D., President of Yale College, and a general Introduction by the editor of the Philosophical Library. One vol. 8vo, cloth, $3.50.

These works sent, post-paid, on receipt of the price by the publishers,

SCRIBNER, ARMSTRONG & CO.,

654 BROADWAY, NEW YORK,

PUBLISHERS.

THE BIBLE COMMENTARY

(POPULARLY KNOWN IN ENGLAND AS "THE SPEAKER'S COMMENTARY.")

A Plain Explanatory Exposition of the Holy Scriptures for every Bible Reader.

To be published at regular intervals, in royal octavo volumes, at the uniform price of $5.00 per volume.

WITH OCCASIONAL ILLUSTRATIONS.

The BIBLE COMMENTARY, the publication of which was commenced by CHARLES SCRIBNER & CO., simultaneously with its appearance in England, had its origin in the widely felt want of a plain explanatory Commentary on the Holy Scriptures, which should be at once more comprehensive and compact than any now published. Projected in 1863, the selection of the scholars to be employed upon it was entrusted to a Committee named by the Speaker of the British House of Commons and the Archbishop of York, and through the agency of this Committee there has been concentrated upon this great work a combination of force such as has not been enlisted in any similar undertaking, in England, since the translation of King James's version of the Bible. Of the THIRTY-SIX DIFFERENT DIVINES who are engaged upon the work, nearly all are widely known in this country as well as in England, for their valuable and extensive contributions to the Literature of the Bible, and in this Commentary they condense their varied learning and their most matured judgments.

The great object of the BIBLE COMMENTARY is to put every general reader and student in full possession of whatever information may be necessary to enable him to understand the Holy Scriptures; to give him, as far as possible, the same advantages as the Scholar, and to supply him with satisfactory answers to objections resting upon misrepresentations or misinterpretations of the text. To secure this end most effectually, the Comment is chiefly explanatory, presenting in a concise and readable form the results of learned investigations carried on during the last half century. When fuller discussions of difficult passages or important subjects are necessary, they are placed at the end of the chapter or volume.

The text is reprinted without alteration, from the Authorized Version of 1611, with marginal references and renderings; but the notes forming this Commentary will embody amended translations of passages proved to be incorrect in that version.

The work will be divided into EIGHT SECTIONS, which it is expected will be comprised in as many volumes, and each volume will be a royal octavo. Typographically, special pains has been taken to adapt the work to the use of older readers and students.

N.B.—The American edition of the Bible Commentary is printed from stereotype plates, duplicated from those upon which the English edition is printed, and it is fully equal to that in every respect.

THE FIRST VOLUME OF

THE BIBLE COMMENTARY

Is now ready. It contains:

THE PENTATEUCH.

The books of which are divided as follows, among the contributors named:

GENESIS...................... Rt. Rev. E. HAROLD BROWNE, Bishop of Ely, and author of *Exposition of the Thirty-Nine Articles*

EXODUS........................ Chap. I-XIX. THE EDITOR.

LEVITICUS .... REV. SAMUEL CLARK, M.A.

" .... Chap. XX. to the End, and

NUMBERS AND DEUTERONOMY........ .... Rev. T. E. ESPIN, B.D., Warden of Queen's College, Birmingham.

Making one vol. royal 8vo, of nearly 1,000 pages, being the only complete Commentary upon the Pentateuch, in one volume, in the English language. Price in cloth $5.00, less than one-half that of the English edition.

Full prospectuses, with division of sections and names of contributors, sent to any address on application. Single copies sent post-paid, on receipt of price, by

SCRIBNER, ARMSTRONG & CO., 654 Broadway, N. Y.